Beat

Slay

Love

. . .

Thalia Filbert

Thalia Press
2015

Published by Thalia Press, USA
ISBN: 978-0-9819442-1-0

Acknowledgements

The authors are indebted to so many people for their help, both literary and culinary in this project.

All of us, and especially Taffy Cannon, thank Melissa Kamenjarin for her expert proofreading. Taffy also thanks Lynne Loeffler and Debbie Besch for their Texas barbecue expertise.

Lise McClendon thanks her mother, Betty, for many memorable meals, a love of curry and hatred of okra, and zillions of cookbooks, and her husband, Kipp Webb, who stayed the course as she learned to cook; also special friends Kate Hourihan, Jay Shepherd, Ana Sims and Fran Read for their special talents and expertise.

Kate Flora also thanks her fabulous mother, A. Carman Clark, who taught her to be adventurous about cooking, and her husband, Ken Cohen, who is willing to eat her experiments.

Gary Phillips would like to thank Adam Richman of *Man vs. Food*, for teaching him, "in all things, moderation, son, moderation."

Katy Munger wishes to thank the many people over the years who have allowed her to shower them with love using food as her chosen mode of expression.

The authors also wish to apologize to Elizabeth Gilbert for co-opting her brilliant idea and to thank her for it as well. May we always eat-pray-love so well. And can we add on "laugh?"

Chapter 1

The Grotto had been a fixture of Little Neck, New Jersey, for over 30 years, famous mostly for its bad lighting and proximity to a low-rent motel where out-of-towners met for sweaty afternoons of illicit love.

Located in a swampy area near a soulless stretch of overdeveloped shore, the Grotto had been a decent place for a home-cooked Italian meal once, but that was years ago. Its owners had died in the 1980s and left the Grotto to their son, whose lack of ambition and money-hungry wife had soon reduced the menu to that of an even lower-rent Olive Garden. Still, competition was sparse and enough people showed up on weekend nights to allow the Grotto to limp along, slowly bleeding the inheritance of its present owner away.

That is, until a miracle occurred in the form of *Kitchen Turnaround,* a popular Food Channel show that was a cross between two even more popular shows— one that featured a psychopathic chef who lived to humiliate kitchen workers under his control, and another with a kindly host who helped failing restaurants regain their feet. *Kitchen Turnaround* aimed for the middle between these two shows: humiliation with redemption.

The star was a lanky and immensely popular Australian chef who went by the unlikely name of Byron Peppers. He could be abrupt and bossy, especially when directing his crew of decorators in their efforts to update a failing restaurant overnight. But he wasn't as vicious as some famous turnaround chefs, nor as knowledgeable about food.

He tried stints as a guest judge on cooking competitions and succeeded only in revealing his lack of taste, both literally and figuratively. But Byron Peppers was charming, good-looking in a rugged way and immensely likeable. In other words— perfect for television. All he really had to do was read the teleprompter in his charming Aussie accent and his competent staff took care of the rest.

It had been the staff's idea to choose the Grotto for the show. They knew the nation would love the comeback story of a failing restaurant hit even harder by the ravages of Hurricane Sandy. The word had come down: the Grotto was their next target.

The whole town of Little Neck watched breathlessly as camera crews moved in and the low-rent motel filled up. Rumors began circulating that something big was afoot, especially when a Closed for Renovations sign went up on the Grotto's weary faux stone exterior. By the time the truth was learned, and residents began planning their compliments about the food in hopes of winning airtime on the broadcast episode, a lot of gossip about the Grotto had already been passed around town. Some said a dead body had been found behind one of the walls during renovations, while others insisted they had heard that Mrs. Grotto, the owner's wife, had been boffing the show's host plus half the crew for good measure.

None of this was true, though some was almost true, and absolutely all of it was rendered irrelevant when the reality of the Grotto's big makeover moment exceeded absolutely all expectations, going down in history as the single most remarkable event in Little Neck's history.

It started out auspiciously enough. The night of October 5 had been a mild one. Some of the town's residents had even ventured out onto the sands beyond the sagging boardwalk to enjoy the solitude of an off-season beach. Others had blatantly cruised past the Grotto hour after hour, hoping to discern whether the hammering and endless deliveries were done so that the restaurant could reopen its doors that night as advertised.

Flyers had gone out promising a grand reopening and inviting town residents to be on the show. No one would have to pay for their meal, the flyer promised, so long as guests signed a release saying that their images could be used. This had been enough to inspire most of the town to declare that they would arrive at the Grotto in their finest knock-off designer duds, ready for their linguine and close-ups.

But by late afternoon, something had clearly gone wrong. Perhaps the renovations had taken longer than expected. Perhaps the wife had thrown a fit over how she looked on camera. That would be just like Mrs. Grotto, most agreed. Maybe there was no hope for the restaurant after all. Perhaps the Grotto would be Byron Pepper's Waterloo.

Whatever the cause, the shades of the restaurant stayed drawn until nearly five p.m. By then, a line had formed outside the Grotto that stretched all the way around the building, through the parking lot, past a convenience store that specialized in alcohol and condoms, and all the way down the block to the entrance to the Dew Drop Inn, where the crew had set up for the week.

It was the crew that finally let the cat out of the bag. Four cameramen arrived and muscled their way past the waiting patrons, looking worried.

"What's the matter?" a fat woman in a velour sweat suit with the word "PINK" stretched wide over her rear end called out. In any crowd, she was always the first to speak up. "Let me guess. You found rats. The Grotto is toast."

She irritated the cameramen. But then, the whole town irritated the cameramen.

This entire episode had been irritating, not only because of the usual complications that ensued when Byron Peppers met a female co-owner whose looks were not outright disgusting, but also because absolutely no one involved in the restaurant, from owners to kitchen staff, possessed an ounce of charisma or had anything remotely interesting to say.

The crew had been searching all week for decent sound bites or someone who didn't look like they worked in a prison kitchen. They were ready to ditch the whole episode and take their sorrows back to the Dew Drop Inn where they could drink the night away.

"Hold on," they announced to the crowd, trying to calm them without revealing their essential dilemma: No one could find the host.

Byron Peppers was missing and there was no way they could film the last episode without him. As eager as they were to wrap and be gone, there was a good chance there'd be no shooting done that night unless they found Byron Peppers soon.

But their low whispers were overheard and the news that Peppers was missing sent a buzz down the waiting line. The cameramen pounded on the door of the Grotto and, soon after, lights flickered on in the restaurant. The crowd grew tense and restless. A minute later, the front door opened and people surged toward it, but a cameraman held them back.

The owner, thirtyish and sporting a Sinatra forelock, motioned to one of the cameramen. His voice quavered and sweat was forming on his pink forehead. "Something's wrong," he whispered. "There's a funny smell in the kitchen. Call the cops. I'm taking my wife out the back."

He shut the door, leaving the cameramen to fend for themselves. Something in his voice had convinced the crew that this was going to be a long night. As one called 911, the others adjusted their gear, firing up their equipment. If something interesting was finally about to happen, they wanted to be ready.

The cops appeared in a flash. Easy enough, since two-thirds of the town's police force were waiting in line for a crack at the new Grotto. The Chief of Police bellied his way up to the front, announced himself, and officiously ordered everyone else to make room. He lived for moments like this one. Hitching up his pants, he ordered the cameramen to open the door then stepped slowly inside the deserted restaurant.

Those craning their necks for a peek behind him gasped— everything they had ever seen on *Kitchen Turnaround* was true. The Grotto had been transformed into an aquamarine and silver palace with fountains built into the walls beside intimate alcoves where tables for two were nestled. Then the door slammed firmly behind the cameramen and police chief. The townspeople waited anxiously outside, wondering what had gone wrong, not yet realizing that their single glance would be all anyone saw of the new Grotto until the evening news aired that night.

* * *

The police chief of Little Neck paused, drinking in his luck.

Here he was, the first customer to enter what was sure to become a famous local landmark once the episode was broadcast. He noticed two cameramen filming him and sucked in his gut, breathing deeply of the aroma in the restaurant. The staff must have been cooking all day.

He could smell short ribs, he thought, roasted to perfection, with perhaps a hint of rosemary and lemon added to the mix. He had starved himself all afternoon in anticipation of his meal at the Grotto. He was ready to tuck in and eat.

The romantic atmosphere was fancy but a bit eerie with empty, forlorn tables, their fake candles dark. Still, maybe he'd take the missus here when everything settled down. He might get lucky.

"Where'd that little prick go?" the Chief asked one of the cameramen.

"Byron?"

"No, the owner of this joint," the Chief clarified, making a note about the crew's opinion of their boss.

"Beats me. He just ran out the back door and jumped in his car," a cameraman answered. "His wife was with him. I got the footage. But if we can't find Byron, there's no show anyway."

"Mr. Peppers ever disappear like this before?"

The two cameramen exchanged a glance. No one wanted to bring up that unfortunate episode in Duluth. The girl's parents were still threatening to bring charges.

"Sometimes Byron gets distracted," one of them finally said.

The Chief had suspected as much. He was a handsome devil, that Byron Peppers. The thought of meeting the show's rugged Aussie host perked up the Chief. Maybe he could get a photo with him that he could show to his friends, not to mention the kids. His grandchildren thought he was an old fogey, but if he could snag a photo with a TV star, they'd have to shut their bratty little mouths.

"Smells good," the Chief remarked, breathing deeply of the fragrant air.

The cameramen shrugged. They'd been let down by too many meals by now to expect anything but disappointment. Most of the restaurants Byron Peppers helped turn around lasted little more than a couple months after the show. The crew could come in and make the restaurant look better, update the menu and draw a celebrity-hungry crowd for a few weeks, but there wasn't much they could do about a restaurant owner who was too cheap to use good ingredients, too mean to keep a decent staff and too indifferent to customers to give quality service.

They were approaching the kitchen. The Chief's feet slid softly across the new white tile floor. It sure was an improvement over the warped wooden floors.

Maybe he could score a short rib or two. He sure was hungry. "Back door this way?" the Chief asked. The cameramen led the way, pushing through two large swinging doors into a gleaming kitchen that was light years cleaner than it had been just a few days ago.

"I see they kept the old pizza oven," the Chief said. The delicious aroma was coming from within its brick walls. "I remember when it was first installed. In fact, my great uncle did the mortar work. They don't make them like that anymore, you know."

He stepped closer, following his nose. He prided himself on his sense of smell. He definitely detected lemon, rosemary, perhaps a hint of thyme and something else … something different. Something almost delicious but a little off. He couldn't quite put his finger on it.

"Smells like your guy did a good job of getting the chef to up his game," the Chief announced with a touch more superiority than his actual knowledge of cooking merited. "I suspect most of the stuff they've been serving here was frozen, at least since the old man died."

The cameramen rolled their eyes. Most of the dishes would continue to be frozen, makeover or not. And no one would ever know the difference.

The Chief stopped in front of the oven and looked around, scratching his head. Where was everybody? Where was the chef? Where the hell was this vaunted Byron Peppers, charming host of *Kitchen Turnaround*? For the first time, it occurred to him that something might actually be wrong. He'd just poke around a little.

With nothing else to do, the cameramen rolled tape as the Chief rummaged around the kitchen, opening cabinet doors and lifting the lids on pots. Thus it was that they captured his gruesome discovery in glorious color and recorded his school-girl scream of terror.

Overcome by hunger and delicious odors, the Chief finally opened the doors of the pizza oven for a peek inside. He was expecting short ribs. What he saw would turn him vegetarian for the rest of his life.

The upper rack of the oven had been removed, creating a large cavern that was heated well above 600 °F. Trussed up like a giant turkey, Byron Peppers lay roasting on the bottom rack, an apple shoved in his mouth and sprigs of herbs tucked neatly behind his ears. His eyes were open, a milky opaque. He was naked, his flesh as crisp and succulent as that of a deep-fried turkey. The delicious smell the police chief had been coveting was Crispy Cooked Peppers.

It was too much. The chief bent over, bringing up coffee and doughnuts for the benefit of the cameras. The cameramen never missed a beat. One zoomed in on their roasting boss then out again, unsure what to do. Perhaps being behind the camera made it all unreal. But once there was nothing new to record, there was nowhere to hide. As one, they lowered their lenses and stared at each another.

"Holy shit," one cameraman said to the other. "Can you imagine what the ratings are going to be on this one?"

Chapter 2

Killing Byron Peppers had been easy.

It was as simple as slipping tranquilizers into his bottle of bourbon—he could always be depended on to have a bottle of bourbon nearby— and then waiting until the others left. Not long after, the obnoxious, ego-stuffed host had collapsed while trying to drunk-dial some ex-girlfriend. Undressing him was a cinch and seasoning him a simple matter of good taste.

Rosemary, of course, along with a liberal sprinkling of parsley and thyme plus a few lemons stuffed up an orifice or two. The apple in the mouth was perhaps a cheap shot, but nothing Byron Peppers didn't deserve.

Moving him afterward had been more difficult.

Byron Peppers was no lightweight and had been as limp as twice-frozen celery. In the end, the only solution had been to prop wooden pallets up on the lip of the oven door at an angle before rolling him up the ramp and awkwardly stuffing him inside. A true chef paid attention to presentation, however. It had been worth it to climb onto the pallets, lean into the still-cool oven, and arrange his arms and legs into a neat bundle, securing everything in place with twine. After that, all that remained was to crank up the oven and leave. Heat would take care of the rest.

There was no chance of detection. Invisibility had its benefits. When you are a plump and unimportant minion, people look right through you. Yes, sir. They look right through you.

Just the same, it was time to look for work in another town. This job was done. Byron Peppers was dead. It was time to move on to the others on the list.

The list.

With a rush, the unwelcome memory of the humiliation to end all humiliations came rushing back. With it, the role Byron Peppers had played in it unfolded as if it had happened yesterday. The cruel cameras that zoomed in on every slice of a knife and highlighted every extra chin. The judges looking so smug behind their table. The oh-so-clever remarks from those who could get by on their looks alone—the cutting digs about the cuisine, the insincere suggestions on how to make what was clearly a perfect dish better, the casual dismissal that came well before the final round.

Byron Peppers deserved his fate.

Another one down. So many more to go.

Chapter 3

There were days when Jason Bainbridge couldn't believe how lucky he was to make money sitting on his ass, watching television and occasionally springing for an unbelievable meal.

He felt like a fool for having wasted so many years with that stupid guitar, thinking he was talented, covering the soundtrack to Twin Peaks every year with a bunch of other over-the-hill hipsters, all the while sounding like a third rate Paul Westerberg. Just like a hundred other thirty-something, overweight losers in his hometown who had dropped out of college to become part of the starving but oh-so-cool underclass.

His palate had saved him from obscurity.

Somewhere along the way, Jason had found he enjoyed food more than he enjoyed music. Not any food, but good food, and not just eating it but listening to people talk about it, watching people make it, writing about the reality show battles unfolding on the Food Channel, the one channel he kept playing around the clock on his sixty-inch, flat screen, high-definition television.

Forget Super Bowl Sunday. Forget Sweeps Week. Forget the premier of new shows. None of that mattered. What mattered was *Cupcake Wars. Cake Master. Chopped. Top Chef. Kitchen Confidential. Kitchen Turnaround. Next Food Network Star. Cookie Monsters.* Even *Cutthroat Kitchen.*

The kitchen was his battlefield and he was a warrior. A warrior of words.

The day he realized he was good at something was a shock. It changed his life.

Telling no one in case it turned out to be a flop, he started his own food blog called Forked Tongue. He covered all the reality cooking shows with the devotion of an acolyte and the wisdom of a master, critiquing every move, dissecting every recipe, even making all-too-educated guesses about the sobriety of the guest judges who drifted in and out of the shows like crazy cousins visiting one another's homes for the holidays.

He discovered he loved the virtual world. He could be anyone out there in cyberspace.

No one cared that he was slightly overweight and on a dangerous trajectory toward fat. No one cared that he was indifferent to getting his hair cut and seldom wore anything other than a grimy pair of jeans and faded T-shirt.

No one knew that his girlfriend had left him the week before, the latest in a long series of girlfriends to leave him. She had been just like all the others, not understanding why he lived in a ratty apartment and drove a clunker while making a big deal out of driving hundreds of miles for the perfect meal prepared by the rare perfect chef.

Screw them all. Life was about food and food was life.

He'd entered the blogosphere as an unknown novice. Almost immediately, Jason Bainbridge's posts had risen to the top of favorability ratings on all of the most popular food blogs. He garnered more stars from other posters than anyone.

With each incisive blog, he grew more famous and each day he attracted more advertising attention. He branched out into restaurant reviews and food articles, but reality TV chefs were his true love. One day he would achieve his dream of writing the next big exposé about the world of top chefs and the crazy men and women who battled for supremacy within it.

For now, he had expanded his repertoire to include original reporting on developments in the personal lives of the best-known chefs and speculation about their futures. He had proved to be remarkably adept at spotting a budding alcoholic, or someone suffering from the pangs of love, or, even more likely, someone trapped in the cycle of drug addiction, soon to unravel before America's eyes.

Much of his success was because he had RSS feeds on all the brand-name chefs for media mentions, followed them religiously on Twitter and Facebook, and was often the first out of the gate with the news of some personal disaster, thus giving him the power to shape the story for the public.

He had become a voice.

* * *

It was a Saturday night when Jason Bainbridge got the news about Byron Peppers. Had he been out drinking micro-brewed ales with his musician pals of old, he would have missed it. His discipline paid off. The report of Pepper's death came in via a Google News alert that was little more than a brief mention by a major news site saying that famed television chef Byron Peppers had just been found dead in an obscure restaurant in some equally obscure Jersey shore town. Filming of *Kitchen Turnaround* was on hold. No other details were given.

Jason Bainbridge didn't need more details. He knew instantly what this latest chef death meant. He was probably the only person in America, maybe even on the entire planet, who followed the lives of virtually every chef who ever appeared on television. He was also probably the only person in America who remembered that a chef in Miami had been found dead on his boat not three months before, killed by a gunshot wound. His murder was still unsolved.

That in itself was not remarkable, especially given what assholes chefs could be and what hotbeds of intrigue the kitchens of high-end restaurants were. But then another chef, the owner of a small bistro in New York City, had been found dead by her staff not six weeks ago, skewered through both her hypercritical eyes.

One chef, not so surprising. Two chefs, a little suspicious. But three chefs in as many months? Something was up.

Yes, and Jason Bainbridge and Forked Tongue would break the story. Why not? There was nothing to stop him. He had a laptop and he could work wherever he could find a wireless signal. He had nothing to hold him here in his ratty apartment. He'd never gone in for cats and a dog was too much trouble. And once again there was no girlfriend to keep him from hitting the road.

Suddenly, his choice was crystal clear: He could sit there on his couch and keep being an observer of life, or he could get off his butt and go out there and make life happen.

It wasn't a hard decision to make. Within an hour of the grisly death of Byron Peppers being broadcast on Entertainment Tonight, Jason Bainbridge had his car packed, his bills paid for the month and his laptop stowed safely in the trunk. He was onto something and he knew it.

He put his clunker in gear and hit the road. This was it. This was his ticket to the big time.

Chapter 4

Jason found the shitty little restaurant in the Jersey swamp by following his nose.

The town of Little Neck was small enough; he could have just followed the crowd that lingered outside the Grotto. But the smell through the propped-open door was enough to convince him. This was a culinary death.

Pushing his way through the onlookers, Jason poked his head inside the restaurant. The odor was strong and not entirely pleasant; no way was he going inside.

A group of cops stood at the far end of the dining room, as far away from the kitchen as they could get.

He waited until one of them broke for the door and snagged her when she stepped outside. "Officer? Can you answer a few questions? I'm Jason Bainbridge from the local paper," he lied. "Can you tell me what happened?"

The cop was wearing a navy blazer and slacks, pretty with short blonde hair and long legs, completely out of his league. She didn't look like a cop from the Jersey shore. He had no idea what the name of the Little Neck newspaper was, if one even still existed.

She ignored him but he kept haranguing her, something he was good at, skipping beside her down the street, winded in no time.

Exasperated, she finally stopped and turned to confront him: "You want a statement? Okay. Byron Peppers has been found murdered in the pizza oven of the Grotto. That gruesome enough for you?"

Jason gulped. "He was— baked?"

"With a bouquet of herbs." She looked closer at him and he tried not to shrink under the gaze of an attractive woman as he usually did. "Did you know him?"

"He wasn't from around here," Jason said to stall for time. He pretended to scribble on his notepad. "Can you spell your name, ma'am? For the story."

"Special Agent Kimberly Douglas. FBI."

Kimberly? The name suited her. She was the kind of goddess girl that guys like him could only dream about. She began walking again, fast. Jason trotted along beside her, every step a reminder that he'd been putting off his fitness program too long. She was going to wear him out.

"Why is the FBI involved?" he gasped. "Is there something unusual besides the, um, baking aspect? Is it related to the deaths of the other chefs?"

She stopped in her tracks. "What other chefs?"

Jason sucked in his lips. Had he said too much? "Um, Fernando Gonzales in Miami last summer. He had that fancy place in South Beach. Then Willow St. Clair in Soho. You know about them, don't you?"

She looked surprised, which was a dead giveaway if you spent your time studying people the way Jason did. It wasn't just feds and narcs who profiled. "What if I do?" she demanded. "What do you know?"

"I figured there was a pattern, you know?" His voice had gotten squeaky. He hated when that happened.

The agent demanded his business card. He wondered if she'd notice he didn't work at the newspaper. But she just pocketed the card listing his blog address and dismissed him, leaving him standing on the grimy Jersey sidewalk with a ripe fishy smell blowing in from the sea.

She hadn't known about the other two chefs, he was sure of it. He was the only one making the connection.

But what was the connection? They were all high profile chefs or, in Byron Peppers's case, a former chef and current cooking show host.

Fernando had a high class joint in Miami and he'd appeared on a few cooking show episodes as a judge, never a contestant. Jason had never gotten to Fernando's restaurant before he had died but he'd heard tales about the late chef's Cuban food that made his mouth water. He'd also heard plenty about Fernando's kitchen tyranny, sexual predilections and unstable temper.

Willow St. Clair had been one of the first judges on some cooking show— *Cupcake Smack-Down*? He wasn't sure. After one meal at her so-called four-star bistro, Jason had labeled her a lightweight and dismissed her from his radar until she was killed.

Back at the Grotto, Jason chatted up a portly policeman or two, hoping for more information. They were all too glad to share grisly details about the murder but nobody had any idea who might have wanted to kill Byron Peppers.

He learned that the camera crew had retreated to the Dew Drop Inn, but reconnaissance there produced little new information. They were all in a lather about the probability the show would be canceled and they'd be losing their jobs. There was surprisingly little mention of the dead chef and even less about the possible reasons for his demise, never mind speculation about the identity of his killer. The closest Jason came to ferreting out any gritty details was when a discussion broke out about whether rosemary was the right herb to use when roasting a human. On that, opinions varied. Some thought there should have been some garlic involved; others felt the killer had needed a heavier hand with the thyme.

Most disagreed about the lemons. "Vulgar," one of the cameramen observed.

Jason was hungry, but there wasn't anything at the Dew Drop Inn that he'd consider eating and though he considered that he could be as cruel and distant as anyone in a fabulously hateful business, it did seem wrong to be eating when a fellow human had just been roasted alive.

"Done to a turn," as the head cameraman had put it. "He was as browned as if he'd been basted."

Had Byron been alive when he went into the pizza oven? It was a question no one had addressed. But it seemed ghoulish to raise it. No doubt that fact would be reported by the papers in due course.

It seemed to Jason that Peppers most likely had been alive, since the others had all been killed in a dramatic, if not symbolic, fashion. And, of course, being roasted alive was the ultimate fate for a chef.

Obviously, these linked events merited further investigation. But Magnum P.I. he was not. There wasn't the slighted bit of Selleck-ness about him. But he had other skills. Foodie skills.

In fact, he knew the cooking scene better than anyone.

Kimberly Douglas might have dismissed him as an annoying gnat, but this gnat knew the world she needed to investigate.

Something was up. He could feel it. Somewhere in the data he'd collected, or would collect, there would be a link between the victims. He just had to find it.

Jason did his best work— aside from eating— in the quiet of his apartment. He found his car and headed back to his little rat-hole in Queens to do some research.

Chapter 5

Charlotte Bernard was in a frenzy.

The smell of warm chocolate surrounding her like a cloud only made her anxious. The taping of the Valentine segment for *Love Bites* was three hours away and she still hadn't finished the huckleberry chocolate pot au crèmes that were the centerpiece of her portion. Worse, the infuriatingly slow assistant the producers had found for her was driving her crazy.

"Dust each one with a very small amount of cocoa, then this berry dust." She showed the assistant how to pinch a tiny dollop and sprinkle it. "Then one perfect huckleberry on top. Can you do that?"

It was unlikely. The woman's fingers were like sausages. She would probably get berry juice all over the place.

Charlotte moved to the other table where the signature martinis were to be assembled. The rambling Montana log house they'd rented for the taping was three times bigger than their NYC apartment— and their apartment took up an entire floor of a very spacious co-op on Fifth Avenue. Dead animals hung on the walls: moose, elk, bighorn sheep and God knew what else. She tried not to look at them. She had to focus on the taping.

This was their biggest show of the year. She and George had been doing *Love Bites* for five years now and each Valentine's episode had bumped their ratings up significantly. George, who called himself Giorgio now, was somewhere, preparing his bison roast. The house was so large she couldn't hear a thing.

It amazed her sometimes how far they'd come.

Good old George and Lottie from Brooklyn, who once owned a Jewish deli and made their own kosher bratwurst, were now stars on the Food Channel with a bestselling cookbook and their own cutlery line. George did love his knives, and he was expert with them. Next up was cookware, in red of course, with a big *Love Bites* heart on the lid of every pot. They'd inked that contract last week.

It was Charlotte's idea to do the Valentine episode in Montana. She had friends who summered here on Flathead Lake. That's how she had discovered wild huckleberries and made it her mission to enshrine them in the Taste Hall of Fame. They were divine and precious, just like the bison that Montana ranchers now raised. She'd made George a fabulous huckleberry sauce to serve with his roast.

He had been reluctant to travel so far from home until she had agreed to let him bring along his bimbo assistant, Marianne. That made him happy.

Everyone knew George and Marianne were on each other like cats in heat, even Charlotte. She'd almost stopped caring. The whole thing was sordid. It had started a year ago when Charlotte left New York for six weeks to judge that stupid cake show. She'd hated that gig but it paid her well to be nasty. She had no problem with that. Anyway, it wasn't really nasty when it was the truth. Nobody knew how to make fine pastries anymore.

She looked over at the martini table. It would twinkle once the candles were lit. Her signature drink, the Berry Drop, would knock everyone's socks off. Huckleberry syrup, made lovingly by hand. Grey Goose vodka. A special, secret lemon liqueur, also artisanal. A bowl of fresh berries. Crystallized ginger. She picked up a glass to check for spots.

"Can I make you one, Charlotte?" The assistant stood in front of her with eager puppy-dog eyes, awaiting her bidding.

"Oh, hell. Why not?" The show was hours away and she felt frazzled. A drink would do her good. "But make it on the counter. The tablecloth needs to stay clean and you've sprinkled cocoa over everything. And for God's sake, don't drop anything."

As the assistant gathered up the ingredients, Charlotte walked into the next room, a library with huge windows overlooking the vast blue water of the lake. She sank into a leather armchair big enough for two cozy cowboys. Her feet hurt. Damn heels. Kicking off her shoes and closing her weary eyes, she called out the recipe. When she opened them again, the drink sat on the table in front of her and the assistant had disappeared.

It looked perfect. The syrup sparkled rich and deep at the bottom, swirling around two perfect, whole berries. The vodka floated on top. The ginger twinkled in the sunlight. It would be gorgeous in close-up.

Charlotte took a sip and licked the ginger off her lips. The assistant had made it strong but maybe that's what she needed right now. She tipped her head back and took a long, luscious drink, feeling the cold slide down her throat as the heat begin to curl in her stomach.

Just what the doctor ordered.

Chapter 6

The camera crew knew better than to bother Giorgio while he was getting ready for the taping. They knew he'd be ready anyway; he always was. There was something almost scary about his way with knives. For a short man he was intimidating. Sometimes they called him Giorgio Scissorhands behind his back.

But his talented hands would be doing something else in the two hours leading up to *Love Bites* tape time. They all knew it, even his wife. Charlotte had let him bring Marianne along so she had to know.

When they heard the bumping and scuffling and grunts from the dining room where he'd set up his bison roast the crew smiled to themselves. Giorgio was taking an extra helping of his lovely assistant, just enough to take the edge off before the show.

It was the *Love Bites* producer, Freddy Maxwell, who started to worry.

It was three-fifteen. The taping was scheduled for four p.m. and nobody had seen Giorgio or Charlotte for hours. They had to set the lights. Freddy knocked on the big wooden doors that closed off the dining room from the hall.

There was no answer. He called out softly, then loudly.

Nothing.

He rattled the doorknob and was surprised to feel it move. Usually Giorgio locked it. Opening it a crack, Freddy called out again. "Ready to set the lights up, George?" Sometimes when he was nervous Freddy forgot to call his neighborhood pal by his new name. He just hoped Marianne had her clothes on.

He pushed the door wide. On the long plank table the bison roast sat on a huge wooden platter, browned to perfection, a fork stuck in its side. Bloody juices ran over the edge of the platter and puddled on the table, making Freddy irritated. What a mess. They were going to be late starting, he could just tell.

All the huge western chairs with their cowhide seats were in place down the table. He looked around for Giorgio and Marianne. Where the hell were they? Then he turned toward the side wall.

Hanging from a huge rack of moose antlers, knives stuck into his ribs, throat sliced clean through, was George Bernard aka Giorgio Bernardi, late of Brooklyn. Late of everything.

The lighting designer bumped into Freddy and the commotion began. Shock, screams, tears, calls to police. Freddy felt numb. What was he going to tell Lottie? Where was she? Could he keep her from seeing it?

Wait, who hated George more than Lottie? He felt cold suddenly. Where was Marianne? Had Lottie killed her, too?

Someone called from the kitchen. Marianne had been found with a bump on her head, out cold in the pantry. Another ambulance was called. They were miles from a hospital. Who knew how long it would take? Meanwhile the camera crew was getting it all.

Freddy slumped against the wall. His career was over. George was dead. Lottie was a murderer.

Love sure did bite.

"Here she is!" somebody cried. "Over here!"

The production crew bunched together, struggling to follow the voice. It came from the library. Freddy had a flashback to playing Clue with George when they were ten. In the library with the lead pipe. But this was no game. George was gutted and hung like a carcass. In the dining room with the knife.

Freddy felt sick as he walked into the library.

Curled into a huge leather chair, tucked under a Hudson Bay blanket with multi-colored stripes, Lottie lay sleeping as if nothing were happening. A martini glass lay tipped on its side on the table.

She'd gotten smashed and slept through it all. Wasn't he just telling George that she had a little drinking problem? The bitch— those were George's words— was putting the show in jeopardy.

Freddy put his hands on hips, prepared to be indignant. But wait. If she was here, passed out, maybe she hadn't killed George after all. Freddy reached out to shake her. "Wake up, Lottie! Lottie!"

Her shoulder was cool under his hands. Her head lolled back against the chair. A white crust had gathered in the corner of her mouth. "What the hell? Charlotte?"

Her eyes were open. And fixed. And dead.

Chapter 7

Jason Bainbridge had just put the final polish on his latest restaurant review. The hip meatball place called Them Balls was located not-so-ironically inside a bowling alley. If the meatballs hadn't been incredible, especially the lamb curry ones, he would have felt no compunction about trashing the twee-ness of it all: the disco ball, the skinny jeans, all that floppy hair. It was such a downtown cliché. But the food won him over and he even rolled a couple games, if only to justify having another order of the lamb meatballs.

That was why he was up at three in the morning, icing down his sore shoulder before he hit "send" on the review. That was why he flipped on the television to find something mindless to help him get to sleep and heard the news about Giorgio and Charlotte Bernardi.

The details were few, just "homicide" and "tragic."

He'd been glued to the news since the Byron Peppers murder, trying to connect the dots. He couldn't find anything besides cooking that connected Fernando, Willow and Byron. It had become a game with him, looking for that one thing they all had in common. But now this one?

It stopped him cold. This was different.

He felt shock, visceral pain.

He knew George and Lottie. He used to live near their deli in Red Hook and stop in for pickles on the way home from school. They were newlyweds then, barely twenty, running her father's deli after he keeled over into the bagels one day. They had so much enthusiasm and were so totally out of their depth. Even as a kid he could tell things weren't the same as when Oscar ran the place.

But they got better, a lot better, then somehow jumped to television.

Their show was a farce, in his opinion, geared for the kind of people who read romance novels by candlelight in silk pajamas, or imagined they did.

But their food was still great. Once a year they had a big blow-out for the old neighborhood and two years ago he'd been invited. Well, his mother had been invited and he went along. Everything was amazing.

Except for George and Lottie themselves. They insisted on being called Giorgio and Charlotte now, even with the old neighbors. George was full of himself, a total prick, and Lottie wasn't much better, flitting around with her pinkie in the air.

Jason's mother had a good laugh about them later. He wondered if he should call his mother now, tell her the bad news. No, it could wait. Bad news can always wait.

Turning his laptop back on, Jason searched for news on the murders. When the info was scarce, he started doing background on George and Lottie, entertainment news about their show, rumors about their marriage (lots), how much they were making, all that dish. There was plenty to read. Two hours later he had a hundred pages printed out.

He wouldn't be getting much sleep tonight.

In the morning, bleary-eyed, he maxed out his credit card booking an evening flight to Montana.

He'd found something in all those pages and sleepless hours. Every one of the murdered chefs— besides having appeared on televised cooking shows as either hosts, contestants or judges— had a connection to a Food Channel producer named Freddy Maxwell.

Freddy was a personal friend of George Bernard's, apparently, and had produced *Love Bites.* His first job in television was as a gofer on a long-forgotten Byron Peppers show. Years before that, he had worked in Miami as a sous chef at Fernando's. And he had been a scout for *Cupcake Smack-Down*, the show Willow St. Clair judged.

Was that enough? Why would Freddy Maxwell kill chefs? Was there some deep-seated hatred there? Jealousy? Envy?

Only one way to find out, and it meant a face-to-face with Freddy, even if that meant traveling to hell-and-gone.

Chapter 8

Jason was a terrible traveler.

He hated airports. Airport food. Airplanes and the slop they called food. The constant and inescapable presence of other people.

Jason was a slob, but at least he'd chosen to be. Too often, he found himself surrounded by mindless slobs, people who had awful hygiene and worse manners and had no clue about it. The snufflers, the grunters, the nose-pickers and phantom farters.

He hated the fact that some ingrained teaching from his proper mother, who despaired over his sartorial choices and sometimes questioned whether he'd been switched in the hospital, meant that he felt like he ought to dress more properly when he went on a plane.

He'd mentally labeled the bottom drawer of his dresser his "Mama's Boy Drawer." In it, he stashed the garments she routinely gifted him— crisp, creased khakis, socks without holes, her version of casual chic shirts still in the package. And recently some black items she'd evidently decided suited a restaurant critic.

He ruined the first shirt because he'd missed a pin that had nearly slashed his throat. He tossed it on the bed. TSA was slow and sloppy, but he hoped they'd be wary of a passenger with fresh bloodstains.

He vetted the second more carefully. Security at the airport was a nightmare, shoeless, half-dressed people shuffling forward in a gloomy line to enter a machine that would finish stripping them naked for the delectation of TSA folks sitting in a room somewhere. Dress with a crowd of others reassembling themselves. And finally, shuffle in another dumb oxen line onto the plane where he was deep in the cheap seats. A middle seat in the middle of the cattle car of coach.

The woman in the window seat— crisp charcoal pantsuit, white shirt, the kind of handbag movie stars advertised in the Sunday Times, a shock of golden hair— looked like she belonged in First Class, except for her obsessive attention to her phone.

He automatically dismissed women who were obsessed with their phones. His last girlfriend had been one of them. He'd been attracted because she seemed to be a foodie. But seriously, a pink phone? With Swarovski crystals?

True, she'd left him. But he hadn't exactly collapsed in a heap of despair.

The only pink he liked was the blush of a perfect pork roast.

He wiggled his duffle into the crowded overhead bin, put his briefcase under the seat, then dropped into his too-narrow space. The blonde woman looked at him. Not some phone-obsessed bimbo.

It was the FBI agent. Kimberly something. On TV, FBI agents flew places in their own private jets. So what was she doing here?

The same antennae that told him when food, despite an elegant presentation, was going to be a little off, sent him a warning message.

"You're not a reporter for the Jersey Shore Gazette, Mr. Bainbridge," she said. "So who are you and what are you doing here?"

There were so many responses to that.

But she was FBI. She was also someone who'd been cold and utterly dismissive the last time they met, a time when he was pretty certain he'd given her information she might never have put together.

He flashed briefly on the possibility that they might work together, she with her investigative expertise and he with his knowledge of the world of cooking and chefs. But the challenge of her words plus her look, again disdainful and dismissive, made that doubtful. He thought she'd even quickly checked his clothes for spots.

"I'm a writer," he said. "I have a blog and write restaurant reviews. Charlotte and Giorgio's deaths are tragic. And newsworthy." Not much sense in lying to her. She could check. The thing was to keep information to a minimum.

"You need to go to Montana to write about some dead chefs?"

What the hell was that supposed to mean? And for that matter, why was she going to Montana?

Jason shrugged. However unprepossessing his appearance, he was not an idiot. He could discern the subtlest of ingredients. Assess the adequate thickness of a port reduction. The difference between a perfectly cooked green bean and one that needed another twenty seconds. He could give you recipes for a dozen different masalas and tell you where you could use each.

If she wanted to stare at him like he was a cockroach under her shoe, that was on her. He folded his arms across his chest and closed his eyes. The humming of the engines was soporific and he hadn't gotten any sleep last night. He'd meant to use the trip to read over his print-outs, fill in some missing information, look for other connections, but he sure wasn't doing that where she could look over his shoulder.

"Mr. Bainbridge?"

Without opening his eyes, he said, "What?"

"Why are you going to Montana?"

Okay. She wanted conversation, he'd give her conversation. "For the story," he said.

"What can a restaurant reviewer write that other reporters won't have already done?"

"Report the details," he said.

"They've already been reported. The few that have been released." Good Lord, she was a snippy bitch. He wondered if she had any idea how she came across.

She seemed young to have been with the Bureau so long she'd lost all touch with ordinary people. Not that Jason considered himself ordinary, of course. But perhaps their basic training did that— swiftly convinced them that they had special inside knowledge the rest of the world lacked.

He'd read some crime novels. Wasn't she supposed to be attuned to nuance? To reading the subtleties as well as the grosser details? Maybe she was trying to aggravate him so he'd spill the beans just to prove he knew his stuff.

Like he'd never sat in a restaurant and had the manager try to get him to admit he was a restaurant reviewer? Like he'd never had a chef who'd served a bad meal try to talk him out of writing a negative review? Like he'd been born yesterday.

One thing reading those crime novels had taught him? Stick close to the truth. He knew what to say.

"Seriously?" he said, repressing a smile.

She nodded, all that gorgeous blonde hair shifting like golden satin against the tailored jacket. What a damned waste.

"Okay. I want to write about the food."

She stared at him blankly.

"The food," he repeated. "*Love Bites.* It was a cooking show. The bites part refers to food."

Oh, yeah. Two could play at treating the other person like a big dope.

"What about the food? They never filmed the show."

Jason imagined the unbelievable frustration the crew must have felt. Cameramen, lighting crew, sound crew. Sous chefs. All those hours of set up and preparation getting ready to tape. Prepping the perfect food and doing the cosmetic tweaks to make it look good for the camera. Light checks. Sound checks. Making the back-up food in case something went wrong.

Someone filmed something. Probably they'd filmed plenty. Possibly even the bodies. No doubt before the police arrived.

And even if the cops had taken their copies, everyone kept back-ups. Everyone had already sent that tape, those clips, somewhere. To the editors. Into the cloud. Onto their own computers. Even if they were in a state because of two dead bodies.

It was the nature of film crews. They were used to working under pressure, in difficult circumstances and with obstructive personalities. Used to finding ways to get the good shots, to make the bad look good, the unlovely look attractive, whether it be food or people.

He wondered if Kimberly knew that. If she'd spent enough time in this little world yet to have a sense of how it worked. Whether she just thought they were cooks, the way she thought he was just a nebbishy food writer. He could be dismissive, but he also knew that few people were "just" any one thing.

"I want to ask them about the menu," he added.

She was giving him that "what a doofus" look again. In another context, she would have been attractive. Here, sitting too close and treating him badly, she looked predatory and self-satisfied. Even leaning forward so he had a glimpse down into that crisp shirt, where something soft cradled in lace could be seen, he wasn't very interested. And for a guy, that was saying something.

"What about the menu?" Suspicion in her voice, like she thought he was hiding something.

He was, but it wasn't really about the menu, though that was important. It was about the milieu. Personalities, contacts, connections. It was about slights and lies and enemies.

He wriggled down in his seat and closed his eyes again. "Sorry. Didn't get much sleep last night. Do you mind?"

She muttered a "Sorry," her voice an exasperated hiss.

Chapter 9

Jason was not surprised to find Freddy Maxwell in the bar.

Crews on location spent a lot of time in bars. The alternative was to sit in hotel rooms, often pretty dismal hotel rooms, and dealing with the talent was enough to drive anyone to drink.

This bar's décor would have given a purist palpitations— it was Downton Abbey crossed with Montana hunting lodge, and the combination of chandeliers and bison heads was likely to get worse as drinking progressed. Unlike a lot of places with animal heads on the walls, the glass eyes here weren't dimmed by dust or grease, but gleamed in the subdued light as if the animals were contemplating revenge.

Freddy was, as the charming expression went, "in his cups," and his manicured fingers were wrapped around a Manhattan like a man who feared someone was going to take it away from him. He looked like someone who'd lost his job, which he had, and like someone who'd lost his last friend, which might also have been the truth.

Jason knew George and Freddy had grown up together. And he knew that producers are often unloved.

Jason introduced himself, expressed sympathy for Freddy's loss, and glanced at an empty chair. "Do you mind?"

He took the producer's nonresponse as an affirmative and settled into the chair. Hardly a second whisked by before a cute brunette in sexy cowgirl attire was at his side ready to meet his needs. Jason appreciated a well-trained staff.

He pointed at the Manhattan. "I'll have one of those." It was hard not to get swept into drinking, especially sorrow-drowning drinking, when the people around you were doing it. He didn't like Manhattans much, so it would help him stay sober.

After he'd offered up his creds, he said, "This isn't just another story for me. I knew Lottie and George. Knew them since I was a kid. Since George's dad died and the two of them had to step up and run the deli. I used to buy kosher dills from them after school."

Exactly the right thing to say. It got Freddy reminiscing and through that drink and into another, and before long, Jason was getting the inside details of what had gone on in that fancy mountain house, from the details of the menu right down to the number of knives sticking out of Giorgio's body and the way his blood had pooled on the floor beneath the rack. Right down to the material of the flooring and who else had been in the room when he found the body. No surprise since details were the heart and soul of food shows and producer's lives.

"And Lottie?" Jason asked. "Was that gruesome?"

"Peaceful as a sleeping baby," Freddy said. "Wrapped up all snug in a Hudson's Bay blanket and curled in an armchair. The only thing out of place was that overturned glass."

"Martini glass?" Jason guessed, having read the rumors of Lottie's drinking problem.

Freddy nodded.

Jason asked, "You think she killed George and then committed suicide in remorse? Because of George's indiscretion with …"

He let it go a beat and Freddy quickly filled in the blank. "Marianne. She's in a state like you wouldn't believe. She really did think that George was going to leave Lottie for her. Lottie was a lot tougher than that. She let George have his plaything because it kept him happy."

Freddy shook his well-coiffed head. "People new to the business just don't get it. Charlotte and Giorgio were a brand. The show depended on them being in love. He might screw around and she might drink too much, but neither of them was going to throw what they had away. It was a goldmine!"

He raised a finger and the attentive waitress scurried away to fetch another libation. Then he leaned in with a conspiratorial whisper. "Did I mention that Lottie's prints weren't on the martini makings? The Valentine's Day signature martini, you know, the Berry Drop. Lottie had gone all gaga over huckleberries, using a special reduction for the bison roast. She was gonna put those little fruits on the map. For the cocktail there would be berries in the glass with the huckleberry syrup. It was spectacular!"

The more Freddy drank the more he talked in exclamations. Soon, though, his words would slur and he'd get too sentimental to be useful.

Quickly Jason slipped in his essential questions, learning who else had been present, under the guise of finding out how everyone was doing, and had things been filmed, under the guise of sympathizing with how difficult it must have been to have their gorgeous set invaded and violated by the police.

Freddy enumerated his crew and assured his new friend that of course they had film and of course that film was safely stored away. As the new Manhattan arrived and Freddy dove in like a man with an unquenchable thirst, Jason broached the ultimate question.

"You must be feeling like that TV character, what's her name? Jessica Fletcher. All of these great chefs you've worked with are dead."

Freddy leaned away from him, a suspicious look on his face. "What are you talking about? Who's dead? Besides George and Lottie? Someone else?"

"Fernando?"

Freddy looked blank.

"In Miami. Fernando Gonzales. You worked with him years ago."

"Oh." Freddy still looked blank. Finally, he said, "Oh. Him. What a rat bastard." He rolled his eyes. "Do you read those books— *Kitchen Confidential,* those things? Well, working with Fernando was like undergoing the Spanish Inquisition. Nothing was ever good enough. Once he threw a knife at me. It's a wonder I survived. But you know—"

He tossed back a sheaf of bright hair that had escaped the clutches of some pretty sturdy mousse. "You know once I was out of his kitchen he was gone from my mind like a grade school lunch." He grinned a toothy grin. "You remember your grade school lunches?"

Jason frowned. "I remember gelatinous mystery meat and a blob of mashed potato served with an ice cream scoop."

"More than I do, dear," Freddy said. "So Fernando is dead? What did he die of? An excess of pâté? He had such a thing for organ meats."

Spoken with a straight face, to his credit.

Jason caught his eye. "He was murdered."

If it was possible to stagger when you were sitting down, Freddy did. His hand went to his chest like some Victorian great aunt.

Jason almost laughed, but it would have been unkind. Freddy had been nice company, and forthcoming. Besides, Jason still had other questions. The man did work in TV, after all, in a world where everything was fake. He might have learned how to fake emotion. Tossed out school lunches as a diversion.

Freddy fortified himself with some strong drink. "Murdered how?"

Jason watched his face carefully. "Shot in the head. On his boat."

If Freddy was involved, he was an incredible actor.

Jason tried out Willow's death and then Byron's without learning anything new. The only result was Freddy's hand wagging for yet another Manhattan, at the end of which Jason had to help him to his room.

Before he passed into drunken oblivion, Freddy gave his sober friend access to his computer, and Jason spent an hour of guilty pleasure tracking down all the film and filth he could find about the set, the menu, George and Lottie's murders— well-filmed details of the food and the bodies— all of which he uploaded to his computer and the cloud.

While Freddy bubbled noisily in the bed, Jason read through his email— when will people learn to password protect their worlds?— and got a greater sense of the problem with George and Lottie and Marianne and how the network honchos were getting nervous about the situation.

Maybe more people knew about this spate of chef killings? Maybe this double murder was a copycat, a cover for getting rid of some potentially messy PR problems? Jason didn't know how he'd ever find that out.

He went back down to the bar to see if anyone else from the show still lingered. No production people, just that FBI agent, Kimberly the Cold, hunched over a glass of warm golden liquid, looking much as Freddy had. Like someone who didn't have any friends. As their conversation had progressed, Jason had been surprised that Freddy was drinking alone. He had been pretty good company. In Jason's limited experience, Kimberly was not.

He had turned to go to his room when she called out, "Jason? Got a minute?"

He had all the time in the world, though probably not for her. Still, his MO, whenever possible, was not to antagonize. He never knew who in his world might inadvertently help him. Who might have an inside tip, a juicy bit of gossip or a fabulous recipe. Or who might be Top Chef tomorrow.

He ambled over to her table and waited for whatever peremptory command would be forthcoming.

She was not the kind of person for pleasantries. She gestured toward the seat across from her. "Sit down, Mr. Bainbridge."

In the time it took to cross the room, he'd gone from Jason to Mr. Bainbridge.

He waited to see what she wanted, grateful that he'd stowed his thumb drives and laptop under the seat in his rental car. He sensed that she'd have no trouble detaining him here while she had an associate toss his room. He also had no trouble imagining her sucking blood from innocents, despite the hair and the blue eyes and her perfect skin.

"In Little Neck you mentioned the deaths of two other chefs," she said. "Where did you get your information, Mr. Bainbridge, and what is your interest in these crimes?"

He decided to take the idiot's path, and simply stared at her.

"Mr. Bainbridge," she said, when it dawned that Jason wasn't going to spill his guts just because she was a cold-eyed Fed, "please answer my question."

He couldn't help himself. Even if food writing, cooking and eating was part of mainstream culture, Jason's countercultural streak went very deep. He pulled out a leaf from TV and said, "Do I need a lawyer?"

"What for, Mr. Bainbridge?"

"Why don't you tell me why you're asking your questions, and then I'll decide whether I want to answer them. Or whether I need a lawyer."

That was never how it worked with law enforcement.

He knew. His sister, an upstanding Brooklyn housewife, was married to a New York cop who sat in the kitchen while she and Jason were prepping elaborate meals and regaled them with stories of the world of crime.

Before they could resolve their stand-off, the adorable cowgirl waitress arrived and delivered a Manhattan. Evidently, she'd decided it was Jason's drink of choice. Since he'd led her to think so, he smiled and thanked her.

When she was gone, Kimberly said, "I'm waiting, Mr. Bainbridge."

He wished he could remember her last name, because "I'm waiting, too, Miss Kimberly," sounded just wrong for this conversation, like an outtake from *Gone With the Wind*. It struck him then that he was very hungry, and that drinking a Manhattan on an empty stomach, even slowly, was a particularly bad idea if he wanted to keep his wits about him.

He waved at his cowgirl and, when she arrived, asked whether the kitchen was still open. When he got an affirmative, he asked her what the chef did best.

Her grin was adorable. "This time of night, sir? I'd seriously advise you to go simple. Have the pea soup with sherry and a grilled cheese sandwich."

Don't ask for advice if you're not going to take it. One of Jason's many mottos, along with "When in doubt, reboot." And anyway, he liked his cowgirl and wanted to believe she wouldn't lead him astray. Well, okay. She could lead him astray if she wanted, but that was not in the food department. "That's what I'll have then." He looked at Miss Kimberly and raised an eyebrow.

"Sounds good," she said. "Bring me the same."

The cowgirl was about to scurry away— she seemed to like moving fast— when she remembered something. "Next time you see Mr. Freddy, can you tell him that Mrs. Bernardi's assistant has gone back to Bozeman? She said she was so upset about what happened and talking to the police and all, she just wanted to go home."

Jason nodded and said he'd give him the message. Somewhere deep in his skull, a tiny bell rang, but before he could give it much attention, Kimberly waded in again with a tiresome repetition of her "I'm still waiting."

If only a commercial break would arrive like on television.

Chapter 10

Back at his rat-hole apartment two weeks later, Jason mounted a map of the United States on the wall over his desk and stuck pins in it for the murders: Miami, New York City, New Jersey, Montana. Beside the map he tacked up a timeline: July, August, October, January.

He stared at the map. Nothing suggested a pattern.

His books on serial killers said that there would be one. The intervals between killings usually grew shorter in these sorts of murders, but that wasn't happening here. In fact, matters had moved fairly briskly with three murders in a four-month period.

In the weeks since his trip to Montana, spring had sprung and a whole new cooking season along with it. He was swamped with the new popularity of fiddleheads, a growing season so short he had to grab and report on them while he could. The hot question of whether pea tendrils were yesterday's news. And there was such an explosion of new vegan restaurants he couldn't keep up. His column about them, entitled "The World is My (Vegan) Oyster" had gone viral.

Back on Flathead Lake, the FBI agent had listened to his explanations of why he thought the murders were connected. She'd then wasted a chunk of his time probing for the "real" reasons only to bat them away. No inclination to learn anything about his world. His world. Fernando's. Willow's. Byron's. George and Lottie's world. It was annoying and condescending. And just plain stupid.

It would be like being a restaurant reviewer who didn't cook, or understand the details of preparation, or care about food. But was ready with an opinion nonetheless.

His pieces on the *Love Bites* murders had gone viral. He had recreated that last show, how incredible the menu would have been. He'd also sold a story about George and Lottie and the deli and growing up eating their pickles, and he had another editor on the hook for a second memorial piece. It might be sinful, but their tragic deaths were turning out to be a huge benefit for him.

As Giorgio and Charlotte would have said, "The show must go on."

Had there been murders he missed? Without something dramatic, it would be easy to kill without attracting attention. And if this killer crossed borders, the potential for missing a murder increased exponentially. For all he knew this killer could be knocking off a chef every week around the globe. Even the most dedicated food writer couldn't keep up with crime news from Manila to Capetown.

Could it be over? Maybe the killer had wrapped up his plans when George and Lottie Bernard cooked their last huckleberry reduction. Maybe a more promising area to explore was what Fernando, Willow, Byron, George and Lottie had in common.

Jason went back to the beginning. By all accounts, Fernando Gonzales had been a beast. A sadistic man who tortured underlings and took all the credit for himself.

Willow St. Clair had been a food snob. Unlike Fernando, she was cold. Indifferent to the people around her, Willow had lived only for the food. She had a deeper relationship with a fresh basket of rainbow beets than with anyone on her staff. Withholding praise had made her staff work all the harder, hoping to earn that single word, "Good," which was Willow's form of high praise.

It felt strange for someone to go from Fernando to Willow, from fire to ice. Even stranger to move on to Australian Byron Peppers, then wrap up with poseurs like George and Lottie.

And how did Byron fit in? He wasn't a chef at all. Not anymore. He was nothing but a talking head. All the styling of those makeovers was done by his staff. Byron was the master of painting crap yellow and calling it gold.

Of course, one thing all of these victims had in common was that they were surrounded by staff and film crews. That led to Freddy Maxwell. But nothing related to Freddy's business with the dead chefs had connected. He might be an unloved lush, but he had everything to lose with the deaths of George and Lottie.

Jason's stomach growled. He browsed the Internet, looking for leads. A click on a Michigan Cherry Festival led him to cherry pies, pie cooking contests and food festivals in general. There were boatloads of them, large and small, and until now he had mostly ignored them, dismissing the concept as small-town boosterism.

But as he made notes on various events, his eyes kept drifting toward Maine on the murder map above his computer. Lobstravaganza on the Maine coast sounded a lot more appealing than a Jerky Dry-Off.

Jason loved lobster. There was something inexorably cheery about the grabby red crustaceans. Besides, last year the festival had garnered huge publicity from the mainstream media and he suspected the public was salivating for more. Word in some circles was that this was the festival to be at this year. If you wanted to be taken seriously as an arbitrator of American cuisine, you skipped it at your own peril.

Would the killer feel the same way?

Lobstravaganza promised a focused weekend, a foodie fest of chefs vying to create the best lobster roll, lobster stew, lobster bisque, lobster appetizer and lobster entrée. It was enough to make a lobster lover's heart sing.

And a killer's.

Jason checked the map. Another draw in the opposite direction: a

Texas barbeque cook-off in the Lone Star state, the Southwest Slam. He'd long nursed a weakness for ribs. But his visibility could use a boost and Maine was where the big food personalities were headed. He reached a decision and booked a room at the main hotel hosting the event.

Relieved at having chosen a direction, he grabbed his cast iron skillet and fixed a quick scramble of organic eggs, nitrite-free bacon, smoked gouda and arugula. He ate it with toasted seven-grain bread rich with figs and indulged himself in a Lungo from his trusty Nespresso machine.

Such irony. He lived in a dump with a crappy kitchen, alley-shopping furniture, dust dragons in every corner—but he had fine cookware and the best coffeemaker around.

Maybe it was time to take a hard look at his life. Maybe a woman invited to share a bed with rumpled sheets and one corner propped up with cookbooks wouldn't understand how deeply invested he was in the world of food and cooking.

Maybe she wouldn't care.

Maybe he'd think about all this later.

Writing an article on lobster would make his upcoming trip tax-deductible and maybe bring in some change. With personal reflection successfully back-burnered, he returned to work. If he was going to be a traveling detective, he needed walking-around money.

Visions of succulent seafood danced in his head as he reread his history of the lobster and consulted his favorite cookbooks and websites for ideas for dishes that hadn't been worn as thin as the soles of a hobo's shoes.

Maine. Lobster. Yes.

Chapter 11

Kimberly Douglas was born impatient.

Much to her mother's consternation, she'd arrived in July instead of the expected September, throwing everyone into a state. While the docs had wrung their hands, popped the little preemie into an incubator and told her mother to hope for the best, little Kim had kicked the thing across the nursery, been taken out of the machine and declared a survivor.

It had been that way ever since. Her porcelain skin, sky blue eyes and honey hair, along with an irritatingly small stature, had led people to assume she was hopelessly fragile and feminine. Ambition, wit and a strong will meant she was anything but.

As an outdoorsy, tree-climbing tomboy, her appearance and the assumptions it led people to make about her had been nothing but an irritation. It was only in middle school, when she was coming into her own on the soccer field and annoyingly girlish things were happening to her body, did she realize it could give her an advantage. Eighth grade boys were fascinated by girls but also terrified by them. That meant when she played co-ed soccer, the field belonged to her.

She carried that lesson forward into her high school, college and professional life. While people were busy underestimating her because of her looks, she could scope out their weaknesses and prejudices— and then kick their asses.

When she joined the Bureau, things got harder. It was still a guy's world, but there were enough kickass women around that she had to use care and choose her spots. Still, her combination of fierce intelligence and ruthless ambition, cloaked in slender blonde femininity, served her well.

With the true sexist pigs, she'd just bat her eyes or stay silent. Guys who liked to throw their weight around and hear themselves talk didn't notice that she was listening attentively, not that they were displaying their weaknesses. She just smiled and took advantage. She could insert a stiletto with the best of them, quick, clean strikes that often went unobserved.

She was also good at seeing patterns, at pulling the relevant data out of the mountain of information collected.

She'd gotten used to winning. She liked being successful. She'd put down some really tough cases. Tracked down some very bad killers. Found and destroyed a nasty nest of would-be terrorists by befriending the leader's abused wife.

And now, faced with something as irritating and banal as someone killing a bunch of TV chefs, she'd been chasing all over the goddamned country and listening to foodie talk shows until she completely lost her appetite. With a whole lot of nothing to show for it.

This bitch of a case was frustrating the hell out of her.

Briefly back home in New York, she sat alone in the conference room with a sea of reports spread out around her, looking for a needle in this haystack. This was ridiculous. She'd have an easier time figuring out the secret ingredient in the complex sauce of the lunch special she'd just ordered in from the Cajun-Thai fusion restaurant on the ground floor.

Wait a minute. Was she thinking about secret ingredients? Complex sauces? These food people were really getting to her.

She felt like she was teetering on a fence and in danger of falling into the stewpot world they occupied. Normally, she liked to stay on the outside, getting inside enough to gather facts and understand the lore of any particular world, but not enough to become a part of it.

She knew she wasn't suited for undercover work. Somehow, protect-

ing herself from guy world and other people's expectations had made her rigid. She wasn't suited to the chameleon characteristics that made undercover
operatives successful. And this culinary world with its own lingo and insider
knowledge was harder to penetrate than a terrorist cell.

As hard to understand as why some reality TV star would grease her
ass, perch a champagne bottle on its vastness, and then show it to the world.

Sweet, sour, salty, bitter, umami.

Umami? Spiralized. Allumette.

And their knives! It was more dangerous to be in a gathering of chefs
than at a convention of motorcycle outlaws. They kept those blades incredibly
sharp and treated them better than many people treated their children. Cared
for them better, actually. She'd even heard about chefs who wore knives in
ankle holsters, much as a cop would wear a backup gun.

Only Giorgio Bernardi AKA George Bernard had been killed by knives,
of course. And he'd been drugged first, then hauled up on the moose rack by
pulley before the killer began turning the chef's own spectacularly sharp steel
against him.

The pathology report had suggested a familiarity with anatomy.
There had been a great many wounds, the report said, but they were deliberately placed, rather than indicating a frenzy. Also, there appeared to be an
element of militarism in the way the knife wounds marched in pairs down the
rib cage, in order of length, the longer cuts grouped toward the center of the
body.

Guns, knives, poison, skewers, roasting alive?

If this was indeed a serial killer, Kimberly had never heard of one
with so many different methods. And so far, other than the connecting thread
of their all having been chefs of some sort, she couldn't find another link.

There had to be one.

The passion and cruelty of the murders fairly screamed this was
someone with a grudge, quite possibly nuts— a term she could never say out

loud to anyone at the Bureau, though her colleagues would all have under-stood. But how could a crazy person have been in so many places and worked with all these people and never been noticed?

Even more disturbing than not being able to find that invisible wacko was that this was the first serial killer she'd dealt with who didn't seem to have a signature. At least none that she'd been able to find.

That was a true rarity in the annals of the Bureau.

One of the profilers had even speculated that perhaps since so much was written and televised these days about serial killers and their signatures that this killer was deliberately refusing to have one. Perhaps the killer's sig-nature was the lack of a signature.

Fernando Muller Gonzales, of Cuban and German ancestry, went pro-fessionally by his first name. He had been shot in the head on his docked boat in Miami in the early morning hours. Bisexual, Fernando had been seen the previous evening spending time with a muscular young man at the popular club Insatiable. The police questioned the young man, but he had a legitimate, if slightly unsavory, alibi.

Shootings, even execution-style, weren't unusual in Miami. Money and a few expensive watches were missing from Fernando's boat, so robbery was initially thought to be the motive. A .32 bullet was recovered from his brain, but the gun that fired it hadn't been found. The feeling was it had been tossed overboard.

Divers found nothing. It was a very big ocean.

The security gate leading to the dock was worthless. Kimberly had popped it open with a screwdriver and figured the killer had too.

Then Willow St. Clair. The poor woman had been killed by skewers through her eyes. But not, as Jason Bainbridge thought, in her swank apart-ment in New York. She had met her end five hundred miles away in her cot-tage on Ocracoke, a remote North Carolina coastal island that thrived during the summer but could be downright deserted during off-season. There had been a struggle in the kitchen of her utilitarian house, which offered minimal comforts beyond the designer kitchen. On that, no expense had been spared. The cottage was a retreat where the chef went several times a year to experiment and try out various recipes.

Isolated at one end of the island, the tiny house had no close neighbors. As a result, Willow's body had languished for days until a concerned Manhattan chef, worried when she missed a scheduled phone conference, called the local police. They found her sitting upright in a kitchen chair, long metal skewers embedded through her eyes. Bruising around her wrists indicated she had been tied to the chair when killed, but no traces of rope were found.

As clinical as a research scientist, Willow cared little for human interaction, and unlike drama queens like Fernando or Giorgio Bernardi, she wasn't shrill with her staff. She would painstakingly explain how she wanted a dish prepared and wouldn't flare up if mistakes were made. For her, the perfection of creating the dish mattered most.

As far as Kimberly could tell, her cooking show was better suited for the Science Channel than the Food Channel. Willow St. Clair had appealed to that section of the foodie crowd who were into micro, macro and dissecting food into its tiniest components.

When her murder happened, nothing had been stolen, Kimberly reflected. The local sheriff had taken good notes and she'd been through them a dozen times.

The North Carolina state detectives believed Willow had opened her door for the killer. Possibly the perpetrator had posed as a journalist— this gleaned from a search through Willow St. Clair's computer. Someone had pretended to be doing a piece for *Scientific American,* which would have piqued the ego of a chef who thought of herself as an alchemist, albeit one who measured meticulously and weighed all ingredients to the gram.

The killer had planned well and knew the quarry in both cases. This killer was working from a list. Kimberly just couldn't figure out how the killer had drawn up that list.

When Willow was killed, nobody had made a connection to Fernando Gonzales and no alarms had gone off. It was only after the roasting death of Byron Peppers that the Bureau got involved. Their cybercrimes people regularly monitored various sites keeping track of everything from white supremacist chatter to women's shoe fetishists.

Several foodie blogs, among them Jason Bainbridge's Forked Tongue, had begun speculating about a connection. Discussions and arguments bounced around cyberspace and the Bureau paid attention. Before long, there were even conspiracy theories.

Her favorite was that the murders were being committed by a group of gluten-free vegans driven crazy by the limits of their diet, a kind of culinary Manson family.

Bainbridge had made another important discovery. The heads of several cooking schools around the country had received a text at the time of Fernando's death. The text, sent from Fernando's cellphone and almost certainly swiped by the killer before being discarded, read: "I Am Shit." The phone itself had disappeared along with the gun.

Kimberly worked through breakfast and lunch, and was running on nothing but a little sugar in her coffee in late afternoon when she pushed back from her desk, disgusted. Nothing was happening. Sometimes the best thing to do was walk away and let her brain do some processing.

Time to take a break.

All of this travel was taking a toll on her wardrobe. A clumsy flight attendant had killed her favorite gray jacket, another passenger ruined her last unstained white blouse. Sitting next to an active child, she'd sustained an assault of some bright pink beverage that had done in a pearl gray silk blouse, and a wad of chewing gum left in the crease of the seat by a fellow traveler had doomed her black slacks.

Was there anyone left in the world who still thought travel was glamorous? She was leaning toward getting those Tyvek suits scientists wore in the clean rooms and donning them before every flight. That would scare the hell out of people, especially since Ebola.

Kimberly hated to shop.

In a perfect world, she would have ordered her clothes the way she ordered take out— phone it in and then answer the door. But women's clothes were designed by sadists— probably male— who had no grasp of the realities of the female body.

She was small-boned and slightly full-chested and that meant that if a blouse fit her shoulders, it gapped just where a federal agent could least afford to have a gap and still maintain her credibility. So she had to try things on. Carry double-sided tape to close those pesky gaps. Never leave home without a handful of safety pins.

Sighing, she grabbed her bag and headed for the elevator. She must go shopping. She paused at the door to glare one more time at the papers that were refusing to yield up their secrets.

* * *

On the sales floor at the glamorous Fifth Avenue boutique, she found herself immediately overwhelmed by the racks of clothing.

She should have been checking out mannequins dressed in current fashion, but instead she swept the room with a gaze trained to spot potential trouble. She was struck by how easy it would be for an assailant to hide herself in such a place. Racks at all angles. Partitions and counters everywhere. She was pondering that, on the verge of giving up and resorting to mail order, when a saleswoman approached her.

The woman was slender and fiftyish, with beautifully cut silver hair and perfect make-up. "You look like a busy person," she said. "Can I help?"

Kimberly hesitated, nonplussed by anyone assuming she needed help.

The woman continued. "Not that you look helpless. Just busy. I'm a personal shopper, you see. I work with people who need to dress well but don't have time to browse. I don't normally work the sales floor but my client just canceled her appointment." She raised perfect eyebrows. "If you'd like some help, that is."

Kimberly liked the way the woman gave her space. "How do we do this?"

After the woman had gathered Kimberly's wardrobe needs, she led the agent to a dressing room. In a moment she reappeared with an armload of black and white and gray, as Kimberly had specified. When she returned minutes later to check on Kimberly's progress, she announced she'd brought another armload of clothes. "For after work," she suggested.

The personal shopper gasped when Kimberly opened the dressing room door to reveal the shoulder holster she was trying to fit under a narrow blazer, but she recovered quickly. "Maybe you need a boxier style?"

When the door closed Kimberly couldn't help laughing at the look on that poor woman's face, and it felt good. She didn't laugh enough. That good humor made her cast a more serious eye on the second armload of clothes the woman had delivered.

It must have been all that lush prose about food. Something strange had come over her. A loosening of some inner coil, a desire for a life outside the office. Somehow Kimberly found herself standing in the dressing room wearing an insanely expensive pair of skinny black jeans, a silky black jersey with a draped neckline that stopped just short of being too low and a black leather blazer.

She swirled before the mirror. The leather was so soft and smelled so delicious she wanted to take it to bed. Actually, things had been so arid lately she'd even had a dream about that nerdy food blogger, Jason Bainbridge. Reading his column on squid ink, and the dark, briny depth just a few teaspoons could add to pasta or risotto, had led her to these interesting dark clothes. It couldn't have been his own dark outfit. Could it?

Jesus. No. The guy was an ignorant slob.

An ignorant slob whose writing had actually led her to taste that dark brine.

Argh!

She swapped the slinky top for the black shirt and stared at the mirror. God. The blazer, black jeans and black shirt made her look fabulous. Not something she could wear to work, but at one of these food festivals or cooking events? This might be just the thing.

With another sigh— sighing seemed to be her default mode today— she realized it was time to head back to work. It had been fun to stay here and be waited on by someone who was so good at this, but shopping was a luxury. It was time to focus on killers and not on how great these pants made her ass look.

However, her personal shopper wasn't quite done yet. The next armload was considerably smaller— a pair of killer black pumps, a sequined camisole, a glittery necklace and jeweled cuff to match, and a scarf she could wear with everything. The woman was good— she'd read Kimberly's longing for something interesting and was playing it perfectly.

Despite her best intentions, along with the work clothes, she left with the black outfit, the shoes and the jewelry— along with a creamy silk shirt and a pair of dark-wash jeans just like the black ones that made her ass look dynamite. Maybe tonight she'd take her ass to a bar?

Her credit card was smoking by the time the total came up. But what the hell? A girl had to cover her dynamite ass with something, didn't she?

Halfway down the sidewalk, Kimberly knew she should thank the personal shopper for the new clothes. But she had no memory of what the woman looked like. Couldn't even recall her name.

Some people seemed to fade away like that. They were there when you were talking to them, but soon after became a part of life's backdrop, invisible to all and remarkable to none.

This thought stirred a distant memory deep in her brain. She tried to grab it the way she usually did. But her thoughts flew back to those skinny jeans and that leather jacket. She smiled to herself as she swung through the revolving door onto the sidewalk.

Not such a tomboy after all.

Chapter 12

Rainbow had been getting a lot of publicity.

It was tough coming up with a new angle in today's endlessly evolving culinary world, particularly in Southern California. Hot young chef Ricardo Z, however, had managed to pull it off. His cliff side La Jolla restaurant called Rainbow, overlooking the Pacific Ocean, was color-coded. All the foods on a given day's menu had a single color in common.

A stupid gimmick, Hannah Wendt thought. She had little use for food gimmicks, or ego-driven chefs. And yet there was something primal and appealing about the notion of having, say, an entirely orange meal. It was like being the world's most indulged little kid.

Rainbow's menu changed weekly, its hues rotating every six weeks through the primary and secondary colors. Any given week's menu would be both iconoclastic and limited, and since freshness was also a Rainbow shtick, when six weeks later a color came up again, the menu would be entirely different.

It had taken nine weeks for Hannah to get a reservation for a Friday night during Red Week, her first choice since it was early summer when strawberries and cherries both were ripe. Even a mediocre chef would have trouble going wrong with fresh local fruit. In a world where people planned menus around Cool Whip, like back home in Iowa, anything was possible.

In any case, Ricardo Z had never been a mediocre chef, and in the ten years since Hannah had last seen him, he'd attained a modest national reputation, bolstered by occasional virtuoso performances on the Food Channel.

There were rumors he was up for his own series, a plan that would soon undergo a sizeable hiccup, thanks to his old buddy Hannah.

She smiled to herself, gazing around his restaurant. She didn't feel jealous of Ricardo's success. They had been colleagues once. Even friends. But that was ancient history.

Junior League Anonymous, that's what she called her look that Friday night. Tousled blonde wig, superb makeup, understated and timeless clothing. In Hannah's case, JLA usually meant black with a very expensive but muted scarf, but she'd switched to her summer look, beige layers—permanently crinkled beige silk slacks that wouldn't crease in a suitcase, a creamy silk tunic blouse and an open-weave beige linen cardigan. Always an expensive scarf tied just so.

Anonymity came easily to Hannah.

She could blend in almost anywhere. Nobody paid attention to a young woman carrying a few extra pounds, a girl with hair-colored hair and hazel eyes and a silver RAV4 with built-ins that Toyota never dreamed about. To be fair, her hair actually wasn't as dull as she'd made it. Back when she had dreams, when she aspired to the same success as the people on her list, it had been brighter, just like those dreams, blonde with copper lights and bouncy curls.

But when you want to be invisible, to minimize the risk of anyone recognizing you or throwing your humiliations back in your face, pretty hair is not an option. Dulling herself down and plumping herself up had definite advantages. Invisibility, for starters. She felt calm, sipping her first glass of red and admiring seagulls swooping out over the Pacific beyond her window table. Then he messed things up, something he was good at.

Ricardo Z, it turned out, was the gregarious sort of chef who liked to believe he was making a Personal Connection with his customers.

He came sauntering out of the kitchen when Hannah was midway through her appetizer, Red Pepper Pesto on thinly sliced artisanal sun-dried-tomato sourdough. She became aware of a slight commotion and turned to see the chef working the room, introducing himself and schmoozing, kissing fingertips as he moved among tables set for the week with red linens. The dark sultry red of Persian rugs in old money Manhattan apartments, or the rich dark red of venous blood, of course. Not gauche like scarlet. This was Cuisine, not Christmas.

The pesto caught in Hannah's throat and she felt a frisson of panic. She was not expecting this, even though the entire purpose of scouting was to learn the unexpected, the better to avoid later surprises.

She began to pay closer attention, and noticed that the interactions between chef and diners seemed to be superficial. She told herself to be calm. There was no reason to expect trouble. He'd never really seen her even when she was noticeable.

Hannah occupied the last view table on the southern end of the building, looking out over La Jolla Cove, with most of the dining room behind her. She made a point of being preoccupied with the view as the chef drew nearer.

He touched her shoulder. "Hello. I'm Ricardo Z and I want to thank you for coming to my restaurant." Friendly but slightly smarmy, with a fake Continental accent.

Hannah glanced up. Despite herself, she wanted a good, close look. And it seemed safe enough. This was a man who had never minded being appreciated, even when he wasn't much to look at.

Bad move.

While Hannah had been occupied with becoming anonymous, he'd been turning himself into something well worth looking at. He had slimmed down and now had a waist under those chef's whites. She noticed a curl of dark hair just slipping from beneath his toque and then was trapped by his chocolate eyes. She watched uncertainty flicker for a moment, followed by a sudden jolt of what could only be recognition. As she wondered how this could possibly have happened, he offered a wide, boyish grin.

"I know you!" he exclaimed. He rubbed two fingers on his right hand against the thumb in a let-me-think gesture. She was reminded what those fingers were capable of. "Got it! From Couteaux Culinary School. Annie— no, wait— Hannah. Am I right?"

This was a worst case scenario that Hannah had never considered.

First, she never anticipated that the prima donna chef would go out into his dining room for a star turn with the customers, even though she automatically had come in disguise. Besides, it had been an entire decade since their... encounter. Well, encounters. Theirs had been a very plural relationship, as in multiple orgasms.

Well, hell. Time to improvise.

"Hannah," she said, with a smile. When you're busted, you're busted.

He gave his head a friendly shake, maintaining the smile. He'd had some cosmetic dentistry done, very nicely. "From... let me think. Ohio?"

She didn't have to feign surprise, though she automatically noted that he was three states and four hundred miles off target. Still, to a Bostonian the Midwest was all interchangeable and one four-letter state with a single consonant was pretty much the same as another. "What a memory you have."

He grinned, pleased with himself. "Do you live in San Diego?"

She shook her head. "Just here on business." If he only knew.

"With your husband?"

Well, that was subtle. When it came to women, Ricky was a heat-seeking missile. Fortunately, he'd also been good in bed, though clearly he had a type of sexual ADHD. His challenge back then had been luring a constant stream of new women into his bed. Not that horny young Hannah had presented much challenge. When she was hungry, she was hungry.

She noted an awkwardness in his tone now. He hadn't progressed all that much with the social skills in ten years. Still clunky. There was no cosmetic procedure for that.

"No husband." Might as well make it easy for him.

"It's lovely to see you." He looked out the window at the clouds on the horizon. "And it looks like you're going to have a spectacular sunset tonight, compliments of the management." He dropped his voice. "Any chance you'll have time to hang out later?"

The smile turned beguiling and Hannah shrugged.

"Either way," he said, "I will make you the meal of a lifetime. And then afterward, if you let me ..."

She got lost at that point, because she was remembering a lot of things she had let him do, back in culinary school. Way back when Ricardo Z was still Ricky Zelinsky, a little bit shy and significantly chunky, but a gifted natural cook and undisputedly the best lay of her life.

Oh, hell— what was the big rush anyway?

Chapter 13

At nearly midnight the evening had wound down— or up— to this: an incredible view of the ocean with gulls and constellations pin-wheeling overhead.

Ricky and Hannah sat in comfortable chairs on a small rooftop deck looking out at the vast dark Pacific. His office was housed in a kind of cupola behind them, and if she had her bearings right, she was directly above the table she'd occupied at dinner.

Pleasant food smells from exhaust fans still lingered in the cool, moist air. It should have been quiet and dark and romantic. The adjacent buildings were empty for the night.

But dark and quiet and romantic only went so far when you were sitting right under a giant neon rainbow. Although as clichéd as the graphic choice might be, it still managed to be striking and in reasonably good taste. Ricky had gone for pastels, and the rainbow was designed to arc out over the ocean as you drove onto the bluff where the restaurant sat in its staid medical research park. On foggy days it would vanish into the Pacific mists.

They sat ten feet from the pot of neon gold in which the rainbow ended. Ten feet in a different direction, they'd passed a daybed in Ricky's office, accessed from the kitchen by a circular stairway. She had a pretty good idea where Ricardo Z intended this evening to end, and had long since concluded that with her cover blown, she might as well just enjoy herself.

Ricky had upgraded her dinner significantly, including some very nice wines, the last of which was a limited edition Merlot from a boutique Sonoma winery. The remains of that bottle now sat by their glasses on a small table between the chairs.

"I can't quite believe this. I never thought I'd see you again," he said, picking up his glass, taking a sip and leaning back. She noticed there was no particular note of regret in his voice. Despite his phenomenal recall during the star turn through the dining room, she was willing to bet she had rarely, if ever, crossed his mind during the past decade.

"Strange things happen," she told him, reaching for her own glass. Oh my, did they ever. "You seem to have done very well for yourself." Matter-of-fact, not jealous or judgmental. At least she hoped it came out that way.

He didn't say anything for a moment. "I guess I have. My old man still thinks I'm a bum, but I'm the one sitting on the roof of my own restaurant on the edge of the world. I brought him out here for the opening and you know what he said?" He assumed a working-class Massachusetts accent. "'It's like a fucking crayon box, Ricky. Who ever heard of blue food, anyway?'"

"Nobody's parents understand them," Hannah responded. Certainly it was true for her. Her relationship with her own father was, well, complicated.

He poured more wine into their glasses and set down the empty bottle. At this rate she was definitely going to have to call a cab. He said, "I've been lucky. Mind you, I think I'm a damned good chef, but good isn't enough. You know that. Great isn't even enough. Luck matters."

"Indeed it does." Assuming that it's good luck, not bad.

Ricky Zelinsky had absolutely no idea of just how lucky he really was. Hannah had begun calculating degrees of risk the moment he first stopped at her table, had felt them escalating with each passing minute and rise in blood pressure after he left. Before the Tournedos Framboise ever reached her table, she had decided to abort her entire San Diego mission.

It was Ricardo Z's lucky night.

"So what kind of business are you in that brings you to Southern California?" he asked.

"Financial management," she said. "I handle investments for a select group of clients." Me, myself and I.

"No shit? You're not doing anything with food?"

"Well, I do eat it now and again. Splendid dinner, by the way. But no, I've never really done much professionally in the food world." She'd had enough wine that she had to consciously resist the temptation to add: Other than roasting and skewering the deserving.

He shook his head. "I just figured the only reason people went to Couteaux Culinary School was to get into the restaurant biz. Too damned expensive otherwise."

He emptied his glass. "I need to hire you. I could use a little financial management."

"Not taking any new clients just now," she said easily. This conversational gambit had come up before and was generally where she changed the subject.

She didn't have to. Down below a door slammed and a moment later, a car engine coughed and caught.

"There goes the last guy from the kitchen," Ricky said. "We're all alone now, if you're worried about your virtue or your reputation."

Hannah laughed. "No longer issues, either one."

"Well, then," he began, and at that moment the neon rainbow switched off. "Was my timing always this great?"

"In your dreams, quick-draw." She saw a momentary wince and knew that he remembered. She had drawn first blood. "But I won't pretend this isn't pretty damned cool up here. Even more so in the dark."

"You were my first real..." He hesitated and she wondered where he was going. Conquest? Punchboard? Not girlfriend for sure, or even friend with benefits, really. And lover would certainly never work. Too much raw, explorative sex. Fuckbuddies, that's what they were.

"And vice versa," she added, leaving the statement unfinished. No reason to be mean. He was like that turkey they pardoned every November on the White House lawn, and he didn't even know it. So what the hell? Might as well celebrate. "We tried a lot of stuff. It was almost like some kind of big science fair project."

"Science was never that kind of fun. But I think we earned a lot of blue ribbons, Hannah."

"Best of show," she told him. "I don't suppose that little daybed in there has wheels on it?"

Even in the dark, she saw his smile widen, a regular old Cheshire cat. "No, but it's really light. Give me a hand."

"I'll give you a lot more than that," she told him, kicking off her shoes and standing up.

Just a little wobbly, not enough to be a problem. Everything tonight had gone very differently from what she'd planned, but this could be an unexpected pleasure. Ricky had become quite an accomplished lover by the time they split ten years ago. If he'd even halfway maintained his skills, this night had a lot of potential.

They really had approached their sex life like a science project. They had talked a lot about it— earnest, grad school-type discussions— and had actually picked up a couple of manuals. Working through those was a challenge, but they rose to it, Ricky in particular.

For a spell, their Hot Sex 101 tutorial had taken a lot more of Hannah's attention than culinary school, which should have told her something right then and there. Food wasn't her only passion. From the dinner she'd just eaten, it was clear that Ricky Zelinsky hadn't been letting his culinary studies slide. Perhaps it was time to check on the progress of his other talents.

"I want your clothes off first," she told him now, unbuttoning the white chef jacket, thinking how nice it was that she'd taken time yesterday to have her nails done, using the fresh manicure to trace a pattern on his soft skin. He helped with the sleeves, and then stood shirtless as she undid the white trousers and slipped them and his boxers slowly to the ground.

Hello again, old friend.

She stepped back and took a long appraising gaze.

"You look real good," she said, slowly removing the expensive scarf.

She knew what he would ask for, and until the very moment of the request she didn't know if she would oblige. The thought, the memory, was a stimulant all by itself.

He began removing her clothes with a finesse she didn't remember, then ducked briefly into his office for a condom. Then Hannah was lost in the give and take of the moment. Ricky claimed to be five-nine but their bodies fit together as smoothly as if they'd never been apart. After a moment, as if choreographed, they pulled apart to bring the bed out. The mattress was hard but she barely noticed.

Lying there with the surf pounding below and a smattering of stars above would have been amazing even if he hadn't been so deliciously exploring her body with his delicate fingers and searching tongue. She reciprocated, feeling ocean breezes caress their bodies in the velvety night.

Then Ricky stood suddenly and pulled her to her feet. "Bend over, Betty Lou." It was the rough drawl he'd always used for the redneck persona he perfected at culinary school. Role-playing in his apartment was a lot more fun than role-playing in the motivational management courses she had taken later in her MBA course.

"Gonna make me, Hank?" Fist cocked on her hip, moonlight washing on her breasts, she matched his twang. Hank and Betty Lou had few boundaries— they had been, they once joked, the poster children for screwing your brains out.

It was all coming back. Hannah realized how wonderful it had been before... well, before he ruined it all so totally. She brushed those thoughts away.

He stepped toward her slowly. "Yeah, Betty Lou. I'm gonna make you. Now!"

He pointed at the railing and God help her, without even thinking about it, she obeyed. Giving the railing a shake to see if it was sturdy enough, she found it sufficiently unyielding, then leaned out over the top rail and braced herself with hands clenched on the outside of the lower bar.

"I wanna hear you howl, Betty Lou."

And there it was. At that moment she knew she would do it.

As their bodies joined she heard his breath intake behind her and after that it was just as she remembered it. But now they weren't in his crummy student apartment with the dingy carpet and battered Salvation Army furniture. Now whitecaps broke down below and the surf pulsed right along with them.

She raised her head and cried out over the ocean, "Ahhh— ooh!!!" and behind her Ricky muttered in a deep low voice, "Werewolves of London." She howled again, louder this time, hearing her wail soar out into the dark night.

It was so good that it took a minute to realize that her blonde wig had flown off into the ocean. That baby was probably halfway to Catalina.

But Ricky didn't want much in the way of explanations, about the wig or anything else. She got lucky there, and what little information she volunteered mostly wasn't true anyway.

She had no office in Chicago or client in Rancho Santa Fe. She did not originally hail from Columbus, nor was she widowed, a line she often used in airport bars.

Ricky had honed his sexual skills as diligently as his culinary ones, and Ricardo Z seemed to be relentlessly randy. He had almost certainly discovered that the culinary world attracted its own sort of groupies, bored rich women who yearned for sex on the butcher block or granite counter, with interesting applications of copper utensils.

They fell into a pheromone slumber on a blow-up bed between silk sheets under down covers, all conveniently stashed in special cupboards in the office. No one could say that Ricardo Z wasn't prepared.

* * *

Hannah awoke startled, unsure where she was or why there were seagulls buzzing her. Then it all flooded back.

The failed reconnaissance. The splendid meal with the corny rubicund theme and the too-abundant wines. Followed by...

Oh, dear God. Had she truly howled into the night with orgasmic abandon, re-enacting scenes that had led to one of her most horrid humiliations?

Well, yes.

It would have been an interesting topic to take up with a therapist, if she had one who was willing to listen to tales of planned and abandoned murder schemes. Failing that, she at least needed to make some new plans.

Ricky, stirring beside her, had gotten an eleventh-hour reprieve. And the hell of it was that he would never even know.

"What a lovely surprise," he murmured, and she wondered whether he meant finding her there, or the night before, or the apparent coincidence that had landed her in his restaurant.

She could smell baking bread, and realized that somebody had already arrived in the kitchen below. She imagined the cook slipping sun-dried-tomato sourdough into the oven and whipping egg whites for a raspberry torte. God, she was hungry.

Then a glance at Ricky made her lose her appetite.

Suddenly everything felt awkward. This was Ricky Zelinsky, for whom she'd made such plans. Desperate, deliberate, homicidal plans.

His body glowed against the silk sheets, a lot more toned than her own. She had broken all the rules of her quixotic mission of vengeance and now his hands were moving on her body underneath the silk sheets. She had lost control. She had no idea what she was doing or why. The truth was that she had been powered by rage for so long that she felt rudderless now that she was briefly content.

That was not Hannah. Hannah was never content.

But existential questions could wait, because now he was reaching for another condom and soon they were gently riding the morning breezes in the missionary position. Which was not enough to elicit any more howls, though it was mighty nice.

Only when she stood on the deck, wrapped in the silk sheet, did she realize that any number of scientific researchers with lab windows overlooking the ocean had been perfectly positioned to watch them start the day with lustful vigor.

She did her own star turn, wrapped in the sheet, then bowed toward the unseen audience.

Chapter 14

There were issues, of course.

After they dressed and went downstairs, she sat at the same window table where she had hoped to avoid his attention barely twelve hours before. He disappeared into the kitchen and returned with shitake omelets, fresh raspberries and an astonishing pot of coffee made from beans excreted by monkeys on some hidden South Pacific island plantation

She had done her best to tidy her rumpled Junior League disguise, but the pre-crinkled pants now looked as if they'd been shoved into an old gym shoe overnight, and her silk blouse had somehow ended up beneath the blow-up bed, picking up a few splinters. The scarf had disappeared altogether and was probably adrift in the ocean with her wig.

Ricky, meanwhile, was dressed in a fresh set of culinary whites, including a toque that she suspected had a condom dispenser hidden inside.

"How long are you in town?" he asked as she lit into the omelet. Last night had offered a lot more exercise than she was accustomed to. She was ravenous.

"Just through the weekend," she told him. "I finished with my client yesterday."

"We're open today for lunch and dinner. Tomorrow, brunch only, and then Monday we're closed. Tuesday, we go purple. Care to stick around and play? You're welcome to eat here, of course."

"I'd gain four hundred pounds if I ate all my meals here," she answered. "And I do need to head back east. But I have a bit of flexibility."

His grin was raw and filled with lust. "More than a little, if I'm remembering last night correctly."

She was ready now. The question was— was he? "About the howl," she said abruptly.

He tore off a piece of baguette, all nonchalance. "Yeah?"

Did he not even remember? Was that possible?

"The party at the Del Rio." She watched his eyes, saw the same flicker of memory she'd witnessed last night.

The reason she was here, of course. Something she'd never forget.

At the conclusion of the third of the four segments of study in the Couteaux Culinary School course, everyone had gathered for a dinner prepared by themselves. Ricky had been nervous about his Funghi con Pomodorini, which went perfectly and was well received.

Task finished, he got drunk in a hurry.

And announced, very loudly, "Ahhh-ooooh, ahh-oooooohh" with his own basso interlude of "Werewolves of London." Which was bad enough, but then he continued, in the same stentorian tone, "That's how Hannah howls when I'm fucking her. Ahh-oooh..."

Everybody laughed. Nervously at first and then full on. They didn't just laugh.

They howled.

As Hannah realized the horror of what had just happened, how her privacy and her pleasure had both been so hideously violated, she did the only thing she could think to do. She walked out the door, abandoning the perfect éclairs she had prepared for the group dessert, and never returned to the Couteaux Culinary School.

As she fled, she could hear the receding howls, and she heard them in her nightmares for... well, far too long.

Now, remembering it all, she surveyed Ricky's face in a sort of split-screen with Then on the left and Now on the right.

"I was really an asshole," he said. Straightforward, no hesitation. A lot of Boston in his voice. "I was loaded, but that's no excuse."

She said nothing.

"I am so... Very. Sorry." He paused a moment and smiled shyly. Those social skills actually weren't nearly as bad as she'd first thought. "Can you forgive me?"

She let a moment pass, then another. Just when it was about to become really uncomfortable, she gave him a tiny smile.

"Maybe."

Hannah's schedule was actually quite flexible.

She had planned her itinerary weeks ago for a Southwest-to-Northeast, corner-to-corner, all-American road trip.

Hannah had discovered, well into adulthood, that she loved to travel, that she indeed possessed a serious gypsy streak. An open highway and an open week were a special kind of joy to her, and she had been really looking forward to the trip.

Now she wondered.

The next place she absolutely had to be was the Maine Lobstravaganza, three thousand miles away. Maine was about as far as you could get from San Diego and still be in the USA. It was a command performance. Someone badly in need of her attentions was going to be there.

Also, she didn't think it would really be too tricky. Maine was such a backward state no one would expect anything unusual to happen.

She had intended to drive the northern route, which was at its prettiest and most passable in summer. She'd skip Montana, of course. No reason to show up in any jurisdiction where she'd been before.

The entire trip would be a joy, and she'd been really looking forward to it. Finding the rhythm of the highway and moving through the vast countryside.

A long drive, from sea to shining sea.

America. It was so heartbreakingly beautiful.

She had no idea where this wanderlust had come from. Until she was twenty-one the farthest she had been from her Iowa home was Chicago.

But over time, being on the move had become ingrained, defining her almost as much as her quest for vengeance.

After leaving the Couteaux Culinary School, she finished an MBA to shut up her father about being responsible for herself, but he didn't really want her in his world and she didn't really want to go back to Iowa.

She particularly didn't want to go back to Iowa.

While she was in college, her financial situation had taken a sharp turn for the better. She now owned a large chunk of an agribusiness created from her cousins' family farm.

This change in fortune had occurred as an out-of-the-blue inheritance from a great aunt who probably feared that her brother's chubby young granddaughter would never find a man and should at least be provided for.

She'd felt herself at an impasse, after B-school, and while she tried to figure out what to do, she put some of her recently acquired skills into practice. She discovered an aptitude for picking stocks that could only attributed to alchemy and managed to make a great deal of money from a modest little pile in about six months.

She rewarded herself with a month in New Orleans, taking a couple of cooking classes and visiting the city's fine restaurants.

It suited her. She didn't have to interact with anyone she didn't want to, ate some astonishing meals, got to fiddle around in somebody else's big kitchen with gumbo and crawfish étouffée and silky pies. Breakfast every morning was café au lait and beignets.

Somebody else always did the dishes.

And then one day she was tired of New Orleans and moved on, deciding that it might be fun to wander around the Puget Sound. Just how much seafood could a girl eat, anyway? Quite a lot, it turned out.

Initially, she returned to her condo in Council Bluffs between culinary excursions. During one of these breaks, she binge-watched the Food Channel, analyzed how the shows worked, developed her own recipes and had an idea she desperately wished she'd kept to herself. That ambition would haunt her always. She could push the memory down most of the time.

Luckily she was as good at compartmentalizing her emotions as she was at picking stocks.

She could handle her finances and investments from anywhere with her laptop. She had her RAV4 retrofitted with camouflaged compartments where she stored things she didn't want the world to see. She assembled a set of cooking essentials that she couldn't count on finding in extended-stay kitchenettes: Japanese knives, special spices, a good blender, a mortar and pestle, quality sauté pans.

She would pick a destination, make a reservation and go. Piece of cake. Or crab. Or habanero chili.

She perfected techniques for reliably obtaining sex on the road. Ricky's initiation had awakened a part of her that couldn't be denied for long. She could usually hook up with a man by visiting the nicer bars in airport hotels. Here she'd have a choice of bored fellows on the road for business, willing to have a little fling. After all, Jenny or Carrie Jean or Piper never needed to know.

She developed a specialized trolling wardrobe: dark silk skirt and ivory blouse with spiky, I'm-not-as-reserved-as-you-might-think pumps that were a little difficult to walk in but accented her legs, perhaps her best feature after the breasts her extra weight had given her.

She'd sit by herself sipping a martini, at a window if possible. It was not uncommon to have to shake off two or three guys before one came along who met her specifications.

Not too good looking, not a super great body, the kind of guy who got passed right by when the young hotties were on the prowl. A wife and a kid or two back in Orlando or Dallas. She tipped the bartender generously in advance and acted every inch the lady.

On her travels, she sometimes took cooking classes or got temporary gigs for cooking shows or prepping at foodie events. She had her authentic resume, which showed her experience at Couteaux Cooking School, massaged a touch to declare graduation, and a second one in the name of Ellen Bartkus, with totally fake credentials.

Ellen Bartkus had a dark bob and tortoiseshell glasses and wore too much red lipstick. She favored shapeless clothes and really knew her way around a kitchen. She could be a competent sous chef or a gifted food stylist, as the situation required.

So far, no one had ever checked either resume. The credentials on both were virtually identical, but experience demonstrated that people treated Ellen far worse than they treated Hannah. Hannah came to believe that brown hair and beige clothes brought out the worst in people, as did smeared glasses.

None of this was what she'd had in mind when she accepted her magna cum laude degree in Finance from the University of Iowa and set off to the Couteaux Culinary School to become a chef.

But there was no reason to be maudlin, not when she was actually having a pretty good time. The world wasn't going to end or her mission go unfulfilled if she skipped the cross-country drive and stuck around San Diego for a while. What was the point of freedom if you couldn't exercise it now and then and change your plans? She could always fly to freaking Maine and rent a car there. She could afford it. After all, she was still in control. Captain of her own fate, and that of so many others.

But enough of revenge, at least for now. Instead she pushed all that out of her mind and took a few minutes to relish memories of newly-toned, still-smokin' Ricky Zelinsky.

Ahh-oooh. Let the howling begin.

Chapter 15

Jason Bainbridge had prepped hard for Maine, immersing himself in lobster, well aware that all culinary eyes would soon be firmly fixed on all things crustacean. If he wanted to be taken seriously as a food blogger, attendance at Lobstravaganza was mandatory. But if he wanted to stand out, he'd really need to know his stuff before he got there. As he boned up on the history of the once-lowly lobster, he kept an eye on the news, almost creeped out by the silence. Things had been too quiet on the killing front. He had a bad feeling something was coming; it felt like the lull in an Italian wedding hall feast— the one right before the long line of waiters entered the dining hall carrying platters of flaming cherries jubilee. Someone was planning a big move.

Happily, his deep dive into the world of all things lobster had been well-received and he was heading to Lobstravaganza with some serious change— and street cred— in the bank. His compilation of innovative recipes, "A New Look at Lobster," had sold to a major Maine magazine, while his blog post, "Pegged," had stirred up controversy about whether current methods of handling lobsters were inhumane. He didn't give a rat's ass about treating crustaceans tenderly, but he was learning where and how to push buttons. Especially effective had been the photos of lobstermen with bleeding hands and the video of unpegged lobsters savagely tearing off each other's claws. Vicious, delicious beasts.

But June in Maine, Jason discovered, was still freaking cold. It hit him the moment he arrived. Maine was a walk-in freezer with no door out.

Boothbay Harbor, site of the preliminary cook-off to determine which chefs would compete in Lobstravaganza, was a peninsula sticking out into the Atlantic Ocean. The North Atlantic Ocean, the one bobbing with icebergs, the one brought to fame by the Titanic.

The sea was a fierce and choppy blue, the harbor dotted with little fir-clad green islands. The wind felt as if he'd accidentally taken a wrong turn and driven to the North Pole.

Despite the biting cold, locals seemed to think it was summer and were strolling around in shorts and T-shirts, eating ice cream and fudge and having a jolly good time. Or maybe they weren't locals. Maybe they were Eskimos who'd come south to enjoy a more balmy climate.

The first thing he did after he'd checked into his hotel was head out to the nearest store and buy a sweatshirt. His choices, once he eliminated all the ones with hideously cutesy sayings, were lobsters, moose or puffins. (The puffins were particularly annoying; he'd have to find some tasty recipes for them.) After pawing through the racks, he found a sweatshirt in basic black— his new signature color— that proclaimed his location: "Maine."

Then he went back to his room, an extravaganza of chintz that gave him heartburn, and logged onto the hotel WiFi to pull up the cook-off schedule. If, like the rest of big-name food world, the killer had followed Jason to Maine, they would likely be targeting someone prominent as their next victim, a chef with some name recognition and, if past patterns prevailed, also some serious personality issues. A visiting culinary dignitary, someone well enough known elsewhere to rate the VIP treatment here. Someone with a reputation as a diva or a dick.

Chefs who didn't work at local restaurants would be using the kitchens of restaurants that weren't open for breakfast, he learned. Starting at nine in the morning, the judges would wander from venue to venue to taste the resulting dishes. Not a bad way to start the day.

If the killer was indeed at Lobstravaganza, the intended victim did not have to be one of the competing chefs, Jason suddenly realized. The killer's target could well be one of the judges, many of whom were local restaurant owners lending out their kitchens to the festival competitors.

Jason thought about the past killings. They had been intimate in a sense. All had hit close to home, or close to the source of each victim's fame, the staging intended to be invasive, humiliating and up-close-and-personal. The more he thought about it, the more he felt he was on to something: If the killer were here and intended to strike, they'd choose someone local and take them down on their own battleground. That meant the next victim was probably local, well-known and a jerk. Now he was getting somewhere. It was almost... exciting to walk in the killer's shoes.

As he pored over the schedule, noting the competitors and judges, even vetting local chefs who were no more than observers at Lobstravaganza, he dismissed many as too unknown, too insignificant, too beloved, too much of a stranger in this strange land. He needed someone local and ripe for humiliation... The moment he saw his name, Jason knew he had him: Buddy Bean. Buddy Bean was the killer's next target. A thrill ran through Jason as he contemplated the possibility that he was right. And then a chill replaced the thrill as he realized how fully he was channeling the killer. He'd chosen Bean because, out of all the celebrities large and small at Lobstravaganza, Bean was clearly the lead contender for Most Likely To Die. He was well known, on his home turf and, most of all, regarded as an asshole. But asshole or not, Jason had to get to Bean first and warn him. No one deserved to die the way this killer liked it to go down.

Jason checked the schedule again. The theme of the day was entrees. According to the write-up in the local paper, Buddy Bean would be lending the kitchen at his eponymous restaurant, Bean's, to a chef from Rockland whose own restaurant was on everyone's "top in the country" list. That had freed Bean to be among the wandering judges.

But where, Jason wondered, would Buddy Bean be hanging out while the signature dishes were being prepared? Who would he be rubbing elbows with? Whose chain would he be unwittingly yanking?

Or, like Byron Peppers at the Grotto in New Jersey, would Buddy Bean not even make it to the starting bell?

Chapter 16

The woman known to some as Ellen Bartkus studied her laptop in the elegant Maine inn overlooking the harbor as she pondered the schedule of one Buddy Bean.

It had been hard to leave the insanely good weather of Southern California behind. But the further away she got from the endlessly blue skies and sandy beaches, the more she could feel her quest for vengeance returning. And the more she felt like herself: strong, determined, unstoppable.

The rich twinkle of the inn annoyed her; fancy places like this paid more attention to their guests and she was in search of anonymity. But the more modest reservation she'd made at a Comfort Inn had been bungled by some idiot clerk, and it turned out that most of the other rooms in town were full and, from the looks of it, full of lots of local tourists. Who would have thought these down east bumpkins would be such foodies?

She had expected the cook-off before the festival to be her best chance to target Buddy Bean, rather than the lobster competition itself. There would be no more than a handful of chefs, food writers and wealthy locals to slip past, she had hoped. Instead, it seemed that anyone with the slightest interest in food in the entire Northeast had shown up. Not to mention plenty of national names.

It was going to make her work much harder.

She'd only been in Maine a few hours. Despite the refreshing salt air and scenic views and a dazzling array of shops selling fudge, she was already sick of it. The entire state seemed to pride itself on bad puns and cutesy titles. She'd seen enough Mainelys, Manelys, moose tracks, Lobstah and other Maine-related brands to last a lifetime.

If she hadn't been on a more important mission, she could have made a bundle here using her financial and marketing savvy to bring these people into the twenty-first century. Now, as she sharpened her knives and mixed up some delicate powders in her mortar and pestle, she amused herself by re-calling the silliness of the shop names: I Scream Ice Cream, Hammer and Claw, Bottomfishers. If it was local color they wanted, she could give it to them.

Her research had turned up lots of information about Buddy Bean as a businessman. The man who believed he was too good for her also believed in vertical integration, dipping his entrepreneurial toe into every aspect of lobstering. He'd started working in a lobster shack in high school, then ex-panded it into a restaurant and added a catering business that did clam bakes and lobster bakes on a nearby island. Then, in order to assure himself of a steady and affordable supply of lobsters, he had himself some boats and hired crews to run them.

Increasingly, she realized, he had come to believe himself invincible and above the law. In an area where lobstermen were extremely territorial and the sacred places where they set their traps handed down from father to son, he had poached, stolen, bullied, bribed and generally done whatever it took to get his hands on prime lobstering territory.

Cleaned up, he might look like a respectable businessman, but un-derneath he was somewhere between a thug and pirate. One who thought he was too good for the likes of her.

Hannah's newest information about Buddy Bean's lobster business had been delivered in an extended monologue from the old geezer who served her lunch. The place looked like it was about to tumble into the harbor and the guy who fixed her food looked about to tumble into his grave, but the fried fish sandwich was fresh and crisp in a batter so light and airy it was like eating crunchy clouds prepared for the angels.

It had taken her forty-five minutes to get the recipe out of him, secret ingredients that included beer and whipped egg whites.

The codger winked at her and said that Buddy Bean had been trying to get that recipe for fifteen years. At that point she had steered the conversation toward Bean's business activities.

Hannah had first crossed paths with Bean years ago at a marketing conference in Santa Fe, spotting him in the exhibit halls towering above most of the other attendees. Later she had instantly noticed him at the fancy bar off the hotel lobby, his tall frame perfectly suited to the elegant fixtures and dark lighting. Back in those days, she was still in the early phases of learning how to pick up men in bars and she had lacked the nerve to make the first move herself. Until then.

Determined to channel her inner power, she had watched Bean sitting at the bar, scanning the crowd, his gaze barely lingering on the women before moving on, as if he were looking for something better. He was handsome, or at least not bad looking compared to her other choices, all men who fell into one of two categories: chubby, hipster chefs with burgeoning beards to cover their double chins, or weary middle-aged businessmen who looked like they knew they weren't getting laid once they returned home and so had pinned their hopes on a miracle happening on the road. Bean was taller than all of them and strong in the shoulders with ruddy skin that reminded her of open air and high seas.

She had mistook his stature for manliness and approached him the moment a bar stool opened up next to his. Excitement coursed through her at the thought she was making the first move. Sliding into place, she let her thigh brush against his hip and playfully raised an eyebrow at him as she slid her wine glass across the polished mahogany toward the bartender, practically inviting Bean to buy her a drink.

He had glanced at her briefly than looked away, bored, dismissing her with a single glance.

Determined, she had touched his arm and asked playfully, "Don't I know you?"

She would never forget what happened next. Bean had let his gaze run slowly from the top of her head all the way down her torso to her feet and back up again, until he was looking her square in the face with a no longer blank, but utterly disdainful, expression. "I doubt it," he said curtly. "I don't have to pay for it."

Then, as if she were contagious, he had given the bartender a dark look, picked up his glass, and walked abruptly away to another side of the bar.

Too shocked to move, she sat there, stunned and humiliated. But the worst was yet to come.

"You can't work it in here, sweetheart," the bartender announced loudly. Several solo men at the bar turned her way. "We're not that kind of an establishment. You'll have to take it elsewhere or I'll call security."

With horror bordering on hysteria, she realized that Bean and the bartender had assumed she was a prostitute, a hooker, a call girl on the prowl for johns.

Putting her head down, she slid from the bar and hurried toward the exit, face burning. But she was not fast enough. A man from the bar caught up with her at the door. He grabbed her by the arm and jerked her to a halt.

"Not so fast, sweetheart," he said with a grin. "How much for the whole night?"

She backhanded him and sent him flying into a chair. He bounced off it and stumbled onto a nearby cocktail table. Its inhabitants looked up, alarmed, and she saw the fear in their faces. She had fled then, anxious to forget Bean's humiliating rejection.

She had never been able to forget.

* * *

She hadn't seen Bean since and doubted that he'd remembered her beyond that one conference but, just in case, she had come to Maine as Ellen Bartkus, the bespectacled brunette who blended into any background. On the rare occasions when she found herself second-guessing her choice of Buddy as her next victim, a few minutes of remembering how he had treated her banished any doubts. Any man who treated a woman like that deserved to die.

Besides, her doubts rose less and less often these days, replaced now by an almost sexual delight in exacting her revenges. Frolicking with Ricky had rekindled other appetites as well, beyond the sexual, until she was just a humming bundle of needs.

Sex and death. They went together so well.

Here was her dilemma: On the one hand, she wanted to dispatch Bean while minimizing the risks of getting caught. On the other hand, she wanted him to suffer. No. She needed him to suffer, to feel the humiliation of being in her power. And there was a second dilemma as well. She had two different scenarios in mind for Bean's demise.

She'd learned online that part of his shtick was that he was personally cooking the lobsters whose meat would be used by the cook-off chefs. He had an apparatus that looked like the cargo net used to hoist large goods off ships. It would be loaded with lobsters before being lowered into a huge stainless steel pot where the lobsters would be boiled. Her plan was to get him into that net among the lobsters.

She knew from things she heard over the years that she wasn't the only victim of Bean's disdain for women. Far from it. He had a reputation of using and discarding women he worked with like last week's Kleenex. So alternatively, she had considered putting him, alive but helpless, into a tank of lobsters and letting them go at him with their big claws. That only seemed fair. Indeed, this had been her favored method— until she learned that all of the lobsters had pegs in their claws. At best they'd only tickle him.

That was when she worked up a third scenario— one that involved cleavers and lobster bait. Chopping off appendages, and one appendage in particular, while Bean was still alive appealed to her sense of justice and fun. But it might be difficult to find a place she could operate. It probably required more planning than simply arriving and watching for an opportunity.

No. It would have to be Plan A. The net. The winch. The boiling water.

Both of her ploys to get in on the inside had failed. She'd emailed from one of her temporary Hotmail accounts to see if participants could watch Bean during the lobster cooking portion of the cook-off, and had gotten the curt reply that Mr. Bean would be doing the cooking at his restaurant around four in the morning and the event would not be open to the public.

Nor had there been any opportunities to become part of the cook-off staff. She'd just have to improvise, something she was getting pretty good at. At least she was well-rested. She had indeed ended up sticking around San Diego longer than she anticipated, then flown into Boston instead of driving cross-country. A rental car suited her needs just fine and was even more anonymous than the murdermobile.

On her way into town, she had scoped out Bean's restaurant. The net, hoisting apparatus and huge boiling pot were outside the back door, next to enormous tanks that held the lobsters. The site would be easy to approach, and the neighboring buildings were all commercial properties that ought to be vacant at the appointed hour. It might almost look like an accident, she thought. Except for the lobster she planned to ram up his ass. Anyone who hated women as much as he did would no doubt enjoy the experience.

Chapter 17

"Baked, boiled or broiled?"

For a moment, Kimberly thought the waitress was asking her about the latest murder. It was a fair question, if a trifle impertinent. And when the waitress repeated the question, it stirred Kimberly out of her musings and back into the rustic room hung with fishnets and old glass floats. In front of her, a fake candle flickered in an amber glass holder.

Another culinary murder, after weeks of quiet. She had arrived in Maine that morning, just hours earlier. After so many weeks she'd hoped the spree was over. Now she felt, well, at sea. Unmoored. Adrift. How many seafaring metaphors were there? She blinked to clear her thinking.

Murder by boiling. Was broiled next? There weren't many cooking methods left.

Also, was she really jaded enough to be eating lobster only an hour after observing the boiled red body of one Hank "Buddy" Bean lying on a morgue slab with a lobster shoved up his ass?

Well, yes. She was. She'd seen some cruel, horrible things. This murder ought to have put her right off her feed, but the fresh sea air, after the flight into Portland then a drive down here, had left her starving. She couldn't wait to tear that red shell apart and dip chunks into lemon butter. She was even prepared to wear one of those corny lobster bibs they foisted on tourists.

When in Maine, she thought, and smiled at the waitress. "Boiled," she said, "and extra sour cream and butter with my potato."

She started to laugh, which seemed to disconcert the waitress. Kimberly recognized laughter as inappropriate but somehow couldn't stop. It beat thinking about what Buddy Bean had looked like, his skin scalded scarlet and peeling off in shreds.

And if a lobster up the ass wasn't bad enough, the coroner had also found a whole lemon shoved down Bean's throat. Probably post-mortem. A garnish, not a weapon.

Were the killings getting more extreme? More personal? All of these crimes felt personal, but surely the insertion of a lobster into a delicate portion of the victim's anatomy added a note of exceptional intimacy and anger. And so far, Mr. Bean was an enigma compared to some of the other victims who had been living in HD, splashed across TV screens from coast-to-coast. Sure, he was well known in some circles, but compared to the television personalities dominating the food channels these days, he was far from the madding crowd.

What had he done to incur such wrath?

Deciding to live dangerously, she asked the waitress for a glass of chardonnay. When the wine arrived she said, casually, "Isn't it awful what happened to Buddy Bean?"

The waitress stopped dead, hands on her ample hips, and leaned back with an odd smile on her face. "You aren't from around here, are you?"

The agent shook her head.

"Because you'd know," the waitress continued in a rush, "when the cops go looking for whoever did this to Buddy, they're gonna have a job of work on their hands. Ain't many people around here didn't want him dead, other than his wife, his mistress and maybe his best friend Jake Pomeroy, and I wouldn't be too sure about them."

Kimberly took a sip of her wine. She was sure the same killer was responsible; this had all the earmarks of a revenge killing. Like the others, Bean had been put on display.

But the waitress's announcement of the general dislike for Buddy Bean was bad news. It could mean a raft of things, starting with the possibility that this was simply a local crime. Or maybe a copycat crime by someone who'd read about the other chefs and decided to use the cook-off as a cover.

"Take a look around you," the waitress said, "Half the town's out celebrating tonight."

Kimberly glanced around the restaurant. She hadn't noticed how joyful the people were. Now she saw smiles everywhere. Big smiles, soft laughter, with louder guffaws coming from the adjacent bar. She'd never seen anything like it. Murder in a small town would normally shock and frighten locals, sending them to huddle behind locked doors. These folks acted as if the home team had just taken a state championship.

While she'd been examining Buddy Bean's crime scene, the whole town was celebrating his ghastly death.

She held her breath, trying to catch conversations from other tables. Snatches came to her.

"That lobstah was a nice touch..."

"It a been me, I'd a used him for bait."

"Ain't a lobstah in that whole ocean'd touch a piece of Buddy. He was mean clear through."

"I heard Susie done it, just purely fed up with him carrying on with Melissa right before her face like that. Not that Buddy ever cared what people thought."

Okay. Buddy sounded like a real asshole, but that wasn't grounds for murder. Despite the fresh air and the views out over the picture postcard harbor, Kimberly was getting a headache. These people were about five minutes away from grabbing pitchforks and holding a dance.

She drank her wine too fast. This case must really be getting to her because Kimberly's rule was one glass, sipped slowly, and she loved her rules. She closed her eyes, wishing all of this away, wishing her boss had given her a decent assignment, something that didn't involve food or yokels celebrating death or a serial killer who refused to act like a proper serial killer.

An assignment that didn't include unforgettable mental images of a boiled red lobster protruding from the boiled red ass of a boiled red man.

She considered canceling the lobster and going upstairs to clean her gun. She liked to clean her gun. The sharp smell of gun oil, the comforting ritual of the process, the heft of it in her hand when it was done. So satisfying.

But she was hungry. She liked lobster. Where else to get them so fresh but Maine? She also liked crisp-skinned baked potatoes swimming in melted butter and topped with lots of sour cream. She licked her lips, practically tasting the tang.

She heard the scrape of chair legs across the wooden floor as a familiar voice said, "Mind if I join you?"

When she opened her eyes, Jason Bainbridge was standing there, looking schlumpier than usual in a baggy black sweatshirt with MAINE in bright red letters on his chest.

"What the hell are you doing here?" she asked, unable to stop herself.

"Same as you, I imagine." Without waiting for an invitation, he sat.

The waitress was at his side in a moment. It gave Kimberly heartburn the way female wait staff catered to male diners. The guy wasn't even attractive and he certainly didn't have charm, but there was that waitress begging for his drink order.

"Think your bartender can make me a Manhattan, Shirley?" he said.

Shirley. Now Kimberly understood. He'd eaten here before. In a ridiculously short time, he'd become something of a regular. No doubt gleaning all the local gossip, a taste of which she'd just gotten from Shirley.

"Have you ordered?" he asked, then grinned.

A grin she had to admit was almost cute. But sheesh, that tacky sweatshirt.

"Lobster," she admitted.

"Brave." He plucked at the sweatshirt as if he could read her mind. "I know. Pretty dank, right? When I got here, it was so frickin' cold. I can tell you a gazillion things about the chefs who are participating in this cook-off, their backgrounds, awards, the names of their restaurants. But somehow I failed to research Maine weather." He eyed her black cashmere cardigan and she felt him register: boring, but professional. "You were smart enough to bring a sweater."

He acted like they were friends, instead of understanding that he was simply another annoying civilian who thought he was smarter than the Bureau. And damned if he didn't read that thought, too.

"If you'd let me, I could help," he said. "I know this world."

"I do not need..."

She paused while the waitress delivered his drink. He didn't strike her as the Manhattan type, but that's what he'd been drinking in the Montana bar after Giorgio and Charlotte Bernardi were killed. Though only one for every three or four drinks that Freddy Maxwell put away that same night. Maxwell was a boozer even when his show wasn't axed due to the double murder of its stars.

Still, he had become so loaded that night that Jason Bainbridge had practically carried him out of the bar.

And Bainbridge had stayed inside the producer's hotel room a lot longer than it would have taken to just dump him on a bed and maybe take off his shoes.

Heaven help her from clueless civilians who want to help.

Surely Bainbridge didn't think that this was some silly mystery novel where the dimwitted police needed—no, sought—help from amateur sleuths. The octogenarian parson. The conflicted grower of exotic ferns. The enthusiastic knitter who owns a cheese shop.

Actually, he seemed more like the firebug who keeps turning up to watch blazes he's set shoot up into the nighttime sky.

Of course, she had checked his alibis for the dates of the other murders, and they held.

They were, in fact, surprisingly solid. Kimberly had been impressed despite herself that he kept sufficiently close track of his time to be able to come up with alibis six months after some fairly random dates. It didn't fit his defiantly unkempt image.

She really didn't want to talk to him right now, but if he actually did have useful information for her, she wished he'd just spit it out and leave. Instead of spoiling her dinner by being chummy at precisely the wrong time. She could find him if she needed him.

She gave him a chilly stare. "I do not need your help. Or want it. I don't even want your company. Tonight or any other night. Excuse me if I'm being too blunt, but I doubt that subtlety works with you."

It came out a bit harsher than she had in mind, and she blamed the wine. She'd swilled it down and now it was turning her into a pig. A rude pig. She stared down at the table, then back at him. He looked insulted, and rightly so. She sighed. "Sorry."

Then, to soften things before she sent him away, and at the same time set him straight, she said, "I'm sure you've heard all the local theories about who killed Mr. Bean."

"Shirley filled me in," he said. "Wife. Girlfriend. Every woman who ever worked in his kitchen. And just about anyone or everyone in town who ever crossed paths with him. Extremely well-loved, our Chef Bean."

"Right." She nodded her head decisively. "This most likely is unrelated, so I can probably give it back to the local authorities." She tried for a smile and hoped it didn't look as artificial as it felt. "So I guess I won't need any insider cooking advice from you."

She really had intended to be softer. But not only was there something squirrelly about a nobody blogger who just happened to be hanging around all these crime scenes, this guy also brought out the worst in her. Even when he barely said a word.

At the same time, she realized that her annoyance really wasn't about him. It was about crap assignments and suspected serial killers who would not let themselves be profiled.

Television was ruining the business.

Every Tom, Dick and Harriet knew way too much about crime investigation, and every jury expected gas chromatography and DNA analysis for the simplest street mugging. You could Google anything and get information about how to evade criminal capture or obliterate your fingerprints or... The list went on and on. Too many retired cops and agents were making names for themselves writing tell-all books.

Even the stupidest of criminals now knew how to erase trace evidence from the scene of the crime and disguise a signature. And there was nothing to suggest that this chef killer was stupid. Far from it.

"Wasn't offering cooking advice," he said mildly, though she noted two spots of red that matched the lettering on his sweatshirt blooming on his cheeks. "I've been doing a lot of research about cooking shows— they seem to be the targets, for the most part, cooking shows and food-related programs— and I've been looking at the credits to see if there are names that consistently turn up. I've developed a database—"

She picked up her wineglass, saw that it was empty and set it down again, settling for water. A better choice, but not what she wanted. She wanted to snap her fingers rudely. Summon Shirley. Throw caution to the wind and order a second glass of chardonnay to drink with her lobster. Maybe even a Margarita.

"Don't you suppose we've already done that?" she said. "We are the FBI, you know. We've run the victim's names through ten different databases. They've crossed paths with each other in a dozen different ways, but nothing that puts all of them together." She sounded like her own grandmother, a woman she hadn't liked very much. For some reason, the way he was making her feel bad about herself was also making her behavior worse.

Why wouldn't he just go away?

One more time, he read her mind.

"I know you don't think you need my help," he said, shoving back his chair and picking up his drink. "You've made that very clear. But just in case you're in the dark about where your mysterious serial killer will likely strike next, here's a thought. Some of the snarkiest, most self-important prima donnas in the culinary world are attending a big barbeque cook-off in Texas very soon."

He turned away, surveying the room for another table, then turned back to her. "I'll be there. And since killing off the unlikable seems to be his— or her— MO, your killer is likely to be there, too. Maybe you want to think about joining us?"

He gave it a beat.

Really good timing, she thought.

"And about the wife. The girlfriend. The townies. Focus on them 'til the cows come home, if that pleases you and the almighty Federal Bureau of Investigation. But I think our... your... killer left a pretty significant clue along with that lobster shoved where the sun don't shine. A lemon and a stick of butter? It's a hell of a calling card."

He sailed off to a distant table, the attentive waitress right behind him to pour him water and take his order.

Dammit! She wanted to back him against a wall and slap him until his head spun and he gave up his source.

Plenty of people in this hick burg probably knew about the lobster. Folks had been there when the net of lobsters was lifted out of the pot with Buddy nestled in their midst. By now, everyone in town probably knew about Buddy's last lobster. But the butter, melted down to its wrapper? And the whole lemon jammed down Buddy Bean's throat? Nobody could see those when the net pulled Buddy to the surface.

Only local investigators and the people who'd been at the autopsy were supposed to know. How in hell had Jason Bainbridge found out?

The hell with it all. She signaled Shirley and ordered another glass of wine.

Then, while she waited for her bright red crustacean to be delivered, Kimberly took out her phone and started looking up barbeque festivals in Texas.

Chapter 18

Hannah spent her final night on the road in Fredericksburg, Texas. Maine was already far behind her. One more down. How many more to go?

She had one more night before she arrived at the Southwest Slam Barbeque Cook-Off, and she was enjoying a splendid German dinner not unlike the ones she had grown up with a thousand or so miles to the north: truly excellent potato salad, exquisite bratwurst, succulent boiled red cabbage with apples, all washed down with a fine brew from the old country. She liked Fredericksburg and always tried to work in a meal when she was passing through the Hill Country.

The air conditioning was cranked to polar levels in the restaurant as she finished up with a flaky strudel liberally studded with raisins. It was refreshing to eat simple food now and again, no gastriques or squid ink pastas or sea urchin egg garnishes.

Outside the restaurant it was hot as hell, despite the late hour. When she'd checked into her hotel earlier, it had felt like traversing a blast furnace just to go the few steps between car and office.

At least it was her car again. She had not liked leaving the murdermobile unattended in San Diego indefinitely. It held her deepest secrets, not to mention the rest of her knives. So she'd flown back from Maine and picked it up instead of going directly to Texas.

While in San Diego, she'd succumbed to her appetites and had dinner at Rainbow. It was now green week, though green mussels felt like cheating. She'd spent two nights in Ricky's place in Pacific Beach, once again putting aside her lust for revenge. It made her feel weak, out of sorts, but she couldn't resist. Ricky was like a luscious dessert after an exquisite meal— she knew she shouldn't have him, but the temptation was too great. With her hunger sated and the Southwest Slam looming, she had finally set out across the broiling Southwest to Austin.

Traveling after dark, she hurtled through the night on empty highways, air conditioner and music on high, sometimes neck and neck with a long-haul trucker, though other vehicles were rare under the incredible starstrewn western skies. Driving at night also avoided the tedium of some of the dullest landscape in the country.

Oh, she loved America. She just didn't love every square mile with the same fervor. A native had once tried to convince her that West Texas landscapes were subtle. But he'd been wrong. Hannah knew the difference between subtle and boring.

Now she was turning her circadian rhythms back to daytime and psyching up for what needed to be done in Austin. Fredericksburg, Texas, a Hill Country town settled by a genuine baron from the old country back in 1846, was just the ticket for that kind of decompression.

She'd stayed in guesthouses here before— the place was lousy with them, all littered with crisply ironed white doilies— but this time she sought anonymity in a chain hotel. When she returned to her room, she found the air so chilled that she suspected that undies set out to dry would freeze first.

Hmmm. Freeze-drying. An interesting concept, though not appropriate for this particular mission. Too many technical challenges. Besides, first she had to learn her way around the Southwest Slam Barbeque Cook-Off.

* * *

The next night, the game was on. Hannah stood holding a draft Shiner Bock along a wall toward the rear of the bar area at Rutt's Rustic Retreat in Austin.

She had assumed her brunette identity as Ellen Bartkus, reinforced by a Southwest Slam T-shirt from a few years back purchased on eBay and a straw cowboy hat picked up in a West Texas truck stop and systematically battered for authenticity. When in doubt, blend.

The place was an upscale version of a honky-tonk, enormous and packed with locals and out-of-towners. A band played at the far end of the room, though she could hardly hear them. All around her, people laughed and talked, men slyly sizing up women and vice versa. Austin was always a study in contradictions, as well as a place with some very definite ideas of what constituted barbeque.

"You from a magazine?" a voice said at her side.

She turned to look at a tall man, a bit thin, but with a pleasant, shop-teacher sort of face. "I do some freelance work for print and blogs," she said, "but I'm not really covering anything here. I had the time and the means for once, so I just came."

She sipped the beer and looked him over, feeling bold. "What brings you to town?"

"I'm a researcher for Chantelle Orion." He switched his Rio Blanco Pale Ale to his left hand and offered her his right. "My name's Cory."

She hesitated then said, "Ellen," and shook his hand. He had a smooth, strong grip and a tingle ran through her. "A researcher for Chantelle, really? How's that working for you?"

"Chantelle gets what Chantelle wants." He looked off, taking a pull from his bottle.

His boss had a well-trafficked foodie podcast and blog. She was popu-lar not just because of her snappy, even-handed restaurant reviews or tips on where to get the best Korean-Mexican fusion taco from which hipster lunch truck.

It was because she dished. She gossiped about who was sleeping with whom, who had stolen whose secret recipe, what business was about to go belly-up and whose pasta had rat hair as the secret seasoning. Given that her inside information more often than not proved to have weight, and she eschewed interviews, her reputation as mystic seer had blossomed.

"Is it true she turned down a multi-million dollar contract from the Food Channel?" Hannah asked.

"Yeah," Cory confirmed. "The blog brings in so much now from advertising, and she loves not having to answer to anyone but her inner circle. So she could shine them on." He smiled at her, brightening. "But enough about the ol' slave driver; what about you?"

Before Hannah could respond, the clamor in Rutt's increased by several notches. They both looked around to see a small knot of people enter the establishment. At the head of the steady moving "V" was Fuller Muddlark.

The one and only Fuller Muddlark. A legend in his own mind.

Muddlark had fled the flat boredom of West Texas for the kitchens of Manhattan at nineteen. He clawed his way up in the food world, initially exhibiting more moxie than talent. He discovered that folks actually wanted him to be a Professional Texan, and that going back to his roots gave him the greatest credibility. Accordingly, he became a meat man.

When it suited him, he could either go full-on gourmand or assume a rugged frontier persona. Both identities had dark sides, colored by a blinding ambition.

He was dressed tonight in his signature look: black stove-pipe jeans, a denim cowboy shirt with cut-off sleeves and silver-toed cowboy boots. Wound around his glistening black hair was a red bandanna, the tail flaring out slightly over his broad back. It was a kind of Willie-meets-Springsteen look. If people noted that his buff-and-rough look resembled a biker with a clothing budget more than a celebrity chef, he didn't mind. It was a carefully crafted image.

Cory was studying Hannah's face, frowning. "Don't tell me you used to work for him?"

"What? Hardly," she snorted. Had she lost her poker face? "I'm not the type for that road show." Two striking-looking women stood at the front of Muddlark's entourage. Both were over six feet tall, bronzed, muscle-toned goddesses, one blonde and one brunette.

"There's nothing wrong with how you look." He studied her as if she were a well-aged side of prime Angus. Choice Angus, anyway.

Hannah felt a shiver of temptation. This guy looked interesting, and the time she'd spent with Ricky had peeled layers off her sexuality, layers that she didn't even realize were there. Rather exhilarating. Two guys in the same week would be kind of nice.

She hoped she kept her growing excitement off her face. "You're sweet. Buy you another beer?"

"Shouldn't I be doing that?" he said.

She offered a coy smile. "You get the next round."

Hannah wedged her way through the throng, wanting to get a closer look at Muddlark and his sidekicks. She knew he was going to be her biggest challenge to date. Not only was he physically fit, but he kept a custom-made, rolled steel knife in one of his boots.

It wasn't for protection so much as a gimmick. He'd made a thing of dropping in unannounced at eateries and proceeding to show the kitchen staff the proper way to slice the rump roast or filet the Dover sole. Of course he'd just happen to have a cameraman in tow chronicling each impromptu lesson.

Hannah had seen Muddlark wield his blade in blurs of precise slicing motions on various YouTube videos. Once there'd been a link to a Piney Woods baton-twirling drill team right beside it, and the moves were surprisingly similar.

Nearer to the horseshoe-shaped bar crammed with patrons, Hannah gauged Muddlark's crew as he gave an interview to one of the ever-present reporters. The two Amazons, rather than appearing vapid and bored as she'd imagined, were alert and on point. Bright eyes under dramatic makeup took in everything as they held their tony cocktails, chatting away. They seemed to glow in the dark, a flash of glitter on their skin.

Their bodies seemed relaxed but Hannah had the impression of cheetahs lazing in the sun, ready to pounce. Despite their decorative air, they acted more like bodyguards than arm candy.

Had Muddlark somehow put the killings of other chefs together and gotten spooked? If the Amazons truly were bodyguards, it would make her task that much harder. And even if they weren't, they were a couple of big, healthy girls with finely toned muscles. Not the kind of people you want between you and a target.

"A Shiner draft and a Rio Blanco Pale Ale," she told a bartender when she finally made her way to the bar. Waiting for her order, Hannah idly wondered if she might take out the Wonder Women with the stuff she'd used on Lottie Bernard. It was a derivative of tetrodotoxin, the naturally occurring poison produced in blowfish.

They looked like the sort who'd always have water bottles at hand, something fancy melted from a glacier in Finland. Hannah could probably manage the sleight of hand once, but having to do it twice in rapid succession was begging for trouble.

She paid cash, leaving some singles on the bar for a tip. This was a cash-only trip, to avoid digital footprints. Hannah walked back toward Cory, careful not to spill her beer despite the ridiculous level of jostling and posturing all around her.

"Pardon me," a tall blonde said, sliding by Hannah in slacks and a pressed shirt. What was she doing here? She was beautiful, no doubt about it, but she didn't belong. She was all business and seemed to have places to go and people to see. With a fluid sidestep she moved on, ignoring the glances the men were giving her.

"No problem," Hannah called after her. Bitch.

Hannah still hadn't spilled a drop of beer when she got back to the guy who worked for Chantelle. Working in kitchens had made her adept with liquids. Not to mention knives. Forks. Skewers. Rolling pins. Pizza ovens. Lobster boilers. It made for an interesting resume.

Chapter 19

Agent Kimberly Douglas wove through the hot, noisy crowd at Rutt's and finally found a pocket of space where she could breathe and still have a view of the room.

So far, she'd been reacting to the killer, playing Janey-come-lately, examining crime scenes post mortem. With little in the way of trace evidence to show for her efforts, as her chief glumly reminded her. Though, to be fair, the first two deaths that the Bureau now linked to the same killer hadn't seemed connected at first and much of the evidence collected was poor quality. By anticipating where a murder might take place she might get the jump on the killer. Even prevent him from acting.

Her expert eyes scanned the room. A muscular man with flowing black hair and a bandanna around his head worked the room as if he were royalty. Who the hell was he?

A man in a red cowboy shirt paused in front of her. "Aren't you with Freddy Maxwell's company?" His shirt was so new that the original packaging wrinkles ran neatly down its front. He seemed to think his smile was endearing. "No, wait. We met at Lobstravaganza."

"No, sorry," Kimberly said. Had they? She couldn't be sure. She gave him the look she used in interrogations— a cobra sizing up the mouse.

"My mistake," he mumbled, moving off.

Kimberly drank her fizzy water and nibbled on peanuts from a bowl on a nearby table. She wished she had brought a sweater. Outside it was absurdly hot. but even in the midst of this large and restless crowd, the A/C was so torqued she could practically see her breath.

Concentrate on the killer, she told herself. With Peppers's death, the unknown suspect had changed up, had made it a tableau. This was not unusual in the evolution of a serial killer. They start out with their central idea, and once they've gotten away with one or two kills, they become emboldened.

They not only want to accomplish their goal, but want to make a statement, make their mark in the world.

Recently one of the agency's profilers, a brainiac with mouse-colored hair and horn-rimmed glasses, had provided his take on her quarry.

It wasn't a stretch to figure out the killer might be a chef or would-be chef who had suffered some form of humiliation at the hands of the victims— possibly a public tearing-down. With myriad reality shows where hopefuls are trash-talked by star chefs, where celebrity judges got in their faces about their awful concoctions, there were plenty of suspects.

What the profiler brought to the table was his conclusion that the person— he was noncommittal on gender— was probably the unassuming sort. Certainly a narcissist, a near universal trait among psychopaths. The killer would believe he or she was more adept and clever than the ones being eliminated. This individual would show them all by removing the competition.

The creativity involved in the details of these murders was also increasing, no doubt about it. And the variety in disposing of the targets indicated some flexibility in methodology as well as an ability to adapt to any situation.

The goal was to kill the chef but how it was done wasn't important, the profiler concluded. The opportunity to do so was the thing, perhaps with a bit of improvisation.

Opportunity? Chance for improvisation? What better occasion than one that brought so many chefs together in one place, a barbeque cook-off covered by domestic and international press? The killer, Kimberly had concluded, liked her challenges.

There! She'd admitted it to herself— the killer might be a woman.

There certainly wasn't any forensic evidence at this point to support her thesis. And it was also true that plenty of male chefs she had observed were bitchy and insecure. Could the motive be something as simple as professional jealousy? Was the killer going after chefs who had merely been insulting?

Were these people crazy enough to kill over a stolen recipe?

Kimberly scanned the room, spotting the producer Freddy Maxwell with his shimmering silver mane. He was a connection between a couple of the chefs, but so were several others, and at least for the Fernando homicide, he had an alibi. Maxwell had been in Seattle pitching a grotesquely wealthy computer executive about the exciting potential of documentary film financing. They had eaten at a legendary seafood restaurant with dozens of witnesses. The computer exec hadn't gone for the pitch, however. Kimberly had checked. She moved a little closer to Maxwell.

In open collar, but wearing ostentatious iron and jade cufflinks fastening French cuffs, he held a squat tumbler of amber liquid and ice. He was saying something to one of the tall, scantily-clad women in Muddlark's entourage. Head back, laughing heartily, she seemed to be genuinely amused by the older man. Freddy was giving it his all, the contents of his drink sloshing over his hand as he laughed and joked with her.

Spice and sex were in the air.

People were in the process of coupling up; hands fluttered across arms and eyes drank in the other. Kimberly had a momentary stab of jealousy. Her relationships, what few there had been, had taken second and third place to her drive to excel at the Bureau. A woman had to be so much more circumspect than her male colleagues to be considered a peer in law enforcement.

She jiggled the ice in her glass, glaring at the liquid, willing it to be something more exciting than water with bubbles. She was on location, not vacation, she reminded herself. This was business.

But that didn't mean she couldn't at least observe and admire the locals. Because once you got past the poseurs in the bar area, the hoity-toity chefs and their self-important followers, a lot of the folks here seemed comfortable in their jeans and well-worn boots, as if for them a Friday night at Rutt's was a regular kind of thing.

Truth was, the crowd in the bar had that local look to them, young and hip but with an overlay of cowboy. Kimberly had good cowboy associations, after a childhood spent watching *Butch Cassidy and the Sundance Kid* over and over again with her mother, a major Robert Redford fan.

Now here she was, deep in the heart of Texas, surrounded by cowboys, and all she could do was enjoy the scenery.

Chapter 20

The barbeque arena, located out in the country west of Austin, was where cooks set up their portable rigs to smoke meats away from the tender population. Some rigs were considerably less portable than others, which didn't matter much in a state where just about every family owned a pickup truck with a tow bar. Hannah saw the smoke from miles away, thick and intoxicating, seeping out of a range of smokers. A surprising number were simply 55-gallon oil drums turned sideways. Others were far more fancy, and a couple appeared to have begun life as water heaters.

In-town smoking was not yet a reality, even in Texas. The Austin city government had long been noted for its progressive streak, but that didn't extend to barbeque pits on Sixth Street. Instead the street was lined with booths where the meat would be available to both passersby and wristbanded Southwest Slam ticket holders. Sixth Street was where the action was. Chefs smoked meat out here, then shuttled it into town.

The process of smoking brisket was protracted— hours and hours, over special blends of hardwoods. There was a whole lot of nothing to be done through most of those hours, beyond occasionally tending to the briskets, ribs and fuel. Consequently, folks tended to hole up in air-conditioned RVs behind their smokers, taking turns keeping an eye on things, answering questions and sometimes offering samples.

It was pretty easygoing, and since brisket was expected to emerge from smokers with a uniformly crisp black exterior coating, nobody even really needed to worry about burning anything.

A handful of daring up-and-comers were actually smoking pork, which in other parts of the state would probably have been regarded as antisocial, un-American and quite possibly a hanging offense. These heretics were identifiable by the vats of mopping sauce beside their smokers, and a couple of them looked suspiciously like out-and-out hipsters.

Hannah wandered through the arena, eyeing the misguided porkers. They had to know they would never win anything. Pork barbeque, AKA pulled pork, was simply not done in Texas. It belonged in those wimpy eastern states like the Carolinas. Texas barbeque was beef brisket, pure and simple.

Ribs were also a fairly universal favorite, and Austin being cosmopolitan and progressive, a lot of folks liked chicken. The Southwest Slam, in fact, offered competitions for a fairly wide range of meats, as well as beans, coleslaw, potato salad, cobbler, rubs and sauces. Recipes were handed down from pioneers and conjure women versed in Yoruba arcana, weaving spells through their roots and herbs.

Hannah realized she was hungry. Really hungry. What with breathing air thick with hardwood smoke and the intolerable heat and the fact that she'd eaten only a Greek yogurt for breakfast, she was about to buckle at the knees.

"Ma'am, would you like to try the best doggone beef west of the Brazos?" A beer-bellied man was pulling meat from a stainless steel smoker the size of a minivan. He held a paper plate toward her, offering a charred, smoky rib with a splash of deep red sauce. "Expectin' Best of Show for this baby tomorrow in the Ribathon."

She recognized the "ma'am" for Southern politeness and chose not to believe he thought she looked old. She thanked the chef, took the food and a wad of napkins, bought a bottle of ice water, then found a seat at a picnic table set up in the park.

The meat damn near melted in her mouth. She didn't know if it was the best she'd ever had, but it was certainly in contention. Before she realized, she'd devoured every speck of flesh and gristle on the Mastodon-sized rib.

She wiped away a rather shocking amount of grease, sauce and char from her face and mouth, then cleaned Ellen Bartkus's sunglasses. They were the dorky kind that you wore on top of regular glasses. She cleaned the non-prescription lenses, too. Nobody would ever suspect somebody of wearing fit-over shades over clear glass specs.

It was time to go. The beef had given her enough sustenance to get back to the murdermobile and into town, though she was not cut out for Texas summer heat and was, in fact, still dizzy.

It was as hot as, well, as hot as a pizza oven. Or a boiling lobster vat.

Back in Austin, Hannah parked the murdermobile at her hotel, iced down the back of her neck, and then went for a stroll down Sixth Street. The bustling street fair was crammed into a few blocks closed to traffic for the Southwest Slam. Entrepreneurs offered everything related to barbeque from fresh bison to five-pepper relish to sauces, from cookbooks to arcane herbal and fermented concoctions. Every other booth seemed to also offer chilled water or lemonade. Folks wanting something stronger had only to step inside one of many bars, often with live music as a bonus.

Stopping to buy another water, Hannah was passed by a pretty young woman in a retro cigarette girl outfit and short skirt. Instead of cigarettes in the open tray strapped around her neck she had dozens of miniature cupcakes in a rainbow of colors and toppings. Some of those cupcakes had perfect little red chili peppers perched atop white icing.

When Chantelle Orion moved across her line of sight, Hannah jerked herself back to reality. The tall, handsome woman with ash-blonde hair wore a flowing black caftan. She was issuing some kind of instructions to a busty young woman covered in tattoos. The assistant tapped her boss's golden words into a small tablet.

Cory Mangum trailed behind the two. He paused next to Hannah, a sly grin on his face. For a skinny guy, Cory had some impressive credentials. Last night he'd demonstrated that he knew how to use them. He had held his surprisingly strong hands on Hannah's fleshy flanks as he went to town and she had loved every moment of it.

Killing had awakened her sexual appetite with a vengeance. Now, even just the thought of it made her hot. It was as if sex was the appetizer and murder the main course. She was remembering that Travel Channel show she had watched post-coital, with an adventurer biting into the crunchy, sautéed tarantula in the Vietnamese countryside.

What would be the right wine to go with spider legs?

Cory nudged her with his elbow now. "Whatcha up to?"

"Went out to see the smoking," she answered. "Ate one of the best ribs of my life. You?"

"Doing my boss's bidding. Hey, listen. Chantelle is having a party out at Delight's tonight. I put you on the list."

"Cool." She purposely brushed her hand against his. "Any chance Fuller Muddlark and his entourage will be there?"

He raised an eyebrow. "I didn't take you for a star fucker."

"Puh-leaze. I just want to interview him for Jin-Wah." The foodie site had a huge hit rate. But it was, of course, a lie.

"Let me see what I can do." He smiled lecherously and she licked her lips in reply. "Duty calls."

Hannah turned her attentions to the food booths. Her wristband entitled her to try just about anything she wanted, and so she did.

Her first brisket was dry and stringy, so she went rogue and sampled hipster pulled pork, which turned out to be superbly seasoned and splendidly moist. Then she tried a venison sausage slathered in cole slaw. Stuffed, she sipped lemonade on a bench under an umbrella.

She was just about to move on when she noticed a well-tailored blonde who seemed spectacularly out of place. In a crowd wearing cargo shorts, cut-offs, jeans and cowboy hats, this woman's crisp white blouse and snug gray slacks were "bandbox fresh," an annoying expression of Hannah's grandmother.

Only an idiot would wear a white shirt to eat barbeque.

The woman strode along the perimeter of the benches carrying a plate that appeared to hold only vegetables. Hannah could see broccoli and zucchini and what appeared to be Japanese eggplant, sliced lengthwise. Probably from the vegan stand down the block, manned by true believers with few customers. They'd told her they "represented opposing viewpoints," as if their booth was a segment on Fox News.

Hannah saw the woman in profile and a tickle of recognition pricked her. She'd seen this woman before. Where? Had she been at the bar the night before? When you spent as much time in unfamiliar locations as Hannah did, a world of strangers swarmed in the background all the time.

But there was something about her that really didn't fit the Southwest Slam. When she walked past Hannah, her shoulders were as tensed as if she were a shot putter ready to spin and release.

There was a hungry quality about the woman. Not for barbeque, that was for sure. She didn't give the impression she was looking to leverage a celebrity chef sighting into a pitch to the Food Channel either. She didn't even look like she wanted to eat those vegetables.

Hannah felt the oppressive summer heat bearing down on her again. Time to go back to her room for a nap. As she lay in the cool, dark room, she realized that something about the woman had been a kind of catalyst.

Something about that woman had struck a nerve. Was she a sister predator? Hannah suddenly realized she was addicted to fear. It was dangerous and delicious. Was this somebody she needed to fear? Where had she seen that crisply dressed woman?

Hannah closed her eyes and drifted into delicious memory. With her first killing she'd discovered there was a chemical reaction, a substance the dying gave off, if only for milliseconds. Fernando had given it off first.

It had been hot in Miami in July, the Florida humidity oppressive. She remembered her hands moist inside the gloves, sweat dripping off her brow.

It was still hot when she crept onto his boat in the dark. Attempting to surface from his pool of drunkenness, blinking rapidly and focusing on the muzzle of her gun as it glimmered in the spill of moonlight, Fernando had suddenly understood what was happening. She chose to believe that he also recognized who was administering the long-overdue justice.

As she watched the wave of fear flood over him, her pleasure had been palpable. She'd consumed that fear, charged as if someone had plugged her into a massive energy source.

When she squeezed the trigger, Hannah had been practically light-headed with the rush. She wondered now if the tailored blonde was also a killer.

Or was she some other kind of hunter?

Chapter 21

"Sorry, Ellen," Cory said, a look of disappointment on his long face. Hannah could barely hear him above the din of the celebrity-studded gathering.

The party was well underway at Delight's out on Interstate 35, a barbeque joint with an international following. Its fine eats had been featured on various programs, even a credit card commercial when a famous sushi chef from Japan had visited. The restaurant was a large wooden, shotgun type structure with thick planks for flooring. 1950s vintage overhead fans whirled, augmented by twenty-first century air conditioning.

Cory leaned closer, almost nuzzling her neck. "I didn't get anywhere with Fuller's people on setting up an interview. They thought I was trying to hook up a discussion between Chantelle and him. But," he added in a downbeat tenor, "I had to say it wasn't that and the glazed curtain descended behind their eyes." He shook his head as if it somehow amazed him. "They are such snobs."

As if that didn't apply to every single person at this party.

Hannah put her hand on his shoulder, feeling his wiry heat through the thin cotton, and suppressed an urge to drag him out back into the weeds. "That's okay, sweetie. I appreciate you trying. I'll show you how much a little later."

He bent down and whispered something lascivious in her ear. Such a pity how people in this business used each other. She liked this guy. But just like the suck-ups, hangers on and wannabes, Hannah was here for a reason.

And that reason wasn't to get laid— at least that wasn't her priority.

Hannah nursed a dirty martini while Cory talked with fellow staffers about technical problems for Chantelle's broadcast tomorrow. A woman in jeans and a tank top skidded to a stop in front of Hannah.

"Hey, haven't we met before?" the woman said. She was short, like Hannah, with hip purple glasses and Ellen's nondescript hair.

"I don't think so," Hannah said.

"I was a production assistant on *86ed*. Did you work it, too?"

Shit. A knife of panic sliced through Hannah. "No. I mean I know the show but I wasn't on it or anything."

The other woman studied her. "Your name's not Hannah something?"

"No. It's Ellen." She returned the woman's stare, casual but steady, blinking a little behind the phony lenses. "Ellen Bartkus."

The other woman hunched a shoulder. "My mistake. You look so much like her."

Hannah drained her drink, already craving another one. This was unexpected, running into someone who remembered her from perhaps the most humiliating incident in her life.

The crucible of shame from which she'd emerged as the Phoenix of Death, formed in fire and knowing what she must do to right the wrongs done to her. This was why she was in Austin and this was why she was going to be successful in eliminating Fuller Muddlark. She got herself another drink, put the 86ed woman out of her mind and examined her problem dimensionally, looking at all the angles.

How to get close to Fuller? What gambit could she use? Then she saw the opening she'd been waiting for and hurried across the room. One of the she-wolves from Muddlark's crew had just brushed off a guy in a five-hundred-dollar cowboy hat and was standing alone. As Hannah slipped into the cowboy's wake, the woman shook her long, dark, highlighted hair.

"Don't mean to bother you," Hannah said, craning her neck up at the tall creature, "and this may sound crazy, but I couldn't help wondering. With all this damn food around here, how do you stay in such great shape? What's your workout regime like?"

Muddlark's assistant showed brilliant white teeth and cocked her head, clearly surprised.

"I know I shouldn't be so bold," Hannah continued, trying to look embarrassed, giving it her all for the game. "But I've kind of let myself go and I want so badly to get back into shape. Obviously I don't have your height or bone structure, but I bet you have some useful tips. You must work out every day."

The bronzed woman smiled with the smug self-assurance of somebody who has never had an unattractive moment in her life. "Diet plays a big part. I'll confess I've slipped since we've come to the Slam. God, I love pulled pork." She drew out "pulled pork" as if describing a sensual act. Though maybe she was just drawn to hipsters.

"I hear you. I'm Ellen."

"Audra." She offered her hand. Audra had a grip like steel. Hannah would be wise to remember that.

As Muddlark's assistant shared tips about exercise and body maintenance that Hannah had no intention of following or even remembering, Hannah nodded as if she could feel her life turning around. When it seemed to fit, she remarked, "It must be tough to maintain your workouts on the road."

"Well, yes, it is," Audra told her, "but that's why we're particular about the hotels we stay at. As much as possible, we want a facility with a good gym. Like what we have at the Grant."

Hannah inwardly rejoiced. Muddlark was staying at the Grant Hotel. She was one step closer to her goal. Chatting more, she learned that Audra was developing a line of organic super foods under the Muddlark banner. Also that the other fabulous assistant, Calista, along with Audra and Fuller himself, would be working out in the morning in the gym at the Grant. This was their regular regime, every morning.

"A slave to the iron," Audra joked.

Hannah giggled and tried to appear interested as she heard about the various juices and liquefied vegetable and mineral concoctions Audra cycled through on a weekly basis. Boring. Rotational legumes, sprouted wheat bread every third day, an intricate combination of road work and kenpo and free weights. Hannah hoped she was showing the proper amount of enthusiasm for Audra's discipline.

The she-wolf explained that she considered it part of her giving back to help women like Hannah. "You just needed some pointers," she added cheerfully. "You'll drop your extra weight in no time."

Extra weight? Hannah tried to smile as she thought: *Bitch.* She would remember that.

* * *

The next morning, Hannah left Cory's hotel, where she had enjoyed another night of romping, and walked the three blocks to the Grant in the dawn's early light. She wore a designer track suit and Nikes, carrying a stylish and voluminous purse, all in the same shade of deep purple.

"Good morning," the doorman said, pushing the door open for her at the Grant Hotel. He was no stranger to welcoming guests back when they had been out all night.

She murmured her reply without actually looking at him. She'd make the Walk of Shame vibe work for her.

The hotel was old school and comfortable, a 1920s Beaux Arts beauty with dark woods and deep carpeting. Loitering in a lobby chair and leafing through a copy of Edible Austin she'd brought with her, she made a show of checking her watch, looking occasionally toward the elevators. Finally the early risers started coming through, some wheeling suitcases and ready to check out. Not everyone in town was here for the Southwest Slam. In fact, a number of these guys had the business traveler look of fellows Hannah might have picked up in a hotel bar in Omaha or Atlanta.

She moved toward the front desk, waiting for the sole clerk on duty to answer one guest's question while another guest dropped his key card on the counter and headed out the door. She set her purse on the counter as if she were waiting her turn. Its designer bulk blocked her hands as she palmed the key card and turned away.

"Something I can help you with?" the clerk called after her.

"Just digging for my phone," Hannah answered sweetly, holding it up.

She rode the elevator to the second floor. The gym was glass-walled at the entrance and she was in luck. The two Amazons and Muddlark hadn't arrived yet. She swiped the purloined key card and joined two other guests inside. One was exercising on the pectoral fly machine and the other kept a steady pace on a treadmill.

Neither paid attention to her as she quickly scoped out the room and found a side door to another hallway. Excellent.

Hannah went through a light workout, going from one machine to another, half-heartedly using pulleys connected to weights. She wore light-weight workout gloves. As she moved around the room, she planted a few smoke devices, mostly under the bench seats of the weight machines.

It was truly amazing what you could buy off the Internet.

She heard murmured voices and turned her head as she sat on the preacher curl seat. She saw the two women and Muddlark in the main hall-way, absorbed in conversation. All three wore shorts, tank tops and neon-colored athletic shoes. Good news. Muddlark had no room to tuck his signa-ture boot knife into that kind of exercise footwear.

She rose in no particular hurry, strolled to the side door and left the gym as the front door opened. The hallway outside was empty. She could hear their voices through the door. They all sounded far too perky for the early hour.

She drew out a remote control device the size of a disposable lighter from her pocket and depressed a button. This set off the smoke bombs inside the room. She could hear gasps and darted back inside the gym, a handkerchief pressed to her face.

"Fire, fire," she yelled, squinting.

She couldn't have asked for a better setup. The smoke was thick and ubiquitous, not unlike the barbeque field yesterday, but more confined. Audra and her doppelganger were at the front door, helping the other two early exercisers stumble out ahead of them. What lovely people they were. Saps. Muddlark stood off to the side, behind them.

"Mr. Muddlark, this way, please," Hannah said in an authoritative voice with just a hint of a Texas twang.

Used to underlings attending his whims and wishes, he followed her through the side door, the smoke eddying around them like snake spirits.

Out in the hallway, Hannah moved briskly to the stairwell, holding the door ajar for him. He willingly complied. The door clanged shut, echoing in the metal and concrete cavity.

Hannah dropped her purse and handkerchief quickly. Then, twirling on the landing, she held aloft two knives. One was an eight-inch Forschner fillet knife and the other a seven-inch boning blade with a tapered end for close trimming.

Fuller stopped, eyes wide. "What the hell?" he asked, surprisingly calm.

"Are you ready for the big barbeque in the sky, Fuller?" She came at him, articulating the knives about her like a samurai. She'd practiced for weeks for this moment, wanting to get it perfect, wanting to paralyze him with fear and awe.

But Muddlark wasn't like the others. He was shocked but hardly frozen. He kicked her in the stomach and she doubled over. He snatched one of the knives from her.

"Come on, bitch, let's see what you got." He had reverted to a thick Texan twang. Bee-itch.

She straightened, getting her breath back. "Like a challenge, do you?"

He came at her and she blocked with her knife, steel ringing on steel.

Hannah countered, slashing at his exposed arm and leaving an angry, red gash across it. He jabbed at her again, backing her down a couple of stairs. She couldn't let him force her down the full flight. If their fight spilled out into the lobby, she was done for. But the section of her brain not consumed with staying alive told her he was too macho to call out for help. He must have figured he could take this pudgy nut-job by himself.

"What, did I give some prized dish of yours a bad review?" he taunted, thrusting at her like a fencer. "I didn't autograph your first editions of my cookbooks?"

She grimaced as the tip of the knife nicked her hand. He was not going to be an easy mark.

Muddlark pressed his attack and backed her further down the stairs, slashing her forearm badly. He had a gleeful look on his face. Hannah had seen it before in his television kitchen, whenever he presented the results of an original recipe to his fawning accolades.

He twisted his wrist in an evasive move and aimed the blade between her ribs. But she jerked away before he could sink the knife home.

Hannah stumbled onto the landing, holding onto the railing for support.

"What, no clever repartee?" Muddlark asked as he bounded down the steps, his knife coming at her in a sideways swing.

Hannah rallied and moved aside with a speed she didn't know she had, avoiding the fatal thrust. Swinging her knife upward, she sank it into his gut with all of her weight behind it.

Muddlark gasped and let go of his knife, his smile fading. "Now hold on, dammit," he wheezed, holding a hand to the wound. "I've got money."

Hannah sneered at him. "You think I want your money?" She tried a backhand stroke, cutting open the cloth of his shirt and the flesh of his chest area. The abdominal wound was bleeding profusely. As he faltered, she sank the blade into the base of his neck.

He dropped to his knees, looking at her quizzically. "What did I ever do to you?" he managed, blood gathering in his mouth.

"You were better than me."

He fell over onto his back, convulsing before he stopped moving. She straddled him, using both knives to hack at his face. When she was done, she hopped to her feet, wired and ready for more. She took a fast look around. Most of the blood was his, but some of it could be her own. She removed the stains that might be hers using cloths soaked in bleach solution she'd packed in her bag.

Running on sheer adrenaline, she climbed several flights up the stairwell to avoid exiting into the lobby where Muddlark's Amazonian entourage and who knew else might be looking for him. She exited onto the fifth floor.

To her left, one of the rooms opened and a couple stepped into the hallway. Hannah kept her wounded arm down, grateful that the deep purple jacket was absorbing the blood from her injury.

She nodded politely at the couple as they passed her on the way to the elevators. They went around a corner and she looked around frantically. Clear in both directions.

She could hear sirens now. They'd found Muddlark's body.

Concentrating hard to keep from appearing panicky, she walked along the hallway and stepped into the alcove that held the ice and soda machines. No door. She was exposed, but she had no choice.

She stripped off her gloves, pants and jacket. Underneath she wore yoga pants and a loose long-sleeved top, both in black, the better to disguise bloodstains. Her arm wound was long but had mostly stopped bleeding. She dug out a scarf from the bag, one she'd intended to be a distracting fashion accessory, and wound it tightly around her forearm, then pulled down the sleeve and twisted it so the slashed portion faced inward, toward her body.

She was just shoving the tracksuit into her bag when a housekeeper in her uniform walked by.

"Can I help you, ma'am?" the employee asked.

"Just checkin' out the drinks," Hannah twanged, glancing at her over-sized bag. Nothing showing. Good.

As soon as the maid was gone, she ripped off her fake glasses and black wig and shook her own hair loose. She slipped on a pair of big designer sunglasses and headed for the elevator. Just another well-dressed Texas woman about to begin her day with Pilates and a latte.

Would the cops question that maid? Would she come forward to tell them about the dark-haired woman acting odd in the vending room? She probably saw a lot of weird shit working in a hotel. Hannah had kept her head down, avoiding eye contact. She was pretty confident the woman hadn't got a good look at her.

Tamping down her anxiety, she waited by the elevators, pressing and re-pressing the button until she heard voices in one of the descending cars. She got on with three other passengers and rode down to the lobby. When the doors opened, Hannah saw two uniformed officers doing impromptu crowd control, holding people back as the EMTs hurried Fuller Muddlark out on a gurney, an oxygen mask over his face.

Hannah sucked in a breath. He couldn't be alive, could he?

The Amazonian sidekick, Audra, was standing right in front of the elevator, her back turned as she talked into her phone. Hannah shrank back into the elevator, letting the others exit, then tapped the button for the basement. As the doors slid closed, Audra turned and looked directly into the elevator. Rather than shrink further into a corner, Hannah stared straight ahead as the gap between the elevator doors decreased, her face concealed by her huge sunglasses. She willed herself to look different, to set her jaw in an odd way, to appear taller.

If Audra recognized her, it wasn't apparent. The doors closed with a sigh.

Walking with her head up as if she were a major stockholder in the hotel, Hannah walked into a basement corridor, passing several workers who glanced at her but didn't interfere with her progress. She exited through a service door, careful to use only the side of her hand on the latch.

Outside, she stepped into sunshine, pedestrian traffic and the smells of breakfast in nearby diners. She melted into a wave of people moving away from the hotel, where news crews and onlookers had clustered outside the main entrance, and started back toward her own hotel.

"Sorry," a man said as he rushed past, knocking against her shoulder as he ran toward the hotel.

Hannah startled. She recognized him. A food blogger. What was his blog? Forked Tongue.

Actually a pretty darned good food blog. His name sprung into her overheated mind: Jason Bainbridge. He knew his stuff and, while he could definitely be critical, he didn't write with the cruelty and arrogance so common in the business. He'd been writing about her exploits, making crazy guesses, but had been complimentary.

Bainbridge bumping into her had started her wound bleeding again. She kept her elbow tight against her side, hoping no one noticed the blood dripping onto her clothing.

Another time, she might have tried to meet him. He could prove useful to her.

She winced, pulling her injured arm closer. Ah, well, another time.

Right now they were heading purposefully in two very different directions.

Chapter 22

It was always a surprising discovery, Jason thought, when women who looked like goddesses turned out to be as human as everyone else.

Audra DeFord was proving it right now. When he'd seen her the night before, one of the glittering decorations in Fuller Muddlark's entourage, she'd appeared as unapproachable as a queen. That high, proud head and exposed skin dusted with some sort of fine golden glitter. She'd looked like an Egyptian goddess.

Now she huddled across from him on the brown velour banquette of the Yellow Rose Lounge at the Grant Hotel. Without her gold powder and makeup, with her hair askew in a messy ponytail, dabbing at her eyes with a tissue, she looked exactly like what she was: a woman who'd lost her job and her employer and was totally at sea.

She'd downed her first vodka martini— stirred, up, two olives and a twist— like a kid taking disagreeable medicine. As she stared with teary eyes at the empty glass, he signaled the waiter for another round. Jason wasn't much for hard liquor, especially in the middle of the day, but as he'd learned from Freddy Maxwell in that bar in Montana, people were more likely to trust you— to be more forthcoming— if you were drinking with them.

He'd been sitting here nursing an unwanted cup of coffee and thinking about what he'd seen and heard at the Grant when she wandered into the lounge, staring around blankly. Jason had become very good at seizing the moment. He introduced himself and made up a story about having met her at a New York food festival.

He suggested a drink, which he would be glad to provide. Leading her to his secluded booth in a dark corner had been easy.

Clearly she was stunned by what had happened and needed someone to talk to. Jason decided he was just that someone and surreptitiously set his smartphone to record their conversation. She told him, in a peculiar and disjointed burst of words, that she rarely drank because it made her gain weight and that she was a vegetarian, but she didn't protest when he ordered that vodka martini.

Vodka was made from potatoes, he figured, and a couple of servings of olives would inject some green vegetables into her diet. He took a long appraising look as she sipped from the glass.

From a distance, Audra DeFord had always looked fabulous. Up close and distraught, not so much. She was on the cusp of anorexia, he figured, despite the muscles under her sleek skin, and she looked almost too tired to move. Shock could do that to a person.

He waited until she was well into her second martini before he asked the questions that really interested him. Until then, he offered only gentle chat, designed to put her at ease.

Even when he began in earnest, he proceeded slowly. "How long have you been... uh... were you with Fuller?"

She looked at her oversized watch as if it might hold the answer and then stared down at her gold-tipped fingers. She wrapped those fingers around the stem of the glass and paused before speaking. "About six months. Calista has been with him a lot longer, and he really doesn't need both of us— there isn't that much to do as a personal assistant— but he likes the way it looks. Looked. The way we framed his entrances and exits and gave off a kind of Victoria's Secret Angel/ bodyguard vibe. And we were a team, the three of us. We made a great team."

Jason was acutely attuned to details, nuances, the subtle touches that made food great, and he unfortunately carried that into encounters with women. He studied women with the same attention he brought to assessing food, and had to admit he was attracted to women who seriously outclassed him— at least in terms of physical appearance.

Now he couldn't help staring at the perfect ovals of Audra's nails, painted in an opalescent gold that matched the shimmery stuff she usually dusted on her skin. People didn't look at her and Calista and think "goddess" because they were beautiful and statuesque. People thought goddess because they were buffed and trimmed and dressed to evoke that reaction. They had a deliberately contrived golden glow.

"Did you enjoy that?" he asked.

She shrugged. "It's a job. Pays better than being an aerobics instructor, that's for sure."

"That's how you met him? In an aerobics class?"

She shook her head, her ponytail swinging. Her hair was lustrous and wavy, brown with lighter streaks. That gold theme again. "I met him through Calista. The two of them were at a food festival in San Francisco. He was one of the judges. Calista wanted to take an aerobics class and the hotel suggested mine. At the end of the hour, she said Fuller was looking for a new assistant and was I interested?"

Another shrug.

He loved the way her shoulders moved, and the delicacy of her bones moving under that perfect tan. He wanted to run his hand up her throat, and run a finger over those lips. Collagen could really make a woman's mouth look sexy. A man didn't just think about kissing when he looked at a mouth like that. It was amazing what the right ingredients could do.

Stop it! he told himself. Just stop. "And then?"

"Fuller liked me, and he said he really liked the way that Calista and I looked together, so I got the job. You know, everyone thinks he's such a snob and he's not, really, he's just a very sweet guy. People don't understand. His job is to project that image." She stopped. "That was his job. Once he was on

TV, being a judge on *Windy City Chefs,* he was expected to act like a star. But underneath that biker chic, he was really just a big old teddy bear." Her eyes went wide, like someone telling a story they don't expect anyone else will understand. "And he's a total genius with food."

Jason struggled to keep disbelief off his face. He didn't know Muddlark well, but he'd never seen anything that suggested teddy bear. Or genius. Muddlark struck him as someone who paid more attention to the styling of his hair than to the styling of his plates.

Also the venue where he was wielding knives and flashing pearly-whites was Chicago, which flattered itself that it was a foodie town. The truth was something else. Chicago, once glorified by Carl Sandburg as the "hog butcher for the world," still had plenty of Midwest in its roots, enough that many of its residents could be fooled by a really fine piece of meat. Fooled enough to believe that Muddlark's sauces and reductions, and even his signature red port foam, were brilliant, when it was usually the high quality of the beef that was making them happy. Not to mention a long list of sides which invariably included multiple forms of potato. There was no more powerful driver of restaurant sales in the heartland than spuds and beef.

Jason had twice seen Muddlark prowl his restaurant, Larkspur, like a big jungle cat, his gorgeous feline concubines in his wake. He oozed sex appeal from every pore as he strode through his dining room, shirt unbuttoned almost to his waist, thick gold neck chains flashing as he gave the big spenders his attention. Especially the older women. He was careful to hold their gazes, to let his hands slide down their backs seductively, to stare down their blouses as if he couldn't wait to taste what they were hiding.

It was a strategy that paid off. Soon Muddlark could afford as many gold chains as he liked.

Jason could admit that Muddlark had done some things with caramelized fennel that were worthy of a Michelin star, and he'd once offered a complex toasted quinoa dish that was close to orgasmic. But Jason had eaten a dozen other things at Larkspur that were simply mediocre. In his book, two out of fourteen was not a genius score.

Still, you play the cards you're dealt. And he needed to keep Audra talking. "I've had some amazing dishes at Larkspur," he lied.

That won a faint smile from her. "You've been there?"

"Many times." Twice, anyway.

"I never saw you there. I work there as a hostess when I'm in town."

Because Muddlark wouldn't trouble himself with a peon like me was the answer. Also Jason required a certain level of anonymity to write his blogs. But that answer wouldn't keep the conversation going.

He shrugged. "Are you there every night?"

"Oh," Audra said. "No, I'm not. And now that he's doing the TV show, Calista and I are over on the set pretty often. So I guess that's why." She had slipped back into the present tense when she talked about him. Jason suspected it would be a long time before she lost that habit.

She dabbed at her eyes with a tissue. Despite the heavy mascara she wore, even at a time like this, still in her workout clothes and with her boss carved up like one of his prize roasts, she managed to avoid smudges on her face. How did women do these things?

"I just can't believe he's gone," she moaned on cue.

Time to start dragging out the clichés. Jason put a gentle hand over hers. "It's a terrible loss for those of us who loved his food. How can a bright light like that become extinguished in a moment?" He managed not to gag and gave it a beat. "Did he have any enemies that you know about?"

She shook her head, sending her heavy gold earrings jangling. "Everyone loved Fuller."

Obviously not everyone. "So he never felt threatened?"

"Of course not," Audra said, rushing to her boss's defense. "Why would someone want to do something like that?"

"Every successful chef has enemies, I've heard, people who are jealous that they've made it. People in the kitchen that Fuller yelled at? Maybe someone he fired?"

She shook her head. "The police asked me all those questions, but I don't know. I just don't know." The ponytail flapped back and forth as she protested. "Where did that person come from? The room was full of smoke but there were only a couple people in there. Maybe he was waiting outside the door? Because when that woman from the hotel yelled for Fuller to follow her, he should have been okay. Calista and I tried to follow him, but he was across the room, and then we kept tripping over equipment, and everyone was yelling and you couldn't see a thing, and it really smelled awful. We went back to the other door just to get out and breathe."

That woman from the hotel, Jason thought, his mind lighting up. What woman would that be?

Chapter 23

Kimberly Douglas didn't learn much from her questioning of the people who'd come to Austin with Fuller Muddlark.

Audra DeFord recalled someone calling out for the chef when the smoke filled the gym but she couldn't see who the person was and assumed it was one of the hotel staff. Calista, the other tall, glamorous assistant, didn't remember anything at all. They were a strange pair, those two. The first one, Audra, had been tearful and subdued, yet Kimberly had sensed a strength in her that she was, perhaps, concealing. As for Calista— she had been nothing short of a basket case, truly upset, so hysterical that Kimberly had actually thought about calling in a psychologist. It was disconcerting for a woman who topped six feet to be so fragile.

Neither one of them had told her anything useful.

But it hadn't all come up snake eyes for Kimberly. Austin PD's crime scene people knew their stuff and had recovered fibers not belonging to the dead man from his clothing.

It wasn't much, but you built the investigation step by step, little by little. Eventually those fibers would match something. Unfortunately, not much else had been found at the crime scene. Plenty of blood, but all Muddlark's so far. Some wet spots on the carpet contaminated by carpet cleaner or, possibly, bleach. Damn those forensic crime shows.

But best of all was Muddlark's last words in the ambulance before he died: "Bitch," followed by a number. "Eighty-six," he had whispered, and then lapsed into unconsciousness and, eventually, died.

"Bitch" firmed up the suspicions Kimberly already had: that the killer she was chasing was a female. A surprisingly strong woman, granted, given what she'd been able to pull off so far. And impressively adept at remaining under the radar.

Women were much better at being invisible. Put on a little weight, get a little old, a few wrinkles, a few gray hairs... hell, the world looked right through you anyway, without any more effort on your part. Kimberly was too smart to jump to the ordinary conclusion that the killer had to be a man. More to the point, she could smell it. This killer was clever and deliberate. Given the number of victims who had been murdered, the killer had to be operating on a long hit list, and that meant a very long memory.

Women and elephants. They never forget. Kimberly knew that better than anyone.

But it didn't matter. Kimberly was going to catch this killer and serve her up good. Gutted, trussed like a Thanksgiving turkey and picked clean. Her professional reputation depended on it.

Kimberly Douglas didn't like to lose.

Chapter 24

The thrill of the chase, of almost getting to the killer in time, of guessing which chef might be next— twice now!— it was crazy. Jason wiggled on the leather booth bench in the back of the hotel bar, trying and failing to restrain himself.

He'd stayed on in Austin after Muddlark's murder, just as he'd lingered in Maine after Buddy Bean's close encounter with the lobster pot, hoping to pick up a few clues from the locals. He'd sampled barbeque wherever he could, wrangled an invitation to a press junket party at one of the bars on Music Row and walked for hours. He might have actually lost a couple pounds, what with all the excitement. His mind churned with theories, connections, people, chefs.

Revenge.

He'd come so close this time. The only thing that took the shine off was the crime scene photo someone had tweeted to him. Old Muddlark was unrecognizable. She'd done a real hatchet job on him.

"She."

The notion of a woman serial killer was growing on Jason. He took a sip of white wine and popped a duck-fat fry into his mouth. Something about Texas made him want to drink white wine. Could it be the heat, the sunshine and the barbeque? Or was he getting off-course on his food choices?

Just before Jason had left Maine, the case had circled back to the scorned wife, Susie. The girlfriend, Melissa, was all too eager to point her lobster-scarred finger at Susie.

The FBI thought it unlikely, and so did Jason. Susie could have done Buddy in any ol' time with that shotgun she kept by the back door of their house. Boiling him and especially the coup de grace of lobster insertion, a tidbit that authorities managed to keep out of the papers, was something else. Doubtful the act of a cheated-on wife.

Not to mention the lemon and butter. That was a serious clue, one slipped to Jason by a janitor in the medical examiner's office. People kept sending him tips. It made him proud that his blog was so popular, so cutting-edge, so to speak.

He smiled. He wasn't opposed to a cornball cooking pun now and then.

Besides, it was all about the cooking. The killer was a chef, someone with culinary experience, with taste, who understood seasoning, like the way Byron Peppers had been seasoned. It was as plain as the nose on his face, all this time. It just took a lobster, a lemon and some butter to make it perfectly clear. These weren't just deaths, they were recipes.

The cocktail waitress circled by and Jason abandoned white wine and ordered a Manhattan. He'd taken to making them at home after being turned on to them by Freddy Maxwell in Montana. His personal preference, now recited to the waitress, involved a lime twist burnt with a match then dropped into the amber liquid. So much better than orange or cherry.

He was watching the taut backside of the waitress sashay away when he saw the woman across the bar staring at him. Was that Kimberly Douglas again? It couldn't be. And why hadn't he seen her before in Austin? He remembered what a bitch she'd been in Maine when he told her about the barbeque slam.

Perhaps it was a long lost twin. Same satiny blond hair, but this woman was wearing something sparkly, with high heels. And smiling? Definitely not the FBI Ice Queen.

His phone beeped. Jason read the text and felt his heart race. A tip from one of his insiders in reality television: "Freddy M. pitch to Food Channel successful. '*A Cut Above*' starts taping in 2 weeks."

So Freddy Maxwell had landed on his feet. Maybe he was still in Austin and Jason could get an interview for the blog. Or pitch an article to one of the high-paying magazines.

He started searching madly on his laptop to find out more about the show. Maxwell had been the one common link between some of the early murders, although he had alibis for most of them. He worked in Fernando's restaurant and on Willow's show. But Jason had talked to the producer after the murders in Montana. He was many things— but a murderer?

His searches revealed that Freddy's new show was a variant on the "cook fast and win" model, an approach that today's audiences, with the attention span of gnats, seemed to love. It was a disgraceful practice. Didn't quality matter anymore? What happened to the Slow Food Movement? The Food Channel apparently hadn't gotten that memo.

Deeper searching revealed a growing lineup of potential contestants for *A Cut Above*, though only one had been confirmed so far: Ricardo Z of Rainbow in San Diego, a rising star with a ridiculous theme restaurant. Speculation about the other three contestants centered on an up-and-coming Hong Kong/San Francisco impresario named Sallie Tam, who was old enough to be his grandmother. The others were still unknown.

His cocktail was set down beside him and he mumbled thanks, eyes glued to Google. Out of the corner of his eye he noticed that the waitress didn't leave. Christ, did he have to tip her for every drink? He looked up, irritated.

"Hello, Jason."

Kimberly Douglas gave him a smile she must have been practicing. It wasn't her usual chilly put-down smile, but this was definitely the FBI agent he'd been encountering around the country. Without an invitation she slid into the bench opposite him. And she was wearing something completely different too.

Jason's mouth hung open as his fingers froze over his keyboard.

Kimberly really didn't look like herself. There was good reason why he hadn't recognized her across the bar. She'd done something new with her hair, which swooped to one side seductively. Her low-cut sequined silver top caught the light under her black tailored jacket. She still wore slacks but now with some rockin' heels.

What was going on?

"You look— different," he said stupidly.

She smiled broadly. "You like?" She touched her sequins sensually. Please stop rubbing your breasts, he thought. She said, "I bought it. I figured I might as well wear it."

He raised his eyebrows and couldn't think of anything to say. He was suspicious. What was her game?

"What are you working on?" she asked, nodding to his laptop.

He closed the lid quickly. "Nothing." He felt protective now, of his information, his theories. She had kept him out of the loop. See how she liked it.

She nodded all too pleasantly. "What about this new one? Did you connect it to the others?"

Well, that was bold, he thought. He squinted at her. "No. But it would be weird if it wasn't connected."

She was still smiling. She was definitely working him. "Did you get a look at those two women Muddlark had flanking his every move? You'd think they could have saved him. Do you think they're what— six-two?"

"Or something," he said sullenly. He was only five-nine. What did he know about tall women except he dug them? "Did you talk to them?"

She nodded. "Calista didn't give me much. She was a mess." Her eyes bored into him. "Did you talk to her?"

"No. Not her."

"Just Audra?" she asked quickly. How did she do that, he wondered. Reading his mind again. "So she told you."

"Told me what?" He didn't want to give her anything. It shouldn't work that way.

"About the woman who called out to Muddlark. A hotel employee, she thought, with a Texas accent. She didn't get a good look at her in the chaos."

He nodded slowly. "She mentioned it."

Kimberly squirmed a little closer to him across the table and lowered her voice. "Do you think it's a woman?"

"Possibly," he conceded. "Do you?"

She wagged her head, uncommitted. "This one feels different."

"Because he fought back?" Jason took a long drink of the Manhattan and felt the cheery burn. The bartender had made it just as he requested. The FBI agent watched him, looking hungrily at his Manhattan. Remembering his manners, he asked, "Are you having something? White wine?"

Kimberly took this as a sign of his friendliness. She relaxed and played with her new hairdo. When her wine arrived, she sipped it carefully while examining him. "He fought back all right. He gave her a fight for her life. Much more than any of the others. She must be really good with knives."

He nodded. "A chef would be."

Kimberly smiled knowingly. "So she's a chef. Somebody who worked for each one of them?"

He shook his head. "No such person, according to my research. And, of course, your big federal database probably told you the same." He didn't want to tell her about Freddy Maxwell's new show. She knew about his connection anyway. Besides, what else did she have to do? She didn't have to write a blog and restaurant reviews and articles. She had manpower and federal authority and a regular paycheck. This wasn't her side job. He downed his Manhattan. "Look, Agent Douglas."

She looked offended. "Kimberly."

"Look, Kimberly." He slipped his computer into its case and stood up. "You made it clear many times you don't want me butting in. I'm just a civilian, a lowly food blogger. What do I know? Are you trying to trip me up, get me arrested for obstruction? I tried to help you. You told me to fuck off. Good night."

He heard her protest as he stalked out of the bar. He couldn't listen. He had to find Freddy Maxwell and get a statement from him so he could break the new reality show story.

Plus, that sparkly top made him a little crazy.

Chapter 25

Poor Hannah.

The words swirled in her brain as she drove through East Texas toward the bayou country of Louisiana. Poor, poor, injured, hurt Hannah.

The wound on her arm looked angry and felt hot. The black stitches she'd finally gotten at a cut-rate urgent care facility marched down her flesh in a jagged red line. The dusty small town doctor, a wizened alcoholic with bristly whiskers and faded tattoos, was perfect. No questions, no lies. "Cut myself with a knife" was all she said. He didn't even tell her to be careful around sharp objects. It was obvious she'd already had that lesson.

Too bad the old wino had shaky hands. The stitches weren't the best, crooked in places with gaps. It would no doubt scar. But who was she to complain? She'd paid cash and gotten out of there with some good drugs. But, damn, it hurt like hell.

She stopped at a barbeque joint just over the Louisiana line. Before she went inside she doused the wound with antibiotic and rolled down her sleeve to cover it, wincing as the stitches snagged the fabric of her jacket. She'd thrown away her bloody clothes at an interstate rest stop, angry all over again about the sloppy way Muddlark had gone down.

She'd given him too much time. She'd let him talk to her, play with her, cut her.

She liked to see their faces, one last time on earth. But his face might haunt her longer than the others. She beat herself up for a moment, then took a breath. He'd paid for his sins, the jerk.

Move on, Hannah.

It wasn't like her to ruminate on her deeds. What was happening to her? For solace she ate an extra-large plate of ribs, making a royal mess at the outdoor picnic table. No one cared. Hell, she didn't even care— about the sauce on her face, the cut on her arm or her many acts of homicidal revenge. She felt better, sated on pork ribs and hot Cajun sauce and warm Dr Pepper.

Back on the road, she turned the radio up and sang, chasing the blues away. What she needed was to get back on the bang-bang train again. She wondered, so soon after Cory. Still, whenever she started to lose her lust for revenge, a little sex reignited it. She just needed to put a little pep in her step. A little meat in her heat.

And New Orleans was just the place.

The Garden District apartment she'd rented years back wasn't available. Too bad. It would have been a welcome sign from on high if it had been. But the agency had another one, not as nice but close to Bourbon Street in case she was in a partying mood. In case, she chuckled as she unlocked the door at the end of a long narrow hall. She would party hard in Nawlins, yes, she would. Get Muddlark's hacked-up face out of her mind for good.

Throwing her bag on the sagging bed, she went to explore the kitchen.

Well, she could eat out. She'd had worse kitchenettes in her travels, though not recently. Precious little could entice her to cook here: a tiny four-burner, a '50s fridge, mildew in the corners, cracked tile and mousetraps. Mousetraps? She opened the curtains on four garbage cans and a privacy fence, the suite's only view.

Changing into her long-sleeved, low-cut, man-magnet silk blouse and a short skirt, she went out for a walk. The afternoon was hot and humid, the scent of swamp in the air. Everything seemed to move in slow motion.

New Orleans had changed since Hurricane Katrina, she was starting to realize, a little more desperation in the air, a little less cash in the pockets. The years had passed though, and the old girl was back, as raunchy and exciting as ever.

Hannah smiled.

She was thinking of the city, but hell, that description fit her to a T.

* * *

Three days later, her mood back to devilish normal from sweaty, anonymous sex and hot beignets, Hannah looked up from her breakfast to see a news program on the television in the corner of the café. She hadn't seen a newspaper for weeks, with all the traveling. And she definitely avoided television news— it could ruin your digestion in an instant.

Besides, who cared what happened on the other side of the world?

But right up there was a photo of Fuller Muddlark and a talking head, some blonde woman. What was she saying?

Hannah walked over to the television mounted behind the coffee bar. She'd chosen this café carefully, for its reviews and its non-tourist trade, and now, at ten in the morning, it was deserted, the powdery crumbs of the morning rush her only companions. Searching quickly under the bar, she found the remote and turned up the volume.

"The murder of the celebrity chef marred the food festival in Austin last weekend. That homicide investigation is ongoing, according to the Austin Police Department. First Muddlark and now this latest tragedy, his assistant, Calista Calhoun. The tall beauty had been despondent since her boss's death and, according to friends, blamed herself for not protecting him. Miss Calhoun was twenty-nine."

The news anchor went to commercial, leaving Hannah staring blankly at a row of shiny pickup trucks. She quickly hit mute on the remote and threw it back under the bar. What the hell happened to that Amazon bitch?

Hannah paid her bill, popping the last bite of delectable pastry into her mouth as she waved to the waitress. Out on the sidewalk, she walked briskly toward a corner grocery and bought a copy of the Times-Picayune. The front page was all about some parade over the weekend, crazy cartoonish floats and smiley people in bizarre costumes. She tucked it under her arm.

Strolling down the avenue, she felt the sun on her face and it felt strange. Really, what was she doing out this early? She was a creature of the night. All chefs were.

Scurrying across the street to a little pocket park, she found a bench out of the sun and scanned the newspaper for the Muddlark story. On the last inside page she found it: Chef Assistant Dies in Fall. She read it quickly, then had to read it again more slowly. What was the deal with newspapers? They don't want to come out and say the word "suicide." Calista had thrown herself off a hotel roof. That wasn't pretty, but it was pretty obviously a suicide.

Hannah set the paper on the bench. Things were happening. Things outside her control. Was it some sort of message? Hell, she didn't believe in signs and messages. It was just that stupid woman, thin and beautiful with everything going for her except her brains. Well, she didn't have to worry about IQ tests anymore.

But it pissed Hannah off.

She walked back to her skanky apartment, musing over the way her moods were all over the place. That guy last night, Larry or Lance or whatever, he had been fun. More than fun. But if she was being honest with herself—there had been that moment, a moment when he was lost in his pursuit of pleasure and she had suddenly imagined herself picking up the beer bottle by the side of the bed, breaking it over the table and then driving it deep into the veins of his bulging neck.

She had seen it all unfolding in perfect detail in her mind and just imagining it had brought her to orgasm.

Somehow she had restrained herself. He was a civilian, not even a chef. And hordes of people had seen them leave the bar together. But, oh, how she had wanted to combine sex and murder. Now that would have been a memorable night.

She had replayed their wild night together in the café as she sipped hot coffee laced with chicory. But then she'd accidentally seen the news about Fuller Muddlark's assistant and pffft. Mood plunge. Pun intended.

What she needed was a plan.

She picked up her pace now, swinging her arms. Yes, a plan. That was just the ticket.

As she unlocked her door, her phone rang in her pocket. Only a small number of people had this number. She'd given the number to Ricky before she left San Diego the second time. But this wasn't Ricky. It said "Unknown caller." She clicked "Off" and set the phone on the table.

It rang again. And kept ringing. Oh hell. Some people, mostly male, could ignore a ringing phone, but Hannah had never been able to do that.

"Yes? Who is it?" she barked.

"Miss Wendt? Can you hold please for Ricardo Z?" Click.

Oh, it was Ricky. Hannah tapped her fingers impatiently. She hated being on hold. She said to the hold music: "No, I cannot hold for Ricardo Z. I can make him squeal like a—"

"Hannah!" It was Ricky, sounding out of breath and hot as an Andouille sausage. "I found you! Where are you?"

"I gave you my number, Papi. I wasn't hard to find." Ricky liked to pretend he was Latin Ricardo for most of all his role-playing. "I'm in Nawlins having a good old chow-down in the land of endless delights. I've got Emeril on speed-dial."

"Seriously?" He laughed nervously as if she really might have the super chef on the other line. "You won't believe what's been happening. I can't believe it myself! Right after Green Week— you know, when you were here— I got a call from a talent coordinator for the Food Channel. It went back and forth for a while, but in the end I got the gig. I got it!"

"What gig?" Hannah asked coldly.

"Freddy Maxwell's new show, silly! You heard about *Fave Flavor*, right? Everybody has been talking about it for weeks. They renamed it *A Cut Above*. And I'm going to be one of the chefs!"

"Great." Why was he torturing her like this? He expected her to be happy for him? Bastard. She'd already spared his life. Some people didn't know when to quit.

"I know!" he exclaimed, missing her sarcasm. "And I need you, Hannah. I get to have a personal assistant to help me with, well, everything, and since you're so organized, and you know money and food and wine and, you know, the sex ain't bad—"

"Ricky!" Hannah interrupted him. What on earth was happening here? She sighed. "I know how great I am, in every way, tip to toe and every curve in between. We fit together in the sack. But me working for you? Have you lost your mind?"

"No— no— no! This is different, Hannah! Wait, will you?" Sounds of shuffling, running, puffing breaths. He came back on the line, voice hushed. "These people are animals. Some of the kitchens I worked in were jungles. But these guys are jackals! Hyenas! This is New York, baby. The Big Time. I'm telling you, Hannah, I'm freaking out!"

"Oh, poor little Ricky," she cooed. What a dick. He was probably peeing his pants. "Are you trembling all over?"

"Yes! You have to believe me, Hannah. I need you to watch my back here. Please come."

She could picture him behind a set, hunched over, shivering. "Where is it taping?" she asked, her curiosity ticking up involuntarily.

"Chelsea Market. Right next to us is the studio where Rachael Ray became a star."

Big whoop, thought Hannah. She couldn't stand any of those stuck-up celebrity chefs. Obviously she had a little harder, ah, hard-on for the bastards who had disrespected her. But really, she hated them all. Ricky was still talking, going on and about the joys of the Market and the Village and Manhattan. Blah, blah, blah. He was such a rube. New York would eat him alive.

He was babbling on when she finally stopped him. "Wait," Hannah said. "What did you just say?"

"The other chefs on the show? I don't know any of them, but maybe you do. Thurogood? She's some Australian ball-breaker. And Willis Covington, an obnoxious snooty Brit. And lastly, the inscrutable Asian. Sallie Tam. She's as old as Confucius."

"Sallie Tam from Chinoiserie? From Hong Kong and San Francisco?" Hannah was impressed despite herself. Sallie had emerged out of nowhere to become an instant legend in Asian-French fusion. Hannah had tried to get into her restaurant on her way down the coast to San Diego but it was sold out for months.

"I guess. She's short, man. She barely clears the counter." Ricky was recovering a little swagger, Hannah noted. He wouldn't need her after all, though working alongside Sallie Tam would be the chance of a lifetime.

Hmmm. This was strangely tempting.

And what did she have going here in the Big Easy? More beignets and rich sauces? Crawfish and roux? Niggling worries about Fuller Muddlark's negativity fallout?

Mad sex and a mad desire to eat every specialty New Orleans offered?

Yes, all that, but she wasn't going to go hold Ricky Zelinsky's limp dick so that he could win some reality TV stupidness. Those shows were such fakes. They were such... and then, suddenly, there it was again: the memory of her humiliation. She shivered. No way. No way could she risk television.

"Good luck, Ricky," she said with a gaiety she didn't feel. "There's some crawfish étouffée down the avenue with my name on it."

"Hannah! Wait," he pleaded. "Don't hang up. You have no idea what's going on here. We start taping in a week and it's balls to the walls. Already the bastards have started. The snide little barbs, the jabs and put-downs. Every day they're trying to undermine my confidence. Yesterday, that skinny bitch Thurogood cackles in that fake Australian accent of hers, 'What small fingers you have, Grandpa.' As if she's not ten years older than me. I'm trying to keep it light, make a joke, and all I can think of is how my hairline is receding and she thinks my cock is really, really small because, you know, fingers and—"

Hannah made a little involuntary gasp. Did he say an Australian accent?

"What's her name?" she asked sharply as her pulse quickened.

"The Aussie? Thurogood."

"What's her first name?" she demanded. Exhilaration flooded through her, and she felt as if she might float off the sofa.

"Gert. Gert Thurogood. She's a real piece of work. She keeps putting toothpicks in my lunch."

It came flooding back to Hannah. Back in Iowa City, the very first French food that ever passed her lips. Hannah's father took her to the restaurant when she made the sophomore honor roll and she had the most extraordinary duck confit. She had no idea the lowly quacker could be so delicious. Until then, all the duck she'd eaten had been shot by relatives during hunting season and you had to be careful not to break a tooth on buckshot.

She met the sous chef, a scarecrow named Trudy who came by the table, carrying something delicious, stopping to shake her boobs in her father's face. Tall, gangly and dismissive, the chef had curled her lip as Hannah gushed with compliments about the food. Then had Trudy looked down her hawk-like nose at Hannah, eyes drifting down her figure, and said, "You like to bog in then, eh, bush pig." She glanced at Hannah's father and exchanged a chuckle with her old man.

There was a pause, then a crushing weight fell on Hannah. It was the worst moment in her young life. She could still feel the stab in her gut, the awful pain of that insult, whatever the hell it meant in Aussie-speak. Trudy's eyes conveyed the daggers. They hurt. The gist of it was one word: FAT. Words meant to embarrass, to hurt, to slay.

And in cahoots with her father, too.

A good-sized man himself, round as a pork pie, her father looked at his plate, agreeing silently with the willowy wench. He said nothing. Nothing. Frank White— White was Hannah's real last name— had abandoned both his baby daughter and the hog farm of his wife's family and escaped to New York where he wrote a food column in *TIME Magazine* for twenty years. He traveled the world, a gourmet of the first order.

But here he was, trying and failing to make amends, embarrassed to be with his own food-loving daughter. In league with a snide, skinny bitch named Trudy— Gertrude, now Gert— who was called Thurogood but was Thoroughly Evil. Through and Aussie Through.

And now, in a wicked twist of fate, it appeared that this wretched, nasty person had made it to the big time. Gert AKA Trudy was going to be a star, a featured chef on a national cooking show, the last check-off on every ambitious chef's list.

Like Ricardo Z. Who was now nattering on like a nabob named Zelinsky.

She blinked back to the present. "What? What are you saying, Ricky?"

"Come, Hannah. That's all I'm saying. I need you. Help me with Gert and Willis and Sallie. I don't give a rat's ass if I win this mess. I just want to have a little fun with food! Fun food, that's what we're about, right? Come on, Handy-girl. Do me a solid here. I'm on my knees."

Hannah closed her eyes, recalling for a moment what Ricardo Z on his knees was capable of.

Then she let herself be enveloped by the warmth of emotion, of pure, unadulterated feeling. She was wrapped in a blanket of possibilities. Fate had put her oldest enemy right smack in her path.

She envisioned Gert Thurogood butchered into bite size pieces. Gert Thurogood tied down on top of a kitchen island and branded with a hot grill until her skinny ass was crisscrossed with a perfect pattern of seared lines. Gert Thurogood locked in a walk-in freezer and preserved in frozen terror.

Hannah's pulse quickened as she felt the rush of revenge, of danger again.

Ricky was still begging. "Hannah, I need you. Please."

She sighed dramatically. "Well, if you put it that way."

Chapter 26

The day after Jason Bainbridge blew her off, Kimberly Douglas stood in front of his hotel room door, fist poised to knock. She took a second to pull down the black leather jacket and pull up the skinny jeans. Jesus, they were tight. But she knew from her long appraisal in the mirror this morning that she looked kind of fabulous in them. Would they do the job?

She knocked and checked her watch. Eight-thirty in the morning. Too early? The door opened and it appeared Jason was dressed. Or he'd slept in his clothes. You couldn't always tell with this one. He pushed up his glasses and looked her over.

She felt strange, and excited. "Mr. Bainbridge," she began, knowing it sounded too formal.

"Jason. Please," he said, folding his arms. "We're beyond the formalities, aren't we, Kimberly?"

"I hope so." She looked beyond him into his room. The morning sun streamed through his window, highlighting a row of tiny, empty liquor bottles above the mini-bar. She hesitated.

He said, "I'd ask you in but it's a mess." He re-folded his arms and waited for her to speak.

She cleared her throat. "Maybe we could have breakfast. In the coffee shop off the lobby. Fifteen minutes?"

"What's this about?" He looked suspicious, like last night when he'd accused her of trying to entrap him on obstruction charges.

"I want to apologize for last night. I didn't mean to come across—however I came across. Can I buy you breakfast? We can talk. That's all I want. Just talk about the case." She kept her voice flat, neutral. No pleading. She was a special agent, by God.

"Off the record?"

"Or not. We can discuss it." She turned slightly and let him see how the jeans hugged her backside. Pathetic, and desperate, yes. But damn, she needed help on this case.

Her heart leapt a little as his eyes glided down her figure. He nodded and shut the door.

Kimberly said a silent "Yes!" and slapped herself on the ass.

* * *

She was waiting when Jason arrived just ten minutes later. The coffee shop was nothing special; the coffee was rank. He'd probably make a stink about the food but she didn't care. He was here and she was going to make him help her if it was the last thing she did.

He had showered. His hair was damp, dripping on the blue dress shirt that matched his eyes. He must wear contacts, she thought. His eyes were very pretty, if you could say that about a man. And he smelled like shampoo. With a little exercise he might be something.

"Thanks for coming," she said as the waitress poured more evil coffee. Kimberly dumped three creams in hers and stirred. Both ordered eggs, hash browns and bacon, surprising each other with the same taste in breakfast: simple, greasy and All-American.

"So what's the big deal?" he asked, obviously still angry.

She smiled and tried to look conciliatory. It didn't come naturally. "I was thinking we could help each other. I really need your help, and I've given you some tidbits for your blog, haven't I?" When he glowered, she rushed on. "I have more stuff, you know, things I haven't told any journalist."

He brightened at the word "journalist."

Encouraged, she rushed on. "I respect your integrity, Jason. And your work. You've filled me in on so many details about this case, things it would have taken me ages to find out on my own."

"So why are you on your own?" Jason asked. "Don't you have a partner or something?"

"It doesn't work that way in the FBI. Sometimes we do, but sometimes we're out there on our own. Like now. With all the travel, the expense of investigations, the Bureau can't afford more than one agent on the scene."

"Our tax dollars at work," Jason said. "Must be tough."

She nodded, smiling. She hadn't smiled so much since college. "That's why I need help from informed citizens like yourself. Jason, you know so much about this world of chefs, and about this case. Nobody has done more work on this case. Not even me."

Which couldn't possibly be true, but she really, really needed him.

They worked on their breakfasts for a few minutes, then Jason set down his fork. "What do you need from me? Theories?"

Oh, thank God. Praise the Lord, he's going to help. Kimberly tried not to look too relieved. "The Bureau's profiler thinks it's someone mousy or nondescript, somebody who blends in well. And you and me, we both think it's a woman, right?"

Jason shrugged.

Kimberly lowered her voice in a conspiratorial whisper. "Can I tell you Muddlark's last word?"

He leaned in.

"It was 'bitch.'"

He sat back, impressed. "So it is a woman." He sipped coffee. "An ordinary-looking, shy woman? That doesn't narrow the field much, I have to say."

"She can't be that shy, can she?" Kimberly said, twirling toast through egg yolks. "She's bold. Fearless really. A psychopath with a very specific agenda."

"People she hates," Jason added. "She's a hater."

"Obviously." The agent squinted at him. "Do you think she's a chef?"

"Maybe. More likely a wannabe chef, somebody who works the back kitchen or some peripheral job but will never have the talent to make it to head chef. And knows it."

Kimberly nodded. "Eliminating competition, that's what the profiler called it. But you said you couldn't find anyone who had worked with all the victims." The Bureau hadn't either, but no reason not to flatter him.

Jason held her eye for a moment as if making a decision. Finally he said, "You know about Freddy Maxwell's connection, right? He's worked with almost everybody."

"Did he work with Fuller Muddlark?" she asked.

"Not exactly. You know his assistants, the seven-foot-tall giantesses? The one named Calista Calhoun worked for Freddy Maxwell before Muddlark stole her."

"A love triangle?" Kimberly said. "I saw them all together, Muddlark and his assistants, at Rutt's in Austin. What did Calista do for Freddy?"

"Production assistant on some of his shows," Jason said. He pulled his laptop out and started punching keys. "You'll find this out soon, so I may as well tell you. Freddy just got a new cooking show called *A Cut Above.* He's the executive producer this time, the head honcho. A really big deal for him, especially after the demise of *Love Bites*. The press conference is this afternoon at the Food Channel booth here in Austin, just before the closing ceremonies and awards."

"Maybe he'll hire Calista again," Kimberly said excitedly. "Do you think she'd help us catch Muddlark's killer?"

He tapped keys madly, chomping on toast. A minute passed. He stopped suddenly, paused dramatically, and looked at Kimberly with a somber face. He spun his laptop around as he said, "Probably not."

The screen was filled with a foodie website named Vittles. The first item at the top was a picture of Calista and Fuller Muddlark, arms around each other, beaming. The headline read: "Muddlark Aide Dies in Fall." The subhead continued: "Despondent over Murder, Takes Own Life."

Kimberly scanned it quickly. "Shit," she whispered. She pulled out her phone and checked for messages or voicemail. Nothing. She called the Austin Police Department liaison she'd been assigned to, a woman detective. She must have recognized Kimberly's number and answered with a cautious, "Agent Douglas, how can I help you?"

"I just heard— on the Internet— about Calista Calhoun. You didn't call me," Kimberly barked.

The detective apologized but didn't sound like she meant it. "It's been crazy here. We haven't even taken the body in yet."

"Where did it happen?"

"At the Grant Hotel. She jumped from the roof, early this morning. There's a lot of hysteria, as you can imagine."

Kimberly covered her eyes. "You're sure it's not a homicide?"

"She left a note," the detective said. "And a voicemail with the other assistant, name of Audra DeFord. A long, teary message. She was in love with Muddlark, couldn't live without him, et cetera. Ms. DeFord didn't get the message until it was too late."

"She didn't confess to Muddlark's murder before she jumped, did she?"

"Afraid not. Just distraught about the love of her life." The detective went into great detail about the note and the messy scene on the sidewalk. Kimberly listened, took notes, thanked her and hung up.

"Definitely suicide," she told Jason. Kimberly stared at the remains of her breakfast and felt ill. She pushed the plate away. "At least we don't have to investigate," she muttered. She looked up at Jason. He was already back on his laptop, typing.

When will it end? she thought. She needed something new, a vacation, a resolution. An arrest.

"Here's the lineup of Freddy's new show," Jason said. Well, wasn't he a man of action? Kimberly kind of liked that in a man. He looked up at her. "Freddy's the only thing we've got that connects these people. I don't think he's the killer though, do you?"

She shook her head. "He has alibis for most of the murders."

"Plus he's not a woman," Jason said. "But what about this? Maybe one of the people on this new show is stalking Freddy. Trying to be near him and lashing out at other chefs. She loves Freddy, like, obsessively, but wants to hurt him by killing his friends and shutting down his shows and closing his restaurants." He frowned then shrugged. "Doesn't make much sense."

No, it didn't make sense, but she'd asked for theories and it was one, however cockamamie. "Who's on the new show?" Kimberly asked.

Jason glanced back at his computer. "Sallie Tam is the big name. Restaurants in Hong Kong and San Francisco. Ricardo Z, from San Diego. Stupid color-themed restaurant but apparently an innovative chef. An Australian I've never heard of named Gert Thurogood. From Iowa now, I guess? And an up-and-coming Brit named Willis Covington. It's a regular United Nations."

Kimberly listened, making notes on her phone of the names. Her heart sank. One of them would probably be dead soon if being a chef near Freddy Maxwell was the key to this case. What could they do? How could they stop the killer before she struck again?

She stared at Jason. He was concentrating as he worked the keyboard of his laptop, clearly his tool of choice. But she had an idea of how he could be even more useful. Would he do it? Would he put his laptop aside for a while, for truth and justice and the American Way? She frowned. He was clearly no Superman. She let a smile twist her lips as she pictured him in tights and a cape.

He glanced at her while typing, stopped and did a double-take. "What?"

"What if—?" she began.

He squinted. "What if what?"

She took a deep breath. "What if you got a job on that show, Jason?"

He frowned. "Doing what?"

"Anything. Food stylist, public relations, production assistant, cameraman— I don't know. The Bureau could get you in there, behind the scenes. We have our ways." She tried to smile for real. "The question is, Jason, do you want to do it? Can you take time away from your other pursuits, your reviews, your blogs? Do you have time? Can you make time to help catch a serial killer?"

"I am pretty busy," he said tentatively.

"I'm sure." She smiled and tried to look gentle. She was starting to get a feel about how to handle him. "It was just a thought. Probably too dangerous. Better to let a professional do it."

He bristled. "Well, wait. I've always wanted to go behind the scenes on a food show. Do an exposé about what really goes on. Dish on the dishes, as it were." Jason cocked his head. "Could I write a book about it? Like, after it's over?"

"When it's done? When you're a national hero? When you never have to pay for a restaurant meal again? Sure. I mean I'd have to run it by my chief, but, yeah. You wouldn't be employed by the FBI at that point."

Jason raised his eyebrows. "I'd get paid?"

"You'd be on the network's payroll. But of course we pay our Confidential Informants. It won't make you rich though." Kimberly leaned in closer. "No blogging during the assignment. I won't be able to sell that."

He nodded. "I could say I gave up blogging for a real job. No money in it or something stupid like that."

She considered. "Or we could use your blog while you're working there, have you write an insider story but also plant things that will upset the killer to try and tip their hand."

He looked appalled. "I couldn't compromise the integrity of my blog."

Integrity? In the same phrase as blog?

She took a deep breath. "Of course not. In that case, you definitely would need to stop the blog. You can say whatever you want, whatever your audience will believe. You just have to shut it down for the duration." She fixed him with her stare. "Are you in, Jason? Can your country count on you?"

She was pretty sure that was too far over the top, but his mouth twitched into a half-smile as he closed the lid to his laptop. He looked taller, laying his hands on his computer, his eyes clear, his chin strong.

"Aye-aye, sir. Er, madam." He gave her a mock salute.

She smiled again, this time for real. It might actually be fun working with this guy.

"Welcome aboard, Jason."

Chapter 27

Audra DeFord began following Jason Bainbridge's blog shortly after the murder of Fuller Muddlark at the Grant Hotel in Austin. She knew he was hot on the trail of Fuller's killer and she wanted to get there first.

The chef's assistant had been devastated by Muddlark's death. She was barely functioning when Jason had talked to her in that hotel bar, plying her with martinis. She'd known what he was doing. Audra was anything but stupid. But she had truly needed to hear a sympathetic voice and see a kind face at the time. She had needed it more than anything.

Besides, he'd been very gentlemanly, or at least she thought he had. Audra didn't encounter many actual gentlemen in the course of her daily life. The southern gentlemen she'd met in her youth in Little Rock had been anything but.

Jason hadn't said anything horrible about her when he wrote about Fuller's murder. She got a little worried about that when she realized she couldn't remember a damned thing about their meeting except that when she stumbled back to her room, she threw up so much vodka that her bathroom smelled like a Russian bathhouse the morning after a bachelor party.

But she didn't blame Jason. He was after a story just like all those people who used to try to get close to Fuller. Besides, he hadn't tried to manipulate her into bed for a self-pity bang. Two other guys had tried that line. Assholes.

That had been a truly awful time, being questioned by so many authorities, in particular that FBI agent Kimberly Douglas. The bitch kept giving her the long stare like maybe she'd had something to do with killing Fuller. As if she could ever have hurt him.

Then, just when she thought things couldn't possibly get any worse, Calista had killed herself.

Audra could barely cope with thinking about it. She had seen Calista's body out her hotel room window, broken and splayed across the sidewalk, and was making every effort to wipe the memory from her mind. She'd played and replayed that so-sad voicemail explanation so many times that she heard Calista's voice in her sleep. If only she had gotten the message sooner. Poor, darling Calista. The delicate flower, the tigress: gone.

Now, after depression and junk food binging, Audra was beginning to emerge from her blue funk. She realized that if she didn't stay focused, she'd wind up a footnote to the Fuller Muddlark murder story. She'd be interviewed on some damn food show when they caught the killer, or during teary re-membrances on anniversaries. The rest of the time she'd be forgotten.

The hell with that. She was still young, tall and stunning. Since she'd returned to her regular regimen at the gym, she was getting her tone and en-ergy back. Furthermore, she had figured out how to capitalize on the late, great body-building chef's death.

If her time with Fuller Muddlark had taught her nothing else, it was that if you gave them the sizzle you better have the steak ready too. Audra was not about to return to angling for gigs as a scantily-clad spark plug model or humping a giant can of malt liquor for a cardboard cutout.

In the past, she'd been happy when she landed those kind of photo shoots. And she got by, supplementing her income by teaching a spin class. But there could be no going back. These tragic, crazy events had offered her an opportunity and she was going to make the most of it.

She was going to be a brand.

Several media outlets had already tried to contact her. She'd ignored them initially, mired in her grief, but now, she was game. She visited a bookstore for the first time in her life and devoured do-it-yourself books on publicity. She boned up on nutrition and diet. To get her spiel down pat, she read articles on self-actualization and tossed in a smattering of Zen.

Calista had been into this sort of thing. It helped Audra that she could recall conversations with her on the subject. Calista had always been very adamant about truthfulness, too, even taking on Fuller once or twice when he wanted her to tell a whopper to blow off some annoying suck-up.

Audra, on the other hand, had no problem with the Social Lie. It didn't bother her one whit when she told everyone she was a salad-eating vegetarian when she regularly downed a chili burger and was addicted to fries doused in ketchup.

Could she help it if she had an insanely high metabolism? She regarded her public diet not as deceit but, rather, as a slightly sinful reward for trying times.

Or, if she was really honest with herself, as a cheap thrill.

Now she was anxious to take a path she had never trod before. What did they say in pro basketball— Audra had played a little ball in high school— go big or go home? She was not going home to that crappy apartment in Little Rock. Not yet. Not ever.

With Fuller Muddlark she'd gotten a taste of the good life and she was going to get her own piece of it. By any means necessary.

Which meant starting in New York.

Audra got herself a room in a fleabag hotel and headed for her boss's former Manhattan office. She congratulated herself for remembering that Muddlark had left behind a valuable asset the executors and accountants were likely to overlook: thumb drives holding the files he had gathered over the years on all sorts of celebrity chefs.

Fuller carried one set with him, but those had been confiscated by the FBI in Austin, along with the rest of his personal effects. But a second set waited in his New York office, hidden in the base of a gaudy trophy Fuller had won at a Rib Roundup in South Carolina years ago. Audra had often seen him stash the thumb drives there.

The FBI had come and gone from Fuller's office, relinquishing it to his estate. The woman who ran the office had already disappeared. But the rent was paid up for months and, given his complicated affairs, would remain that way until his estate was disentangled.

All it took to get inside was letting the seventy-something building superintendent cop a feel. She could take one for the team. The super had met Audra and she knew he lusted for her. He was damned lucky to have gotten his spidery old hands on her luscious breasts and he knew it. He didn't squawk when she slammed the office door in his face after he unlocked it for her.

She retrieved the drives from the trophy base and settled into Fuller's ergonomic office chair. It hurt her back. The computer password was taped to the bottom of the keyboard and the drives were labeled with numbers that corresponded to listings on the office computer. Piece of cake. She'd aced her computer classes in community college and probably would have even if the instructor hadn't been so, well, agreeable to extra credit options.

Since she'd been ten years old Audra had known what it took to get a "A" in life and how to get into places she wasn't supposed to go. Now she was going to put her skills to real work.

Chapter 28

Hannah stood on Ninth Street in Manhattan and gazed up at the tall brick facade of Chelsea Market. Her breath caught despite herself.

The sidewalks and gutters were all New York, dirty and foul in the oppressive heat of summer. But the epicenter of American food stood tall and proud before her. Chelsea Market, where they taped all the hit East Coast food shows. Hannah had waited so long for this.

New York, New York! Chelsea Market was an old biscuit factory where the Oreo cookie was invented. What was more American than the Oreo? The Saltine? The Mallomar? Say no more: It was their home, too.

Tourists and shoppers bumped and bustled by her as she entered into the food hall in the morning rush. But then the old fear fell over her. She slipped into a fugue state as she walked past mounds of baskets and cookware, skirting bakeries and specialty shops. Bagels called to her, croissants knew her name. A spice shop lined with every exotic flavor lured her to its door, but she saw it through a fog.

She barely noticed when she reached the elevators. Once she reached the upstairs, she'd have to face television cameras once again, even if they weren't actually on at the moment.

The memories— would they never leave her?

She came to her senses as the elevator slid open to the television studios, less glitzy and much more utilitarian than the bazaar below. Stained gray carpeting, a glass-top reception desk. A few molded plastic chairs.

She relaxed and took a deep breath. In her black slacks and black-on-black tunic, she was as nondescript as she could get without hitting a sale rack at Walmart. The only thing she'd changed was her hair. She'd made a wild decision on the trip north— her impulses were coming more often now and she was giving into them without question, recognizing that they were a sign.

She had bleached her hair platinum, dipping the pointy ends in bright blue dye, a crisp cobalt. Today she had it cinched into a ponytail off the side of her head as if to say to the world: "Fuck you, here I am."

It was so unattractive and radical she was sure that (with one potentially dangerous possibility) no one who knew her from other jobs would recognize her. The hair was all they'd notice.

She'd debated about her name and worked out a solution on the drive north. She was partial to "Ellen" these days, but Ricky knew her as Hannah and she couldn't see him remembering to call her something else, not in the state he seemed to be in. However, some of Freddy's crew stayed with him and it would be just her luck to have them recall the "Ellen" she'd been in Montana.

"Hannah!"

Ricky skidded around the corner into the lobby, a royal mess of hair on end and panicky eyes. He did a double-take before enveloping her in his arms. "Thank God. I thought you'd never get here." He smelled like onions. No, shallots. "What the hell's with the hair?" He laughed nervously. Before she could give him more than a satisfied smile he rattled on. "Come on, let's go back to my dressing room."

He grabbed her arm and dragged her through a warren of poorly-lit hallways to a scuffed door where "Ricardo" was scribbled on a piece of craft paper and haphazardly taped. He didn't comment or apologize, just looked quickly down the hall both ways, then turned the key and pushed her inside.

Hannah stood astounded, in the middle of a disaster zone.

Fast food bags filled the small room, on dressers and chairs, hanging from lamps. McDonalds, Burger King, Five Guys, Taco Bell and KFC. Boxes and wrappers were strewn everywhere. An overwhelming odor permeated the air: rancid grease and old French fries.

It looked as if a bunch of teenage boys had been partying for weeks while somebody's parents were away. All it needed was a pried-open liquor cabinet and a kid puking in the john.

Was he having a nervous breakdown?

Behind her, she heard Ricky's girlish shriek. Was he just seeing this mess? He began cursing, softly at first, then louder and louder. He ran to a closet and pulled out a plastic bag. Crazed and huffing, red in the face, Ricky grabbed the fast food bags, stuffing them into the big, white trash liner.

Hannah stepped aside as he thrashed by her, madly tossing in the food bags. Things were worse than she thought. He was off the deep end already and the show hadn't even started taping.

Finally he tied the strings of the trash bag and threw it into the hall. He closed the door, slumping against it, agony on his face. He slid down the wall to the floor, hiding his face against his knees, moaning.

Hannah put her hands on her hips and spoke sharply. "What is going on here? Pull yourself together, Papi."

He looked up at her, all but crying. "You see? You see how they hate me?"

"Who hates you?" Hannah asked. But she knew.

"All of them. This has been going on all week. Every day it's some new kind of hazing, some prank. That's what Freddy calls it, a prank. He says it's part of being on a show like this. You have to be able to take the pressure. You have to get competitive, figure out how to win." Ricky moaned again. "I just want to—"

"To what?" Hannah said, her voice hardening to a spot midway between schoolmarm and drill sergeant. "To quit? To run home to San Diego with your dick tucked in, embarrassed that you couldn't stand the heat? 'Little Ricky Zelinsky loved his crayons and his colored food but he had to get out of the big folks kitchen.' Is that what you want them to say? To tattle all over the Internet?"

She realized as she spoke that she had grown genuinely fond of Ricky. She'd been able to set aside his past transgressions to move forward in his occasional company. Maybe she'd even gotten a smidgen closer to some kind of forgiveness.

She wanted him to succeed here because she wanted him to succeed.

Though of course that wasn't everything, or she wouldn't be here at all. She also needed him to participate in the competition on *A Cut Above.* If he gave up and slunk off to think up new recipes featuring Jamaica blue coffee beans and orange mushrooms and purple chard, Hannah wouldn't get her chance at killing Trudy AKA Gert Thurogood.

And she so wanted to get close to the skinny bitch again, to look her in the eye and bring her down. Hard. Gert Thurogood was Hannah's Original Sin. That was how Hannah looked at it. Gert's nasty remark, uttered so many years ago when she was still Trudy, had been the moment when everything started to go wrong.

That was the moment when Hannah saw her father for who he really was, a weak, passionless man. That was the moment she realized she would never live up to his expectations, that he cared more about his reputation than his only daughter, when he had realized she was a poor substitute for the son he never had. Gert had made that much obvious. Maybe Hannah should be grateful to the bitch for opening her eyes. No. Gert Thurogood needed to pay.

Hannah had been fantasizing about it all the way up from New Orleans: As she bought gas, as she studied her map, as she slept in crappy Super 8 motels, reduced to eating Little Debbie cupcakes by the box just to keep her strength up. She had imagined so many different ways to kill the woman and yet still had the feeling that the perfect method was eluding her. Gert's death needed to be special.

Ricky was staring at her with pleading eyes. When she didn't give him any pity he pulled himself up off the floor. He rubbed his face and sighed. "You're right. They won't break me now that you're here." He hugged her again and she thought she might puke. Sniveling worm. What had happened to the arrogant dude in the chef's whites on the roof at Rainbow? She pushed him off her.

"Ricky, this is on you," she snapped. "Get it together." She glanced around the dressing room. It didn't look much better without the fast food. In fact, it looked worse. Also the smell had lingered. "What was all the fast food about? Has this happened before?"

She was starting to wish she'd grabbed a Five Guys burger before he pitched everything. This was not the time or place to admit it, but the smell of fast food often touched a deeply buried and persistent affection for the forbidden.

"Not to me. I figure it must be Willis Covington," Ricky said. "He keeps going on in that irritating limey accent about American fast food, how it's filled with offal and insecticides and cooked in axle grease. Total asshole."

He shoved some food magazines off a broken-down green sofa and gestured for her to take a seat. Hannah sat carefully, hearing springs pop beneath her and doing her best to avoid the stains. Ricky sat beside her and took her hand. "But you're here now. You'll help me. I have to get ready, Hannah. I need four dishes to win this thing. Four incredible dishes."

Hannah examined his face. He looked calmer now, like maybe he wasn't going bonkers. With chefs it was sometimes hard to tell, since they were so high-strung. "What sort of dishes?" she asked.

He smiled, relieved to be back in the game. "I don't know yet. We're supposed to find out today. There's a group meeting in ten minutes. You made it just in time."

"To the rescue," she said mockingly. "Hey, listen, I had a kind of bad experience way back with Freddy Maxwell, and I'm hoping he's forgotten all about it. Do you suppose you could introduce me as Hannah Sinclair?" She let a veil of sadness float over her face briefly. "It was my married name."

She had given Ricky her phony widowhood story their first night together on the roof over Rainbow, and he had never asked for details. Most people didn't, which made it an ideal conversation-stopper. There was something unnerving about the idea of being widowed at Hannah's young age that left people speechless and uncomfortable.

Ricky was no exception. He hadn't asked for a single detail, bless his pea-picking heart.

"Of course," he said, squeezing her hand. "Let's go, Hannah Sinclair."

Chapter 29

The production meeting for *A Cut Above* was held in the studio where they would tape the show starting next week. Hannah really wished that Ricky had given her more time to prepare. But she couldn't have gotten here much sooner, being otherwise occupied in Texas. He had been here a week already, but she was the new kid on the set and would have to really hustle.

The show began taping on Monday and it was already Thursday. They would need every minute of those three and a half days to get the recipes ready. Never mind that each of those minutes was also allotted to the challenge of dispatching Gert Thurogood to oblivion.

The dark, cavernous studio was mostly empty. Spotlights shone on four kitchen stations with stainless steel racks, cook tops, ovens and refrigerators. The stations were stripped of all utensils and food items. They gleamed under the lights. The setup reminded Hannah a lot of the set of... no, she would not think about that. She simply would not. She squinted, keeping her eyes from the harsh spotlights.

Hannah turned her mind to which station Ricky would get and whether it mattered.

Would there be a subtle pecking order in the assignments, or would they be positioned to highlight contrasts? Certainly it wouldn't be random. Nothing about this operation sounded random. And who would the judges be? They had yet to be announced.

All of that could wait, however. She had one important hurdle to pass first: Freddy Maxwell, the person she worried most about recognizing her. Once she got past him, she'd be locked and loaded.

Maxwell stood in a small huddle on a platform across from the cooking stations, his silver mane twinkling with hair gel as he conferred with a short Asian woman. That must be Sallie Tam, Hannah thought excitedly. As they got closer, Sallie's clear atonal voice carried. She was speaking to a younger, black-haired Asian woman in Cantonese. The assistant bobbed her head and turned to Freddy, who looked amused and slightly mystified.

"Chef says she won't be, um, tormented by the other chefs," the young assistant/interpreter said. "She says there is no place in cooking for jokes and games."

"What is she talking about?" Freddy asked, frowning.

Sallie began to talk rapidly, moving her hands around in circles. The assistant listened and began to explain, but Sallie put a hand on her shoulder to stop her. "I shall speak," the chef said, turning to the producer. "Some idiot tape knives to ceiling of my dressing room. Nobody suppose to be in room, only me. Knives cost thousands of dollars, maybe ruined. Knife fall when I go in room. Very dangerous."

Freddy's eyes widened and he didn't look happy. He was probably remembering Fuller Muddlark's last knife fight, and his buddy George Bernard, hanging from the moose rack in Montana with his own fine cutlery studding his ribcage. Hannah restrained a smile. The moose rack had been a nice touch.

The producer stammered an apology to Sallie Tam and gave her a condescending lecture about Americans and their silly prankster ways.

Ricky nudged Hannah and whispered, "That's the same thing he told me. I thought it was bullshit, too."

"Did you get your knives taped to the ceiling?" Hannah asked.

"Not yet," Ricky said. "Maybe it was somebody who takes *A Cut Above* too literally?"

"Ha ha" Hannah muttered, frowning. "At least the junk food prank was edible."

The other two chefs entered the studio now, assistants in tow. Hannah stared at Trudy Thurogood and her pulse begin to race. Trudy— Gert now, Hannah reminded herself— was still tall and gangly with a hawk-like nose and long, piano-playing fingers, but her short blond hair had gone white. She'd combed it mannishly up and back, making her appear even taller. Her face was lined as if she'd smoked or suntanned too much. Probably both. But neither habit made much sense. A chef who smoked paid a huge price in the taste bud department, and that knobby body would be grotesque in a swim-suit. Like giant beef jerky on parade. Human bacon, extra-crispy.

Hannah was starting to get hungry.

Wait— what was he doing here? Next to Gert lurked that blogger, Jason Bainbridge. Was he writing about the show? She'd seen him in Montana before her teary departure, then again outside the hotel when she'd killed Fuller Muddlark. And she'd been in disguise.

Hannah took a breath. Bainbridge was the type to only notice the food. A second fellow stood near him, thinner and nervous in a brown vest, his hair in a Pee-wee Herman twirly hairdo. Probably the host. All the hosts were trying to outdo Chopped's Ted Allen these days. As if that could be done.

What a posse. Hannah tried not to smirk, keeping her face neutral. After the twin Amazons in Austin, this felt like taking on Miss Peabody's Pre-school. During naptime.

The fourth chef, Willis Covington, had a studious British look. Round glasses, bow tie, white shirt and pressed gabardine slacks made an odd get-up for a chef, but Hannah had to grudgingly admit that he totally owned it. His brown hair was longish, slicked back and curling over his starched collar. Hannah had a nagging feeling she knew Willis Covington from somewhere, but surely she would have remembered a man dressed like that?

Covington's assistant was male and rather colorless, a shock of blond hair, ramrod straight, but possibly not entirely straight. He had beautiful lips, probably tasty. A challenge, she thought, her libido never far from her mind these days. Sex and death. It had a certain inevitability about it.

"Ah, everyone's here," Freddy said, affecting an upper class accent that Hannah found repulsive.

This was the big test. Would Freddy recognize her as Ellen Bartkus, who had worked briefly for Charlotte and Giorgio Bernardi on *Love Bites*?

Nope. As Ricky introduced Hannah Sinclair in a too-loud voice, Freddy didn't seem to register either the name or appearance of the newest assistant. Nor did anybody else show much interest.

Business as usual. Anonymity R Us. Being dumpy had its advantages.

By the time the introductions were over, the only names she knew for sure were the ones she'd already known: Gert, Willis, Sallie and Jason Bainbridge, who was apparently now moonlighting as a food researcher. Freddy explained that everyone on the set of *A Cut Above* would be able to tap into his vast knowledge of food and recipes whenever he was free. It was hard to imagine why anybody in this company would find that necessary.

Hannah shuffled her feet nervously. She couldn't be sure that Jason Bainbridge wouldn't recognize her. A prickle of anxiety, or possibly sexual excitement, tingled through her. There was something crazy luscious about him and his springy hair. He was like a Kennedy who'd gone to seed early. As Freddy passed out packets of instructions, Hannah poked Ricky in the ribs.

"Isn't that guy a food blogger?" she asked innocently, nodding toward Jason.

"Failed blogger. Pretty pathetic," Ricky whispered. "Rumor is he lost his shirt. Shut down his blog and reduced to working for a living. But he might be helpful with recipes. Everyone says he knows a lot about food."

Freddy Maxwell clapped his hands sharply. "All right, everybody," he said, "Listen up. Your packets contain all the relevant information for your competition. Please note that this is not an elimination contest like *Chopped*.

Each of you will participate in every portion of the show. Scoring will be numerical and cumulative, and the highest score at the conclusion will win both the competition and a limited-run television series of your own."

Ricky inhaled sharply and leaned toward Hannah. "First time they mentioned a series. Oh, man."

Sallie Tam raised a tiny hand. "We know score?"

"Absolutely," Freddy replied. "There'll be an electronic scoreboard above each of your stations, updated in real time."

As opposed to what, Hannah wondered? Fake time? Freddy always had a tendency toward hyperbole. Unless they were booby-trapped to drop powdered sugar or ice water on low scoring chefs, or to shoot off fireworks for high scoring ones, a scoreboard was a scoreboard.

"We've finalized the judges," Freddy continued, "and we're very excited with the lineup."

He went on to name three chefs from around the globe. Restaurateur Caleb Harrison from DC and the Food Network's own Lorena Martinez. Lastly, Martin Devereaux, a faux Frenchman from Detroit who'd made a splash in the Loire Valley.

Hannah watched the chefs' faces as the judges were announced. Willis Covington cocked his head and nodded approvingly. Sallie Tam never moved but frowned slightly at the mention of Lorena Martinez. Gert Thurogood appeared to have just taken a hearty suck on a cassava-sized lemon.

Freddy continued. "Throughout the past week, you've each had the opportunity to work at all of the four stations. As of right now, you'll be permanently assigned and will be responsible for everything related to that station." He pointed from left to right across the stage as a hush of anticipation fell. "Willis, you're on the far left. Next comes Sallie, then Ricardo, and Gert on the far right."

Excellent.

All of them would rehearse together and cook side-by-side as they got ready for the taping, which could provide just the opening Hannah needed, since Ricky was right beside her quarry. The idea of Gert Thurogood keeling over on national television was just too delicious, but unfortunately cooking shows never ran live.

On a more personal level, Hannah liked the station assignments because when she wasn't involved in her own extracurricular activities, she would be able to observe Sallie Tam for the pure pleasure of it. The woman was supposed to be a magician in the kitchen. Although clearly older than the other chefs, Tam seemed immune to the passage of time. She never appeared to hurry and her exact age remained a complete mystery to the world.

Hannah was theoretically there to assist Ricky, but she hadn't even liked babysitting as a child. If Ricardo Z got too bossy or demanding during the next couple of prep days, she would simply remind him that this was his competition. She was strictly the pep squad and erotic release team.

"And now for the final announcement that you've all been waiting for and asking me about," Freddy said. "The theme." He raised both hands as if officiating at a revival meeting. "The theme for this special premiere episode of *A Cut Above* is going to be Nouveau Nostalgia."

Come again? Hannah saw her own confusion mirrored around the room.

Freddy chuckled. "I know what you're thinking. That doesn't make sense. You can have one or the other. But the premise is really quite straightforward. We're looking for vibrant new approaches to traditional cuisine. Sliders made of chopped calamari, for instance. Or mac-cheese borsht, though I'd caution you all against macaroni-and-cheese in general. It is so last decade."

Kind of like you, Freddy, Hannah thought.

"Now," the producer explained, "you have free rein to take the Nouveau Nostalgia theme in any direction you want, as long as you can justify what you do to the judges. Any questions?"

* * *

After the meeting folks began setting up their work areas and Ricky took Hannah around to meet everyone. He seemed energized by the new information about the theme and judges, and had pointed out to Hannah that his central station meant he would probably get more air time then the chefs on the ends. Even better, he appeared to have bounced back from the fast food prank and didn't mention it to anybody. Hannah knew that would rankle the perpetrator.

Gert Thurogood was cold and dismissive, barely looking at Hannah. Her rudeness hardened Hannah's resolve, as if hardening were necessary. Gert carefully removed utensils from a large case and handed them to the guy with the Pee-wee Herman hair. He wasn't the host at all but Gert's assistant. Interesting. The Pee-wee Herman look was itself nouveau nostalgia.

Even more interesting: The guy turned out to be named Herman, with a German accent, and he lined up Gert's utensils with Teutonic precision. Herman the German. Hannah would have no trouble remembering that. When Gert turned away with a sharp nod, he skittered after her like a lap dog.

Sallie Tam, on the other hand, surprised Hannah by being gracious and polite, and her assistant Kamling professed great admiration for Hannah's blue-tipped hair. Just as well. She couldn't kill everyone, now could she?

Willis Covington and his assistant were also polite. Despite Ricky's belief that the Brit was behind the drive-by burgering of his dressing room, Willis seemed pleasant enough, with that English reserve.

Then Hannah shook Covington's hand and their eyes met for a moment. Her blood ran cold.

She did know Willis from somewhere, and it wasn't a good memory. Not at all. The shock of recognition had clearly hit him too. But where had they met? She didn't know any British chefs beyond seeing them on television and had only been to England once, on a two-week trip when she was in college. Did he know something about her? This had potential for real trouble.

Ricky was introducing her to the maybe-straight assistant. He was yummy in a blond hipster sort of way and despite herself Hannah hoped he'd notice her. But he mumbled a greeting with barely a glance. That settled that. Willis and his entourage stalked off into the shadows.

As Ricky gave her a tour of the studio, the production room, the kitchens and a back kitchen where much of the food was stored or surreptitiously prepared, Hannah searched her prodigious memory banks for Willis Covington. She had run across a whole lot of people in a whole lot of places.

Was he from Iowa? Business school? Couteaux Culinary?

Had she met him on a cooking show? God knows she'd met tons of chefs, production people, stylists, runners and gofers. She'd sworn those days were behind her, that she'd never subject herself to that level of invisibility and abuse again. How she hated pretending to be powerless now.

Because here she was, a gofer again. Holding Ricky's hand, bucking up his courage, telling him how great he was— or could be— all the while sublimating her own personality and ego.

It was going to be a very challenging week. Unless, of course, she found a way to cut it short.

Chapter 30

Kimberly Douglas spread the file folders across her desk.

While she'd been on the road, the FBI had moved her from her airy south-facing office with its view of lower Manhattan and Battery Park to a cubicle in the middle of dozens of other cubicles. That would teach her to pursue an actual lead. She had been livid when she returned from Texas but there was nothing she could do about it except stay out of town so she didn't have to face it. Unfortunately, right now, New York was where she had to be.

The background checks on the four chefs in Freddy Maxwell's new show had revealed some interesting details. Kimberly wasn't sure what they meant yet or where they connected with the killer, but with Jason's help she hoped to crack this case before another gruesome murder occurred.

The big news outlets had gotten wind of Fuller Muddlark's sensational homicide. The suicide of his beautiful assistant had seen to that. Since the food bloggers had been piecing together a connection between the murders for months, she supposed it was only a matter of time before the media caught up. But she hated that outside scrutiny.

She sifted through the background checks. Sallie Tam had the cleanest sheet Kimberly had ever seen, although she'd had some issues with immigration over the years. Since she'd gotten her EB5 entrepreneur green card there was nothing of a federal nature in her file.

Gertrude Thurogood's immigration status was more interesting. An Australian, she'd been in the US illegally for the last fourteen years, ever since her student visa expired. She hadn't paid much in taxes either, something un-derhanded there. She'd run a successful restaurant in Des Moines for the last ten years. Where was the profit?

Richard Zelinsky appeared normal enough, apart from his drug use. He'd been caught with cocaine a couple times and wiggled out of it.

But the last chef, Willis Covington, was a real piece of work.

When Kimberly first opened his file she thought the contents must have somehow gotten switched. The photo of Covington showed what ap-peared to be a completely different man.

That man was named William Clover, known as Bill to his friends in Mobile, Alabama, where he had run a mom-and-pop diner specializing in soup and pie. Bill Clover had ceased to be— at least in the US— six years before. Dropped off the map. Disappeared. Hightailed it out of town.

The diner closed one day and Bill Clover vanished, leaving behind a mountain of unpaid bills, three hundred pounds of rancid butter and a preg-nant girlfriend.

Nobody had looked very hard for him, actually, except the girlfriend. And she had no luck. She really had no luck. Turned out she was carrying twins. Bill Clover's unpaid child support had reached the point that it could land him in jail. If only he could be found.

Meanwhile out of nowhere Willis Covington had started showing up all over the London broadsheets three years ago. A dandy, a ladies man, a dashing young restaurateur. Bill Clover had totally reinvented himself into an exciting chef with a trendy restaurant called Covington Garden that special-ized in fresh and tasty farm-to-table vegetable dishes.

How long would it be before somebody on the cooking show figured out Willis Covington was really wild Bill Clover? And what would happen then? Would anybody even care, or would these nut-jobs in the cooking world just give him props for initiative and reward him with his own show?

Kimberly stared at the soft gray walls of her cubicle. Sallie. Gert. Ricardo. Willis. Which one would be targeted? Who would be next?

Could Willis Covington be the killer? Had he reinvented himself to get closer to the chefs he despised? She had no reason to interview him about anything right now, and there was no way to find out if he had alibis for all the murders without questioning him. Had he just entered the country? She could check with Customs on when he'd been in the US and she could certainly track him now.

She took his file with her to her supervisor's office and knocked on his open door.

"Sir? I'd like to request a tap of a suspect's phone."

Chapter 31

By the end of the first day of preparation, Hannah was exhausted. Her cut still hurt like hell, she'd been driving for days and anxious for weeks. Austin had gone badly and now that she'd seen the set for *A Cut Above* and gotten so tantalizingly close to Gert Thurogood, her mind kept going blank. She wanted to choose the perfect way to kill her but her thoughts kept wandering to other things.

She had made a lot of plans for Gert on her way to New York, but half of them were impractical and the rest were simply half-baked. She had managed to put off Ricky for the evening with a quickie in his still-nasty-smelling dressing room. It was like having teenage sex in a burger joint bathroom. Then she had wandered through Chelsea Market, picking up enough prepared food to last a family of four for two days. Food helped her focus.

By nine p.m. she had eaten every last bite.

Feeling vaguely embarrassed, she tried to assuage her guilt by watching a YouTube video of a girl in Korea who had become a national sensation for binge eating.

Not the sort of binging Americans indulged in, however. There were no football jocks trying to eat seventy-five corn dogs in four minutes, no frat boys getting alcohol poisoning, no children up to their ears in ice cream. This was slow and deliberate, taking place at a leisurely pace, with bowls of tasty-looking dishes and lots of sound effects, including slurping. Hannah watched only the first ten minutes before clicking it off. The thrill of eating wasn't in the eating as in the connection it had to life, and through life to sex, and through sex to death itself.

She ought to make her own video. About food and sex and death. The big three.

Burping with satisfaction, she showered in the marble hotel bathroom and sank into bed. Ricky had offered to share his hotel room, but that was a great deal more togetherness than she had in mind. And she wanted no questions about the cut on her arm. She could always pass it off as a cooking wound, but that was a stretch. Best to keep it hidden for as long as possible while it healed.

Besides, everything was going to have to be planned on the fly now and she didn't need Ricardo Z going boo-hoo in the corner while she plotted. She had three problems to solve: how to keep Freddy Maxwell at bay, how she knew Willis Covington and how to knock off Gert Thurogood in a sufficiently humiliating way.

She had read somewhere that if you concentrated on a problem before you went to sleep, it would resolve itself by morning. She set two balls bouncing before she drifted off—how to get rid of Gert and how she knew the Brit, Willis Covington.

* * *

It was Willis Covington she dreamed about, and he appeared in dozens of different scenarios, none of which included her: on the Silk Road with Marco Polo, preparing the papal breakfast in Vatican City, slopping hogs at her grandfather's farm in Iowa, crawling through guano into a cave filled with rabid bats and sitting by a campfire.

The campfire dream woke her and sent her bolt upright.

Years ago Hannah had made a pilgrimage to the Terlingua Chili Cook-Off in one of the more remote sections of West Texas. Overall the experience was a bust; most of the competitors seemed only interested in how many unbearably hot peppers they could cram into a single serving of chili.

It had seemed like a great idea, a fine fall adventure, but she felt woefully out of place in her rented mini-camper in the middle of nowhere. Everything in Terlingua, with a population in the mid-two figures, was in the middle of nowhere.

She couldn't remember what the guy had called himself, though she knew it wasn't a prissy name like Willis. She remembered eating blistering hot bowls of red with him that they washed down with oceans of tequila. She also remembered waking up naked in his tent with a Texas-sized hangover.

Not-Willis had been not-much as a lover, desperate to get her clothes off and ending the moment with a hearty Yee-haw!

She avoided him the next day, and the following morning she awoke, alone in her mini-camper, to a brouhaha concerning items stolen by a burglar who had apparently taken off before sunup. The thief had stolen guns, which required real cojones in relentlessly macho West Texas, cash boxes from a couple of concessionaires and an assortment of whips from a leathersmith's booth.

Not-Willis wasn't the only person missing, but Hannah had no doubt who was to blame.

The Texas Rangers were called. This didn't require a lot of effort, since several were attending the Chili Cook-Off, but if Not-Willis or anybody else had ever been apprehended, Hannah didn't know it.

So who was he really?

It was still dark out. Hannah couldn't get to sleep again, so she ran herself a bubble bath and turned on the radio in the bathroom. Lying back in the warm suds, she put her mind to Gert Thurogood but felt a jolt as she heard the name Fuller Muddlark come out of the radio speakers.

Seriously? Why was anyone talking about Muddlark's death in New York City? He wasn't all that famous and he was a Texan who had made his reputation in Chicago.

Even more incredibly, she recognized the voice of the woman who was speaking: Audra DeFord, his surviving Amazonian assistant.

Chapter 32

"So, Audra, you've been through a hell of a lot," the host said, her full lips close to the mic in the radio studio. She called herself Beacon.

"It's been a trial, Beacon. It's only through restoring my spiritual and body balance back that I've been able to come through it." Audra felt the lie flow from her lips with just the right amount of pain.

Beacon's forehead wrinkled in sympathy. Audra was pretty sure Beacon would buy anything she had to say. Which was fine with her. Beacon wasn't a bad looking woman, if you liked them butch. She had weight-lifter arms and decent breasts. Who was she kidding with a name like "Beacon" anyway? Her real name was probably Bertha. Despite her New Age pretensions, Beacon had more than a whiff of working class about her.

Her show was called Portal to Potential on WZAP, a late night program on a listener-sponsored station. WZAP was housed on the second floor of a stucco building that was home to a handful of community organizations and a drop-in legal clinic deep in the Red Hook section of Brooklyn.

"You must have worked incredibly hard to regain your balance," Beacon said earnestly, "Tell us about that."

Audra sighed, rearing back slightly as if bombarded by a psychic blow. With just the right amount of quaver in her voice, she said, "As you can understand, I was devastated by the murder of my mentor and friend Fuller Muddlark. And then for my dear friend Calista to succumb to her grief, I mean, it was almost too much to bear."

"Yes, yes, tell it, sister," Beacon murmured.

Audra continued. "Of course, when things like that happen, it's only natural to feel overwhelmed, adrift. After all, no right-thinking person, a person who is in touch with their inner being, can even imagine anyone so callously taking another's life. But there I was, drowning and wallowing in my own pity party. I was lost for a few days, Beacon, not listening to the warnings from my chakras."

"Oh yes, I hear you. The same thing happened to me when Mr. Cuddles, my cat, left this earthly plane last year."

Audra stifled a laugh. Mr. Cuddles? She reached across the desk to pat Beacon's hand. "Traumatic events can be devastating. That's why we must work to regain our inner and outer health."

Beacon squeezed Audra's finger before letting her hand go. But not before Audra saw a hungry look cross her face. She had her.

"Tell us, Audra, about using your regime of super foods to regain your bearings. Well, really," Beacon gushed, "regain your glow. I have to tell my listeners that you radiate such a positive aura."

"That's sweet of you, Beacon."

"I can only speak the truth." The host smiled demurely. "You're the perfect guest for my show. My program usually features recipes that any busy working woman or man can do make. I'm not just talking about kale and shredded carrots sprinkled with lemon juice, either. I'm talking about delicious, nutritious meals for you to enjoy and relight your own glow. I'm about all of us lighting the way for better health and, therefore, better living in other aspects of our lives."

"Well, Beacon," Audra began, "More than anything— it's really about becoming aware."

"And if your body is unblocked..." Beacon said.

"Your mind becomes unblocked," Audra finished.

Audra then launched into her soft sell. "Take, for example, vegetables available from our mother the sea. I'm talking about life affirming plants such as dulse, kelp, nori, wakame and arame. These are high in minerals and a great source of iodine, which is essential for the thyroid."

"The thyroid being so central to the regulation of our core metabolism," Beacon said.

"Precisely. Body temperature, muscle strength, appetite, and the health of your heart, brain, kidneys, even our reproductive system."

Audra went on to extol the benefits of seaweed. "Nori is great for making sushi rolls. Sprinkle it on your salad or soups or add it to your smoothies. Then, of course, there's— *berries.*"

Beacon leaned in, eyes locked on Audra's golden skin. "Sweet... juicy... ripe... succulent berries."

Audra licked her lips slowly and said, "Goji, acai, camu camu, chokeberries and blueberries. My latest newsletter is devoted to them. Goji berries are rich in antioxidants and have been used for centuries in Chinese medicine. Acai berries are known to be energy boosters and have anti-aging effects. Camu camu berries are from South America and are considered to have the highest Vitamin C content of any plant, bar none."

"I understand chokeberries contain some of the highest levels of antioxidants of any fruit as well."

Audra concurred and offered several recipes and morning smoothie preparations for recapturing the glow. "I should mention as well," she inserted, putting a touch of reverence in her voice, "that even though Fuller Muddlark was known for his meat dishes and loved his barbeque, he and I were readying a line of vegetarian-based meals. He asked me to co-write the cookbook that went along with it. Of course, I'll finish that task to honor his memory."

Audra could just imagine how Fuller would have howled at the idea he might publish a book about vegetables. Unless they had been cooked limp in bacon fat, Fuller hated vegetables.

Beacon said, "Your upcoming book in a way is a testament to him?"

"His dream will be realized," Audra murmured.

Who was going to challenge her? Certainly not Fuller, and not his publisher here in New York, either. They'd jump at the chance to profit from his death.

Audra had just turned the page on a new chapter in her life. Being an almost-thirty former aerobics instructor, one-time Charger Girl and aide to a murdered celebrity chef was not going to be her sad sack epitaph. Hell no.

They took calls during the last few minutes of the show then headed out into pre-dawn Brooklyn. The station was located in an area "in transition," as real estate doublespeak liked to put it. It was five o'clock in the morning, and Beacon's Portal to Potential show, which ran after the Tibetan throat-singing hour, had given way to Morning Yoga With Manny.

It was a pretty safe bet, Audra concluded, that Beacon's entire audience was comprised of weirdos, insomniacs, nursing mothers, the brown rice Baba Ram Dass crowd and a few 9/11 truthers. Few of them would have even the slightest interest in improving their health with camu camu, or in buying Audra's not-yet-written cookbook. But you had to start somewhere.

What mattered was that Beacon was a step up on Audra's ascent to the top. Audra had done her research and knew that Beacon was some sort of adviser to a British chef, Willis Covington, who was going to be on that new cooking show, *A Cut Above*. She needed to find a way onto that show and Beacon was her ticket.

She and Beacon went to a coffee shop for herbal tea— Audra was craving steak and eggs and it almost killed her to sustain the allusion she was vegan— but by seven-thirty that morning, she had her legs spread on Beacon's bed and a birds-eye view of the top of Beacon's head bobbing below her.

"Oh, my," Audra moaned, grinding her pelvis as if she were in ecstasy. Truthfully, she'd gotten more excited painting her toenails the night before. She grabbed Beacon's hair and made noises that were far too loud for this time of the morning. Maybe she should have gone into acting? The new Bond movie was casting and she certainly had the look. Audra let her mind wander into a fantasy of living in Hollywood as Beacon continued her almost desperate ministrations.

"I needed that," a breathless Beacon said later, after Audra had faked her climax. Sun dappled through slats on the window across their bodies. They lay side-by-side, Audra nude, Beacon clad solely in black lace panties. Beacon slung her arm around Audra's waist and leaned in for a passionate kiss.

A ring tone sounded in the other room: *Defying Gravity,* a song from the musical Wicked.

"Sorry," Beacon said, "but I need to get that."

"Mom calling?" Audra asked.

"Somebody equally demanding." She wandered off into the other room. "Why, hell-o there, Willis. I kind of figured you'd be calling about now, big boy."

Audra found herself on full alert. Jackpot.

Beacon had to be talking to Willis Covington, a man that Audra now knew was the biggest fake since the moon landing, an event everyone knew actually occurred in Arizona. Thanks to Fuller Muddlark, Audra knew that the chef's name wasn't Covington and he wasn't even English. He was just some cracker from Alabama.

Fuller had been an ambitious man. He'd amassed exhaustive files on his competitors, their likes and dislikes, their quirks and peccadilloes. All the better to get an edge up. And now Audra had all the files. But she'd known about Willis Covington even before then.

One of Fuller's information brokers had uncovered the deception about a year ago. Audra remembered being at the Octagon Tango in Aspen during some food contest her boss was judging. Fuller had made quick work of a few bourbons after a long and irritating day.

On one of the silent big screens in the VIP section of the club, Willis Covington was being interviewed.

"What a cardboard cutout," Muddlark had said. He had rigid ideas about honesty. Being big on working out and staying in shape, Fuller was opposed to steroid use and by extension those who cheated in any way. Maybe that's why he had such a mania to get the goods on his fellow chefs.

"He's a redneck from Alabama." He had turned to Calista. "No offense to you rednecks." Calista was related to the seventh US vice-president, John Caldwell Calhoun, an ardent defender of slavery.

"None taken, honey pie," Calista joked, putting the country in her Connecticut voice.

"But you gotta hand it to him," Muddlark said, taking another sip of his Maker's Mark. "He's reinvented himself and as far as the world is concerned, the nobody diner owner known as Bill Clover has given way to the famous Willis Covington." Muddlark had saluted the screen with his glass and downed his drink.

But there was another aspect to Covington that Audra didn't known until she retrieved Muddlark's secret files, an aspect that very much involved Beacon.

The radio host returned to the bedroom. "Sorry, that was one of my clients."

"You do life coaching?"

"In a way," Beacon said, getting back under the sheets with Audra. "I like to think of it as advising on how to develop the energies within us. But in this case, I had to refer him to a specialist. He had other needs." She rubbed Audra's washboard stomach. "I teach people how to achieve the fullness of a mind-body connection so as to reach their full potential. Are you interested in such a connection?"

"Sure." Audra needed to ensure her entree into Willis Covington's world, so she might as well lock in Beacon's help. Slipping a hand inside the other woman's panties, she heard Beacon moan with pleasure as she murmured, "I could always use some more mind-body connection myself."

Chapter 33

Jason met Kimberly in a tapas bar near her office. Tapa the Morning was owned by an Irishman, and Jason had liked the place very much a few years back when tapas were taking the culinary world by storm. The place hadn't fared well after the foodies moved on, however, and he was frankly amazed it was still in business.

Even so, it seemed a safer bet than the other place she had suggested in the same area. Mongolian Barbeque? Puh-leaze. Leave it to the Mongol hordes.

Honestly, did the woman have no taste buds at all? He pictured her sliding a Chicken Divan Lean Cuisine into an immaculate microwave in an antiseptic apartment, where the maid came to clean an already spotless kitchen and you could perform appendectomies on the kitchen floor.

Still, he didn't want to dismiss her tastes entirely, and it was to his advantage to ease her carefully into real cuisine. If their joint venture had any success at all, he was seriously considering asking Kimberly on a real date one day. He had not yet figured out what she would consider a real date, of course, and it was so long since he'd had anything worthy of that name himself that he didn't even know what his own idea was.

He did know that it would involve extraordinary food: the aphrodisiac menu which had been his first blog post to go viral.

Oysters were at the heart of it, of course, both raw as an appetizer and then as an entree in a gratin with asparagus and almonds. A simple arugula salad with avocado slivers dressed in extra virgin olive oil and a sherry and honey-dressed fruit salad that included cherries, strawberries, bananas, figs and pomegranate arils. Dessert would be a chocolate soufflé, right out of the oven with freshly whipped organic cream from contented, hand-milked cows.

It occurred to him that the only kitchen where he could currently prepare that meal was in his grubby Queens apartment, where a few of the dust dragons had recently morphed into dust dinosaurs. Since he'd begun his climb into the food world's major leagues (despite his current humiliating role as gofer on a TV show he despised) he was starting to realize that he needed a serious upgrade in living quarters.

Well, the six-figure advance that his inside story of the chef murders was certain to bring would make a good start toward that goal. He hoped that it wasn't bad karma to be wishing for another murder so that he could be an eyewitness. Probably, but he was willing to take that risk. He knew, with an unsupported certainty, that there would be a killing on the show. He just hadn't sorted out killer and victim yet, though he hoped neither would be Sallie Tam. Watching her cook had already been amazing.

"Tell me everything that happened this afternoon," Kimberly was saying as she sipped an almost undrinkable sangria. She'd ordered a pitcher to share, made with a harsh red wine that allegedly hailed from Andalusia but was probably Two-Buck Chuck.

He nibbled Pimentos Fritos con Ajo and winced. The garlic tasted raw and the badly-roasted peppers were leprous with flecks of charred skin. That would have been bad enough, but the whole dish seemed tired, as if it had been prepared last week, and had been waiting in the back of the fridge for some sucker to order it.

Luckily he had a murder investigation to attend to. "The contestants were peeing their pants they were so excited. I don't know why Freddy was stalling about announcing the important stuff like judges and theme. Maybe he had trouble nailing down the chefs to judge. What did you find out about them?" He had texted the names to Kimberly from the set to give her a jump-start.

She pulled some white index cards from a pocket. "So far they seem to be exactly who they claim to be. I don't have much on the French guy, Martin Devereaux."

She pronounced his name with a Francophile relish which surprised Jason. Was she a linguist, or had she just aced high school French?

"Devereaux is descended from French royalty in a vague way, and he used that as his calling card when he set up shop among the Chateaux of the Loire. Something like coming back to the land where his people once lived."

She shuffled her cards. "The judge from DC, Caleb Harrison, lost his driver's license for a bunch of DUIs a few years back and apparently decided it was easier to just take taxis than to stay off the sauce. He went through rehab at least four times, once with Lindsay Lohan. He had a restaurant in Washington called Quid Pro Quo that burned a few years ago, and he named the new one Phoenix."

Jason snorted. "His food is nearly as original as that name." He'd been doing his own research. "Anything else about him?"

"A sealed juvenile record in Maryland. And a couple of messy divorces, though that probably ties into the drinking. No kids. Actually, the only one who turned up anything that's current is Lorena Martinez. She's a Southern California native with a gold-plated birth certificate, and she's been active in immigration rights since she was a teenager. A couple of arrests at demonstrations over the years, and she brought truckloads of food to the border when there was that problem with children coming unaccompanied into the country a few years ago. She's also lobbied extensively in Congress."

"That surprises me," Jason said. "The Food Channel usually steers way clear of political controversy. There's no problem if chefs or judges are assholes— they seem to prefer it, actually— but the network really doesn't want to be associated with politics. I remember a guy who had a weekly show during the last presidential primary season. He took a leave of absence to go on the road with some rich candidate and when his guy flamed out, he couldn't get his job back. He was reduced to occasionally judging *Chopped*."

"What about the contestants on *A Cut Above*?" Kimberly asked. "Anything new? I've got people down in Mobile looking into so-called Willis Covington's life as Bill Clover."

Jason shrugged and pushed the sangria away. "I doubt that will help much. If you want the goods on Willis Covington, you're probably better off trying to figure out how he got the money to go abroad and reinvent himself. He's just biding his time, as best I can tell. I can tell you that Gert Thurogood is working on being the world's bitchiest scarecrow, but that doesn't necessarily make her murderous, just impossible to be around.

"Ricardo Z's assistant finally showed up this afternoon," he continued. "Ricardo's been the subject of a lot of hazing, and I suspect it isn't so much that he's more disliked as the fact that he hasn't had anybody watching his back. The assistant is named Hannah Sinclair, and she's got that California edgy look: blond hair with blue highlights, acts like a ditz. Don't know why she wasn't here from the start, but he seemed more comfortable this afternoon after she arrived."

"Have you figured out who's behind the hazing? The business with Sallie Tam's knives sounds pretty dangerous to me. Who's missing at critical times? It ought to be simple enough to figure out."

"Unfortunately not so simple," Jason said. "When the chefs are working at their stations, the assistants come and go, running out for exotic ingredients and special gadgets. There's also the possibility that somebody's hired an outsider to sneak in and do it. I'm inclined to rule out Sallie Tam as the hazer, mostly because she's Sallie Tam and as big as a gnome. And she seemed genuinely upset by what happened to her knives. Ricardo Z was so freaked when his toilet seat was greased that I don't know about him. There was a big nasty garbage bag outside his dressing room this afternoon that smelled like the dumpster behind a fast-food burger joint. Hard to imagine him doing that to himself. If I had to put money on it, I'd say it was Willis Covington."

"Everybody's been targeted?"

"Or so they claim. Of course if there are only four people and one of them isn't being bothered, that's a little obvious. Willis Covington said there was chili powder in his shaving cream, but I didn't see any splotches on his face."

Kimberly nodded and tasted some glazed chorizo, smiling with an appreciation that the dish simply didn't deserve. Jason would have to teach her a few things. "Nobody suspects you're there on the FBI's account?" she asked him. "You're sure your cover is still safe?"

Literally on the FBI's account, Jason thought smugly. His hotel room, paid for by Uncle Sam, was bigger than his Queens rat-hole. He shook his head. "These people are way too self-absorbed to be paying attention to an assistant. If anything, they're flat-out disdainful. I'm supposed to be a total failure now, remember?"

She smiled again and shook her sheet of golden hair. He felt stirrings first in his heart and then, sudden and insistent, a bit lower. Hmm. Best to draw out this meal, execrable though it might be, or he'd have to clutch his laptop to his waist when he stood up, like a teenage nerd who'd just been chatted up by the head cheerleader.

"And Freddy Maxwell?" she asked. "He still acting jumpy?"

Jason considered as he took a taste of the cheese. Finally, here was something that the kitchen hadn't screwed up, though it would definitely taste better at room temperature.

"Freddy's always hyper, and whatever was going on that delayed the announcements of judges has probably been making him even worse. But I can't see anything that makes him likely to kill one of his own contestants, particularly after *Love Bites*. Apart from the possibility of enhanced ratings. And that assumes that the show would go on and not be canceled outright. Which I'm certain it would be."

"So what happens now?" she asked.

"They've got two days to work up their first show menus and arrange for ingredients. This isn't like *Chopped* where they surprise the chefs with a bunch of oddball ingredients like toad sausage and Fruit Loops and then give them twenty minutes to prepare an appetizer. Everything they cook for this competition will be worked out in advance and there's time to practice repeatedly. The actual cooking time for the taping will have about a two-hour limit, because of the taping schedule, and probably the only reason it's that long is that traditional cooking— the Nostalgia part of Nouveau Nostalgia— tends to take longer. Lots of simmering, roasting, that kind of thing."

"Has anybody asked for your help with recipes?" Kimberly had seemed to think this was a big deal, Jason being touted as a food expert. He knew the reality was a lot different. All the chefs had been around kitchens forever and the last thing they wanted was pointers from a food blogger they didn't know or trust.

Especially a failed food blogger. Even though he knew the label wasn't true, it rankled him. God, but he hoped he got a bestseller out of this.

"I had some requests for fried chicken recipes this afternoon, but I think that may just be a smokescreen. And I think there may also be some smokescreen practice cooking going on."

Kimberly looked confused so he decided to keep it simple.

"Say I plan to fix steak for the judges," he explained, "but I practice sautéing fish in front of the other chefs so they won't know what I have in mind. Meanwhile, the guy who's going to prepare fish is frying up pork chops. The actual menus don't have to be announced until the taping begins."

"I'll be in the audience for that," Kimberly told him. "Assuming something awful doesn't happen first." But she sounded as if she almost wanted something awful to happen.

At last, Jason thought. The two of them had something in common.

Chapter 34

Hannah felt as if she'd been in Manhattan for a week by the time Ricky finally agreed to stop cooking on Friday evening.

He had fiddled around with everything you could possibly characterize as American nostalgic or comfort food. Hannah had hauled and chopped and sampled and critiqued through endless rounds of meatloaf and oatmeal cookies and ten-bean salad and (despite Freddy's caveat) mac-and-cheese. While Ricky fried chicken and six kinds of potatoes, he'd sent Hannah downstairs to the food shops in search of every conceivable type of chocolate chip. She wanted him to stop messing around and go with the meatloaf and a traditional Cobb salad, but he was too busy being in a white hot panic to listen to her.

Hannah had been in plenty of high-pressure cooking situations in the role of assistant, but enough was enough. When he started talking about the infinite possibilities for Jell-O molds, she whispered in his ear about her plans for him that evening and, with that, he had finally agreed to pull the plug.

Willis Covington had left hours ago without preparing so much as a cup of Earl Grey tea. Gert Thurogood was long gone.

Only Sallie Tam remained, apparently prepared to pitch a tent beside her station to save on transit time. Hannah enjoyed watching Sallie at work, because her approach offered a decidedly Asian cast to Nostalgia, experimenting with what seemed to be four hundred types of noodles and some truly odd but intriguing ingredients.

It was still light when they emerged from the building. Hannah was grateful for the long days of summer. She was anxious to reconnoiter Gert Thurogood's hotel room, a task made possible by the floral deliveries she'd arranged on her morning break. Hannah had purchased three small but elaborate baskets of flowers and hidden a tiny WiFi camera in each, tucked amidst the fragrant blooms. The baskets came with a congratulatory card from Chantelle Orion, the popular food blogger Hannah had seen in Austin. In the card Chantelle apparently was thrilled that Gert was chosen for *A Cut Above*, whether they'd met or not. Hannah had paid a street musician to carry them into the hotel and had watched him deliver the flowers to the front desk while she held his trombone as collateral.

The WiFi cams would provide live streaming picture and sound, and once they were delivered she called the desk, identifying herself as Chantelle and giving very specific instructions on placement in Gert's suite. It seemed unlikely that Gert would have the time to call Chantelle and thank her, given the taping schedule.

And if she did find out about the WiFi cams later, after Hannah had learned whatever they might reveal, it would only ratchet up Gert's paranoia very nicely.

Deliciously, really.

First, however, she had to take one for the team, and since their particular team included only her and Ricky, that wasn't too hard to manage. They taxied to his hotel, filled the Jacuzzi and hopped in. By the time they were finished an hour later, about the only thing in the room that wasn't wet was Hannah's clothing, which she had carefully removed and placed on a hanger when she started to draw the tub. Lots of suds for cover, but he'd been so busy concentrating on his own body parts, he'd never noticed any of hers. The cut on her arm had gone unnoticed.

Ricky lay on sodden sheets, barely moving. She wondered if she ought to put a mirror under his nose to be sure he was still alive, but by the time she dressed, he appeared to be reviving.

"I need to spend some time in my own space to recharge," she explained. Recharging was the least of it. Hannah had plans for the rest of the evening that very definitely did not include Ricardo Z. "I'll be back here at seven tomorrow morning and we can have room service before we go to the studio."

He frowned. "Room service? What could they possibly offer that we can't do better at Chelsea Market?"

She leaned over his body and offered a brief close-up demo, though after two rounds in an hour, he wasn't in any condition to respond.

"This, for starters," she said. "Now get some rest. Though I have to tell you, Ricky, if you send me out to get Jell-O tomorrow, I'm going to bring you some hog hooves and tell you to make your own. You can throw some acai berries in it and sweeten it with fresh stevia leaves. That ought to satisfy their urge for Nouveau Nostalgia."

Chapter 35

Surveillance recording A-04, Friday

Subject: Willis Covington AKA Bill Clover in conversation with "Beacon," AKA Betty Mantlo.

On Saturday morning, Kimberly Douglas finished reading the file designation and pressed play on the tape recorder. She leaned closer.

A woman's voice answered. "I figured you'd be calling about now, Willis."

"I know this isn't our agreed upon time, Beacon. But I'm feeling the pressure, you see."

"That's all right. It's this new show, right?"

"Yes, I, my God, you'd think that these days I wouldn't have performance pressure but there it is. I can't seem to get myself centered. It doesn't help that Sallie Tam is out to undermine me."

"Why do you say that?"

"We got into it at a country estate in Sussex a few months ago. She and her staff had flown in from Hong Kong as this was a big to-do ramping up for the Queen's Festival of Food and Ideas."

"And...?"

"You know me too well, Beacon." He sighed. "Well, I did also have a thing with one of her young assistants. This lovely creature had the most fantastic ass. We went at it in the gardener's shed. Mind you, luv, I say shed, but those confines had more square feet than these over-priced apartments they're cramming hipsters into here in New York. Let me add, too, that I am so happy to be in the same city as you for once. I've come to rely on you for your insight and guidance, Beacon."

"Let's schedule some in-person time, Willis. In the meantime, do you still have the number I gave you? Call. I think it will ground you. Clear your mind. Stop fighting it if that's what you want."

"Yes. I have it. And you're right. I need it. I'll make the call."

They set a time to touch base again, and the FBI agent clicked and fast-forwarded through several mundane retrievals from Covington's smartphone, pausing briefly to listen to him make an appointment with a tailor or chat with a friend. Then she came to a retrieval that intrigued her. In it, Covington dropped his British accent and talked in his normal voice, All-American with his Alabama roots evident.

"Hello, Aunt Tizzie's," a woman answered to begin the phone call.

"Look here, y'all got some rib tips left?" Covington demanded.

"Better get down here quick if you want some. Once we run out, we run out," the woman said.

"I heard that. Oh, say, there's plenty collards left though, huh?"

"Of course, we make ours with garlic and fresh chilies," the woman replied.

Covington continued, "How about shortnin' bread, like in the Carolinas?"

"We've got amazing shortnin' bread," the woman said saucily. "Good enough to make you cry."

"Momma's little babies like shortnin' shortnin'," Covington sang, evoking the memory of an old song Kimberly had heard in her youth.

"If they don't, we spank them." The women laughed, though it sounded more like a bark.

"I'll be good. Eighty-second street exit?"

"Yes, sir, the R train."

"I'll be there soon," Covington said. "Save me some of that shortnin' bread."

"Always."

The call ended and Kimberly tapped off the recording and sat back in her chair.

Now why would Covington revert to his true voice to ask about menu items at a Southern food place? And what was with his obsession about shortnin' bread?

Kimberly searched online and discovered that shortnin' bread was just another name for shortbread, a deliciously buttery cookie. But why would anyone be so obsessed with it? She also discovered that there were three Aunt Tizzie's Down Home Kitchens dotted across the City. Apparently the original was in Harlem, the second in the Bronx and the third one was in Queens. Covington was headed for the one in Queens, even though the one in Harlem was closer.

Maybe he was doing research for Nouveau Nostalgia?

Covington had made a splash in England introducing new takes on Southern dishes, no doubt learned at the hem of his Southern grandmother's elastic-waisted double-knit polyester pants. Kimberly's research indicated Bill Clover had been close to his nana. Southern food would certainly qualify for the first show's theme.

"Save me some of that shortnin' bread," he'd said to the woman. And she'd replied, "Always."

Something wasn't sitting right. Besides, no New Yorker called the "7" train the "R." But maybe the woman at the restaurant had said that because Covington was from out of town?

Kimberly replayed the recording, trying to discern the words and ambient sounds. She heard the din of conversations, silverware clinking against plates and the tinkling of glasses.

So what was it? What was gnawing at the back of her mind? Something about the way the two talked, like they were having one over on each other.

Kimberly swore to herself. This case had reduced her to chasing her own shadow. But she had to follow her instincts. She had nothing else to go on. Inside the Bureau, the killer was being called the Chef Slayer and the Slicer and Dicer. Wait until the media got a load of that.

She opened another app on the computer. Soon she'd backtracked the number Covington had called. She checked that number against the two listed for Aunt Tizzie's in Queens. It didn't match. She looked up the number and it was listed as a company called Xana Holding. She called the number and it picked up after the fourth ring. A recording came on asking her to enter her access code. She hesitated too long and the line disconnected.

Okay, she decided, when in doubt, reconnoiter. She asked a colleague to look up Xana Holding and left her Manhattan office to take the subway to the restaurant.

* * *

Aunt Tizzie's in Queens was located on a bustling commercial street in a converted two-story brick and wood building that had probably been built in the 1930s. Many businesses had come and gone in the structure, and no doubt it had been rehabbed several times. It was only 11:30, but there were already a fair number of people getting a jump on lunch. A heavenly blanket of smells greeted her as she stepped inside. She stood there a moment in her professional dark suit and rubber-soled flats— they were better for running or kicking a chump in the nuts— and took it all in.

Up until this case, food had been a necessity to Kimberly but not something she'd paid that much attention to beyond liking her steaks medium rare and her asparagus crisp. But over the last few days, it was if a hidden switch had been flicked on inside her for the first time. She craved food.

As she waved off an offer of a table or booth and made her way to a diner-style counter, Kimberly tried to make sense of this new sensation. Of course, she had read Jason's blog posts, along with other foodie sites, as part of her research. It had been routine background work and a hope she might somehow stumble across a lead to the killer.

But now she had read countless recipes and watched videos and live demonstrations on preparing everything from seafood gumbo to Smith Island cake, a concoction with so many thin layers it looked like a frosted stack of pancakes. She now knew the simple act of chopping green onions could be an undertaking of care. It was part of the process of making the whole— the meal as nourishment for the body and the soul.

Even the lowly grilled cheese sandwich had taken on a peculiar beauty for her. She'd seen a video of a chef preparing one the night before and could not get it out of her mind.

Apparently, you had to heat the olive oil in the pan just so, use the right white bread, something airy like sourdough or ciabatta that would toast to a golden hue with a sensual crunch. She'd learned it was preferable to grate the cheese for better melt, say a combination of Parmigiano Reggiano, throw in some extra old cheddar, and two parts Swiss Gruyere, plus generous amounts of unsalted butter spread across the bread, spread across all the bread.

In her imagination, she lovingly grated the cheese in a steady back and forth, back and forth rhythm, like two hearts synced as one. Her hands sliced a loaf of bread fresh out of the oven with a precision and efficiency she'd never demonstrated in the kitchen herself. Oil gurgled and popped in a hot pan, like a primordial soup from which all mankind had emerged with a reptilian need for good food. The smell of cheese filled her nostrils and bloomed, ripe and pungent.

Breathing hard, Special Agent Kimberly Douglas realized she'd become aroused as she sat at the counter, enthralled at the food porn unfolding in her head. Being a woman who had to contend with the old boys' network, she'd gone out of her way not to be proficient in any way in the kitchen. They weren't going to hang that stereotype on her. So she'd never realized how sensual food preparation could be. Oh my. Her face was warm and her sensible white cotton panties were starting to stick to her. She squirmed, getting her breathing under control. She had an uneasy feeling her reaction might have something to do with that slovenly blogger, Jason Bainbridge, and that was something she was not ready to admit, not even to herself.

"Get you some water, hon?" the waitress asked. "You look a little parched."

The waitress, a forty-something brunette with horn-rimmed glasses and wide hips that stretched her blue and peach-colored uniform, was back quickly with her glass of water.

Kimberly gulped it down. "Sorry," she said. "I know I don't look it, but I feel fine, great really."

"Good to hear." The waitress looked less than thrilled at this news, handed Kimberly a menu and left to attend to another customer.

Number one rule was not to draw attention to yourself unless warranted, Kimberly admonished herself. But what the hell? Woman did not live on bread alone.

She eagerly studied the items on the menu, wondering which dishes Jason Bainbridge might recommend. She loved the way he cared so much about food. It spoke of his deliberate nature, and that was an approach that might pay off in other areas. Whenever Jason first tasted a dish, he would hold his fork carefully in front of his mouth, inhaling deeply, then tentatively touch the tip of his tongue to the food before tipping it into his mouth and swallowing. It was as if he wanted to make sure that all of his senses were engaged before he took the plunge.

He had potential, she thought to herself.

She wondered what would happen if she asked him to make her a grilled cheese sandwich.

Chapter 36

"I'm sorry, Mommy," Willis Covington pleaded, his voice a high-pitched Southern twang. He wore nothing but a large plastic diaper bound with old-fashioned safety pins for show. A big, plastic pacifier was affixed to a cord looped around his neck, and he clutched a raggedy teddy bear to his chest, stroking its fur with an unconscious rhythm. He was breathing hard, acutely aware of the way the thick diaper lining seemed to caress his raging erection every time he moved. He stuck the pacifier in his mouth and began to suck hungrily as he eyed the bare breasts of the woman before him. She had dark brown hair, just as he had requested, and enormous breasts that looked soft and natural.

She wore a light blue house dress unbuttoned down to the waist, exposing the huge, pink orbs that mesmerized him. Her hair was half-pinned in a bun on the top of her head, though strands of it tumbled in curls to her shoulders, making her look irritated and overwhelmed. Just watching her stand before him, angry and all-powerful, made him flush with desire.

"You've been a bad boy," she scolded him, reaching for something on the apartment floor. She wore black spike heels, despite the frumpiness of her dress, and as she bent over to pick up a flyswatter, the tight cotton skirt rode up to reveal nothing but bare skin.

Willis caught his breath and flung the teddy bear to the floor. He cupped his hands over his groin, squeezing intently.

"I said not to touch yourself," the woman said sternly. "You dirty, nasty boy." She advanced toward him, her breasts jiggling with a fullness that made Willis lick his lips. "Do you know what Mommy does to dirty boys like you?"

"What?" Willis whispered, his voice hoarse with excitement.

"She spanks them." She grabbed the edge of his diaper and pulled him toward her, then sat on the edge of the bed and forced him across her lap. She jerked the diaper down around his knees and ran the plastic flyswatter up the back of his legs before flicking it lightly across his buttocks.

He groaned and she smacked him harder, and harder still, the flat rubber head bouncing off his flesh and leaving a dimpled welt behind.

"No, Mommy, no. I'll be good, I will," Willis pleaded. He was fast approaching the ecstatic moment he had been waiting for. He had been very specific in his needs.

"What's this?" the woman demanded as her head reached between his legs and cupped his erection. "You bad, bad boy. Mommy needs to teach you a lesson."

Willis whimpered as she flipped him over and pushed him down on the bed, stripping him entirely of his diaper.

She bent over him and dangled her breasts just out of his reach. "Bad boys like you get none of this. None of this at all." The woman ran her fingers over her nipples, squeezing them, and Willis was sure he saw droplets of milk trickle down her flesh. "Not even a tiny little drop."

He ran his tongue over his lips, unable to take his eyes from the hard, pink points of perfection.

"But I'm hungry," he whispered, his eyes sliding sideways to a small jar waiting on the dresser top. "I'm really, really hungry, Mommy."

The woman straddled him and leaned toward the dresser, letting her breasts drag across his bare chest. He gasped and froze at the sensation. She reached for the jar, unscrewed it and stuck a finger inside, digging out a glob of sticky, pale goo. The room smelled suddenly of peaches.

"How hungry?" she demanded as she smeared the baby food on her upper thighs, then dipped her fingers back into the jar and daubed some of the pureed mixture on the cleft between her legs.

"I want some," Willis pleaded. He stuck the pacifier back in his mouth and began to suck at it mightily. His hips had begun to buck beneath her.

"Bad little boys have to wait their turn," she snarled at him. The woman overturned the jar of baby food and let it drip across his belly. He groaned at the sensation. It was cool and sticky. He sucked harder on the pacifier.

She bent over him and began to lick the peach-flavored apple sauce off his skin with short, delicate strokes of her tongue, before alternating bursts of flutters with agonizingly slow long strokes, lapping at him as she carefully, methodically cleaned every morsel of the baby food from his belly.

He was crying now, tears running down his face as he sucked at the plastic nipple embedded in his mouth and eyed the heavy breasts just out of his reach.

"Your turn," the woman announced when she was done. The tip of her tongue emerged from her mouth and she delicately licked the edge of her lips clean of a leftover speck of pureed peaches. "If you do it right, I'll let you have a taste of these." She cupped her breasts and leaned forward until her thighs were positioned in front of his mouth. "Now be a good boy and clean your plate."

He grabbed her muscular thighs and pulled her toward him, lapping hungrily at the baby food that had dried in sweet trails leading to the place he loved best. She smelled of peaches and musk. Willis forgot about all else and left his troubles behind. He felt a deep peace flood through him as he surrendered to her power.

Their entwined shadows were splayed against a nearby wall. A breeze blew the curtains over the open window apart momentarily, revealing a glimpse of the entrance to Aunt Tizzie's across the street and three stories below. It was three o'clock in the afternoon. Willis Covington had found his heaven.

Chapter 37

Kimberly sat at the counter for hours, enjoying a steady stream of newly ordered food, experiencing the textures and smells as if she'd just been graced with hyper-transplanted taste buds.

But she was not so enraptured that she forgot why she'd come. She observed and made mental notes, trying to figure out where Willis Covington was and what activities Aunt Tizzie's masked. From where she sat, she could watch the entrance and the street in front. She had not spotted Covington at all. She did see a familiar woman, plump but shapely, enter to pick up a to-go order. She'd had a platinum bleach job with frosted blue tips.

Where had Kimberly seen her? The woman wore slacks and a man's style Oxford cloth collared shirt, the sleeves worn full length and buttoned.

She had stood at the counter, a few stools down, speaking to the waitress with the horn-rimmed glasses, discussing a take-out order. Kimberly heard a mention of Ricardo Z. Maybe that was it. She must have seen the woman at one of the food cook-offs. She'd ask Jason.

Soon after, post-Aunt Tizzie, Kimberly was back in her hotel room, taking a quick nap. She had an apartment she sometimes got to visit, nearby in Brooklyn. But she'd talked her chief of station into setting her up here in Manhattan for the taping of *A Cut Above*. She lay on her back on the huge, decadent bed and closed her eyes, reliving the deliciousness of her lunch.

Kimberly had enjoyed the fried catfish with greens, seasoned with minced rabbit livers and jelly. She'd indulged in the carbs of Hoppin' John, which turned out to be rice with black eyed peas and a fantastic brown gravy shot through with chicken broth and enlivened by chunks of extra crisp bacon. Now she was discovering the meal should have been billed as including an obligatory nap, rather than the cobbler dessert she had self-righteously declined.

She was just dozing off when her eyes snapped open.

Shortnin' bread.

A male customer had come in early in the afternoon, asking the counter girl about shortnin' bread. He had hummed the same song Willis Covington had tried to sing. The first waitress he spoke to looked at him like he was daft and told him they didn't have shortnin' bread on the menu, recommending the blueberry pie instead.

But then the waitress with the horn-rimmed glasses had hurried over to assure the customer that they did indeed have shortnin' bread. He had sung the same tune Willis Covington had: "momma's little babies love shortnin' shortnin'" and the helpful waitress had beckoned him closer, whispering something in his ear. He'd left soon after, grinning, and heading somewhere in a hurry.

Shaking off the grogginess of her nap, Kimberly typed in the phrase "momma's little babies love shortnin'" on her laptop browser again, broadening her prior search. This time, she came up with a lot of very bad, some might even say offensive, recordings of the old Southern song on YouTube. But beyond that she had nothing.

Was it a code phrase? Clearly. But she couldn't just go back to Aunt Tizzie's and ask the waitress in the glasses, could she? She could ask one of her male fellow agents to go instead, but the woman had looked savvy, and might well be able to spot an agent. There was a reason that the ATF could go scruffy in a meth-dealing biker gang but not the FBI.

Kimberly sat back, unconsciously rubbing a hand across her breasts. What about Jason? A curious smile spread across her face as she thought of him.

Her phone rang and she answered at once when she saw it was a colleague. "What?"

"I found Xana Holding for you. Are you ready for this?"

He explained that Xana Holding had come up in a couple cases involving international drug cartels. But not for smuggling. Xana Holding specialized in kinky sex for the big money crowd, especially S&M— with your choice of whether you wanted to hurt or be hurt.

Kimberly blinked. Which side of the equation did straight-laced Willis Covington fall on?

Chapter 38

As the day of the taping grew closer, Hannah felt strong and prepared for anything. But during the trip from Austin to New Orleans, she had been scared, hurt and unsure of how she could possibly continue her crusade. That was when she got the gun.

She had stopped for gas and food at Rusty's, a roadside joint close to the Texas-Louisiana border that included a mini-gun range just behind the kitchen, nestled between a pair of storage areas for propane tanks. Personal freedom in Texas apparently extended to the right to decimate your business and your customers with a heady mix of live rounds and flammable fuels.

Maybe freedom was just another word for the right to blow your ass up.

It wasn't hard to talk Rusty himself into giving her some hasty firearm lessons. Hannah had observed some world-class flirts in her day, and had just been hanging out in a state where Advanced Flirtation was probably a grad course at the state university.

Plus, Rusty made his own version of Ricky's star turn through his place, a true joke in this dump. Still, she had let him massage her shoulder absent-mindedly while she choked down a dry burger that had probably been picked up in the pasture at daybreak. She'd even complimented him on the fine flavor of the cow patty.

It worked. He allowed that he'd be more than happy to show the city girl how to shoot a gun and protect herself against the unspecified horrors of urban life.

"Self-protection is what it's all about," he told her, pushing back his straw hat. "Self-protection— and being the last one standing."

Still guns made Hannah queasy. She had managed to shoot Fernando Gonzales in Miami, but found the entire experience off-putting. It was loud, for one thing, and the gun kicked like that half-broke horse her uncle kept because he claimed it kept him humble. The same uncle had convinced her to shoot one of his duck-hunting shotguns but after that, she'd sworn off firearms.

But in Louisiana, her arm still throbbing from the knife wound and her heart still pounding from the narrow getaway, Hannah realized she needed some backup. She wasn't going to bring a knife to the next gunfight. Time to start packing some heat. The FBI was after her, that blogger Jason Bainbridge kept turning up, and she could never be sure just who might remember her from the past, like that woman at the roadhouse in Austin.

Rusty was happy to sell her a Colt Defender for cash. He took her out on the range and taught her how to hold the weapon correctly. Apparently, this required him to lean his skinny bowed legs into her and press his hard-on into her backside. She endured.

He was an excellent instructor in any case, despite racist comments that popped out almost every time he opened his mouth. No matter, he was in the distant past.

She smiled to herself now as she walked along a sidewalk on a Manhattan summer Sunday afternoon, nearly as hot and sweaty as she had been on the bayou a week earlier. Hannah Wendt was packing heat in New York City. She had a gun and she knew how to use it.

More specifically, she was following Herman the German, during a break from test cooking caused by a problem with one of the stoves that was now frantically being repaired by a maintenance guy who kept swiping food samples off the counter as he worked.

She needed to know Gert Thurogood's schedule. She could afford no slip-ups in killing the skinny bitch. Muddlark would be her last mistake. Using an app obtained from a spy tech site, Hannah had stood near Herman the German yesterday and cloned his smartphone, just like in the movies.

Herman was now several yards in front of her on Flatbush Avenue as late afternoon fell, both of them on foot. Earlier that afternoon, she'd helped Ricardo Z with one of the recipes he intended to roll out on Maxwell's show. Taping would begin in the morning. Ricky had been sending her on various errands across the boroughs all weekend, even to Aunt Tizzie's right here in Queens. He had wanted to taste their meatloaf.

Hannah returned her attention to Herman, who was also apparently doing some advance work for his boss. Gert's assistant turned a corner and went into a coffee shop.

Hannah followed him inside. The place was crowded and she didn't think he'd spot her; she was wearing a watch cap with the *Walking Dead* logo and a black wig. He'd seen her at the studio but his gaze usually swept past her. Flunkies didn't have much in the way of camaraderie, as most were angling to parlay the drudgery they were undergoing into their own futures as celebrity chefs.

Herman glanced around before heading toward a man sitting on a stool by the diner's picture window. Hannah eyed the new man with appreciation. His head was large, his jaw chiseled like a Mount Rushmore profile. Black hair curled around his ears. Large biceps were evident under the tight material of his broadcloth shirt tucked into designer jeans that caressed his groin. Hannah imagined she could bounce a silver dollar off his tight abs—though why waste time with that when they both were stripped naked and the clock was ticking.

Be still my loins, she admonished herself. Because that's who this guy had to be. An "escort" as they'd put it on the six o'clock news.

For Herman? No, it had to be for Gert.

With a paper cup of coffee before her, Hannah commanded a stool along a side window. Her earbuds in, she used the spy app to hijack Herman's phone as a listening device. She'd seen him pull his phone from the inside pocket of his Dolce & Gabanna blazer, consult it, then tuck it back away. He was probably expected to keep it on 24/7 in case Gert needed him to run out and pick some fresh juniper berries.

"You come well-recommended for your discretion," Herman said carefully.

"I pride myself on being tight-lipped," the muscle man responded.

"Ms. Thurogood is demanding. But in return, she understands the need for proper, dare I say, exceptional, recompense," Herman said delicately.

"Very good. I'm aware an artist needs certain releases, as it were. But be assured, while I have a high tolerance, I have limits as well."

They were speaking so formally, as if finalizing plans for the duchess's garden party instead of setting apparent ground rules for kinky sex. From where Hannah sat, she couldn't see Herman's expression. The stud-for-hire would take the money and do whatever trashy things Gert wanted him to do to her. That's what sex workers did. But he was also letting her go-between know that he would turn the gig down if his rules weren't honored.

"My mentor is stern but fair, sir."

Beefcake sat back, spreading his large hands wide. "Good. Let's set the terms and time, why don't we?"

Hannah was impressed at the price he named. They set a time to meet in Gert's hotel room.

As they talked Hannah used the spy app to look though Herman's emails on her smartphone. She found an exchange between the two men indicating that Gert's need for control in the kitchen did not extend to the bedroom. She wanted to be punished and forced to do certain things that the public Gert would never consider. Which meant that when the escort said he had limits, he didn't mean he was worried about Gert hurting him— but the other way around. He was telling Herman he refused to get so carried away that he couldn't reel it back.

Hannah laughed aloud, not caring if it made her look like a crazy bag lady. She didn't want to miss a moment of the upcoming festivities. She hurried out of the coffee shop, her mind racing with images of all the things she would do to punish Gert if she ever got the chance.

An hour later Hannah spread her takeout dinner on the desk in her hotel room. She plugged her phone into her laptop and tapped into the feed from the hidden cameras in Gert's room. The instructions she'd included with the flowers had said to put one arrangement in the bedroom, and one in the front room.

The concierge had placed them precisely. Good man.

It wasn't quite show time yet, but forking in some of her food, Hannah tuned in just in time to see Gert cross the front room in a black robe embroidered in carmine Chinese lettering. She was on the phone to an assistant, lecturing about the proper way to prepare the crust for shepherd's pie. That was a bonus: Hannah now knew Gert's game plan for the morning. Shepherd's pie. Nice choice.

Hannah noted that the chef was sporting some wicked-looking Jimmy Choos and she could tell from the way she walked that they were new. Would they fit her? Hannah wondered. Gert wouldn't need them after tomorrow.

The chef clicked off one call to take another and walked out of view. Hannah assumed it was the clerk in the lobby announcing her gentleman caller. Shortly after, a knock at the door announced Beefcake. He looked every bit as scrumptious as he had earlier in the coffee shop.

Hannah ate more of her salad as she overheard parts of their conversation, all formal and banal. They were out of view briefly but soon the two nestled onto the couch, holding drinks Gert must have mixed for them. Beefcake had taken his shirt off and, as predicted, his abs were epic. There was precious little small talk before Gert let her robe fall open. She reached down to rub between her legs, but the hired stud slapped it away. "Don't be such a slut," he said as if following a script. "If you can't control yourself, I'll have to punish you."

Gert groaned and sat upright, but her hand crept downward again. Beefcake grabbed both of her hands and stretched then above her head, then pinned them against the wall behind her.

"If you're going to be a dirty little girl, then you deserve to be treated that way."

Gert thrust her pelvis out, her bony hips emerging from the folds of her silk kimono.

Hannah ate and watched with wanton interest, her physical hunger feeding her sexual appetite and vice versa. It was getting harder and harder to keep her basic urges apart.

Gert was writhing on the couch as if she were a snake trying to distract a snake charmer. Her companion knelt on the sofa, clasping her hands, and attempted to pin her against the cushions with one of his masculine thunder thighs.

"Do you have no shame?" he demanded.

Apparently Gert did not. She pushed her head forward and began licking at his nipples, murmuring for him to take her. He responded by standing and throwing her over his shoulder as if she were a sack of corn. He marched out of camera range with her.

Dammit. Hannah fumbled with the settings of the camera feeds and brought up the image of the bedroom. She waited anxiously until the stud kicked the door open, Gert dangling over his shoulder, and literally threw her onto the bed.

"I see you will have to be punished," he said in a cold voice. He unbuckled his belt and let his pants fall to the rug. He had gone commando this evening. Hannah saw at once why Gert was paying top dollar. She gasped and leaned forward, hoping for a closer look, her food forgotten.

Gert was crying, "No, no, no. Please, no." But she didn't sound very convincing, not even for role-playing. Not to mention that she had spread her legs as she scuttled back across the bed, as if to get away from her attacker.

Gert and her friend had prepared carefully for this moment. There was a whip and a rope coiled on top of the dresser. Beefie grabbed the rope and stepped toward Gert, smiling.

"Please, no!" Gert pleaded. She was breathing heavily and had unconsciously started to thump her body against the headboard. "I'll do anything. Just don't touch me."

"It's too late for that," the man growled. He grabbed her legs, dragged her to the foot of the bed, then bound her feet together. "Lie on your stomach," he ordered her. "Now."

"I'll be good, I swear I will," Gert begged as she rolled over and thrust her ass in the air.

"It's too late. You're going to get what you deserve." He grabbed the whip off the dresser top and began to lightly flick her naked legs as she started to groan. As her moaning filled the room, his strokes grew heavier. Small welts began to bloom on Gert's legs.

"I'll be good. I'll be good," she repeated as she clearly presented herself for entry. Talk about your mixed signals.

"I said, it's too late!" the stud roared, causing Hannah to drop her spoon. "You brought this on yourself and you'll get nothing you don't deserve!" He snapped the tip of the whip against the wooden bathroom door, the sound reverberating like a gunshot. Gert screamed, from either fear or delight. The man began whirling it above his head as if he were a lion tamer in the center of the ring.

Hannah felt herself flush.

Was she excited because she was aroused or because she wanted to be holding the whip? Boy, what she wouldn't give to have Gert bound in front of her like that, helpless so that she could flay the flesh from her very limbs.

Gert's words to the stud earlier on the couch had raised old memories she'd like to forget. Somehow that pleading was tangled up in the memory of when the chef had insulted her in front of her father. The embarrassment and anger from that night, from all of those nights, came roaring back inside Hannah now and turned to rage—focused solely on Gert.

The escort slashed the whip across Gert's back while muttering insults: Gert was a slut, a whore, a tease. She was going to get what she deserved. Suddenly, he dropped the whip, leaned forward and pulled Gert's legs apart as far as the ropes would allow. This was it. The denouement.

But unexpectedly, the man picked the whip up again as he positioned himself behind Gert and wrapped the leather strip around Gert's throat. He began choking her as she bucked against him, pleading for him to stop. Her veins bulged in her forehead; her face turned scarlet. Gert twisted to look at the man. Her eyes looked as if they were starting to pop out of her head. She was choking but still bucking furiously against him.

Hannah leaned forward, praying the stud muffin wasn't going to snuff Gert in front of her eyes, cheating her out of her much more authentic revenge. Gert's eyelids fluttered as her face went purple, then she groaned as the man entered her from behind, his body thrusting in time to the rhythm of the headboard pounding against the wall. Gert's gasps had turned to groans— but her glory was not to be.

Before she could get what she had paid well for, the door to the bedroom burst open and what seemed like a half dozen men and a lone woman exploded into the room with guns drawn, screaming, "FBI! Freeze! Hands above your head! Get down on the floor! Get away from the bed!"

"What the hell?" Hannah screamed, disappointment flooding through her.

In the chaos that ensued, three FBI agents grabbed the male escort, threw him down on the ground, and handcuffed him before he could say a word. Another picked up the whip and backed slowly away from the bed, bumping into the flower arrangement and secret camera.

As Hannah shouted, "No!" in her hotel room, the bouquet tumbled to the floor, taking the camera with it. She saw shadows and the blur of legs and hands, then heard cursing and the gurgling of water.

Abruptly, the scene went black.

Chapter 39

Kimberly knew at once that they had made a terrible mistake.

As usual, testosterone had catapulted the other agents forward and they pushed her out of the way. The male agents had pulled the pair on the bed apart and been so busy trussing the big guy up that they missed the obvious: No one was being killed here, unless you counted her own career. It was just more kink she couldn't quite fathom.

Were all of these culinary people nuts?

Kimberly locked eyes with Gert Thurogood, who lay on the bed desperately pulling the covers over her lashed body. She looked like an angry parrot, her face screwed up in such outrage she couldn't manage a single sound. Her mouth hung open in noiseless outrage.

Just as well. Kimberly did not think she wanted to hear what the celebrity chef would have to say, and she had no doubt that eventually it would be said to someone far above her on the food chain. She'd pay for this. Oh, how she'd pay.

She had no one to blame but herself. She had made the call to get the manager to open the door and given the directive to burst into the bedroom. But how was she to know that the sounds the two agents tracking Gert had heard from the room next door were sounds of sexual pleasure and not torture?

Celebrity chefs were dropping like flies. She had panicked, certain that Gert was meeting her maker. When she gave the order to go in, she'd been trying to save the damn woman's life.

No matter. Kimberly knew she would be demoted and transferred to South Dakota once this got out. Hell, she'd be a laughingstock from here to San Francisco.

Gert Thurogood began to open and close her mouth like a fish gasping for oxygen in the air. Her face was bright red. Kimberly was suddenly genuinely afraid she might be having a heart attack. She stepped toward the apocalyptic woman, prepared to do CPR.

"Get away from me!" the celebrity chef screamed, regaining her voice with shocking ferocity. "And uncuff my friend immediately!"

Kimberly could have argued. She could have at least pretended to confirm that this was, indeed, consensual sex. She could even have apologized and thrown herself on Thurogood's mercy. She did none of those things. She was tired, sick of the entire cooking world, and she felt like a damn fool.

"Let him go," she barked at the other agents. They stared at her in protest but sensed her mood. They uncuffed the naked man pinned to the floor.

He hopped to his feet with impressive agility and marched from the room, head held high. Without saying a word, he scooped up his clothes from the floor and strode through the open hotel door, buck naked.

"We didn't even get to see his ID," one of the agents complained.

They'd seen everything else. "Shut up, Bucky," Kimberly snapped.

The agents filed reluctantly from the bedroom, disappointed that their bust had been, well, a bust.

Alone in the bedroom, the two women stared at one another. Kimberly wanted to apologize but the words would not come. She really had only wanted to save Gert's life. She had expected to leave this hotel room a hero.

"I suppose you think I'm a slut," Gert finally snapped at her. She was breathing more easily, but her face remained bright red. Kimberly realized she was mortified at having her humiliation needs discovered. This could either level the playing field or make matters even worse.

"I thought you were being murdered," Kimberly answered more calmly than she felt. She took a deep breath and forced herself to say, "You have my deepest apologies."

"I suppose you think this is funny?" Gertrude Thurogood challenged her. "I suppose you're going to be telling this story all over the FBI... locker room or whatever you call it."

Kimberly was not a stupid woman. When she saw the edge, she took it. "I won't say anything if you don't say anything." She offered the chef her hand.

Gert stared at her for a few, long seconds, considering her options. Was she willing to swap her pride for her righteous anger? Kimberly could only pray she was.

"Fine," the chef said curtly. She shook Kimberly's hand, letting the sheet drop to do so. Her breasts looked like sweet potatoes. They were long and tubular and tanned an unnatural orange. Kimberly forced herself to look away and headed for the hotel room door.

Thank you, Jesus, Kimberly thought as she hurried down the hall, desperate to put the whole debacle behind her.

Chapter 40

Jason knew it. He should never have eaten that second burger. But everyone knows that when you meet the perfect burger, you have to go for it.

Who would ever have dreamed that a Korean guy with an address in Hell's Kitchen and a store the size of a closet cooked the best hamburgers in New York City?

The meat had been freshly ground, flavorful and fatty, charred just right, and nestled in a buttered homemade bun sporting grill marks. He couldn't wait to go back.

Jason lay on the couch in his hotel room, savoring the meal he'd just enjoyed almost as much as the fact that he wasn't paying for his suite. He still couldn't believe that it was all going on the FBI's tab.

Which was only fair. He deserved plenty for stepping away from his blog with the appearance of failure. Momentum was everything when it came to hits. He only hoped he would be able to regain his readership once this episode was over and his insider status revealed. If he got a book deal out of it— if he could be first with the definitive true crime on the chef murders— then he'd be golden. But if he couldn't? He'd be screwed.

Reluctantly, Jason admitted that he might have thrown away his entire writing career just because Kimberly Douglas was the hottest FBI agent he'd ever seen. Hell, the truth was that she was pretty much the hottest woman he'd ever gotten close to. But who was he kidding? He was an overweight, aging millennial desperately trying to hold on to his moment of dubious fame.

She was out of his league.

He flopped back, intending to nap, since it was technically still too early to legitimately head for bed, but a furious pounding at his hotel door made him sit bolt upright.

His stomach dropped. No one pounding that hard was bringing good news. Either there had been another killing or the hotel was on fire. He wasn't sure which would be worse.

"Coming," he shouted as he shuffled to the door. Jason was a cautious man, but he was so groggy with burgers and beers that he was slower than usual unfastening the chains and deadbolts on his hotel door.

The pounding intensified as he fumbled with the hardware. "All right. Christ. Hang on," he complained, peeking through the peephole. When he saw who it was, he flung the door open.

Kimberly stood in his doorway looking simultaneously more angry, more upset and more attractive than she ever had before.

"I need to come in," she said, shoving past him. She crossed the sitting area in a couple of steps, threw herself down on the couch and put her head between her hands.

Jason was speechless. He followed her to the couch and stood there, staring down at her. She smelled like peppermint with a hint of basil. Delicious.

"Is everything okay?" he asked tentatively.

She looked up at him with a fierce glare. "What the hell's the matter with you people?"

"My people?" he asked faintly, his mind racing—what did she mean by "you people?" Jews? Bloggers? Foodies? Oh God, was she was another foodie hater?

"In the cooking world," she explained angrily. She shook her head, perplexed. "Can you not have normal sex? Do you all want to be beaten or spanked or humiliated in some way? Because I've read the jackets, and I've seen the surveillance, and a whole lot of you are seriously kinked."

Now Jason was really confused. "To be perfectly honest, I don't know. I haven't had sex with many of these people."

She didn't seem to be listening. Her forehead wrinkled. "I'm going to be the laughingstock of the Bureau. My career is over. I can only imagine the nicknames they'll have for me now."

"What happened?" Jason asked. He chanced sitting next to her, closer than he would ever have dared had she not been in crisis. She was too upset to notice. When he realized she wasn't paying him any attention, he dared to put his hand over hers and squeeze. Her fingers were long and delicate and incredibly soft.

Oh God, he was starting to sweat.

He willed himself to stay cool. He visualized his sweat glands shutting down. He prayed that he could somehow suck the perspiration back into his pores. Because now that she was there, just inches from him, he realized that, unsuitable or not, snooty or not, he wanted to be near her.

She was staring at the opposite wall, lost in the memory of whatever had happened. If he could keep quiet, he was pretty sure she'd spill it all. Women in the movies always did. And the women in his own life had certainly never hesitated to explain why they were unhappy, though they were usually unhappy about him.

"A couple days ago I put some guys on watching the chefs," she explained. "All they were doing was sitting around on their asses. I figured it couldn't hurt. I put one of my best guys, Bucky, on Gert Thurogood. She's pretty high strung and she has the longest history in the US. I figured that if the killer was going to target anyone, it might be her. I just had this feeling."

"And did someone attack her?" Jason had no idea where this was going, but she hadn't pulled her hand away so he didn't really care what direction she was headed.

"Yes. I mean, no." She rolled her eyes and groaned. "A couple agents were stationed in the room next to hers and they heard her moaning and begging for mercy. There was the sound of hitting, muffled screams..." Her voice trailed off.

Wow, Jason thought. How long had it been since this woman had gotten laid? Or, for that matter, the other agents? From her description, and the fact that it was a hotel room, it sounded clearly like rough sex. Did they teach these people nothing in the FBI?

"Anyway, the other agents called me. I was down in the lobby and I came up to join them as fast as I could. I didn't even wait for the elevator. I yelled at the manager then raced up twelve flights on the run. I listened to the sounds coming from her room. I agreed. She sounded like she was choking, strangling. I thought her life was in danger. So I gave the order to go in. The manager arrived and he opened the door. We went barreling in."

Jason realized, at last, where this was all going. "Let me guess— she was getting the hell beat out of her, but she was enjoying every minute of it? It was all consensual?"

Kimberly nodded. "We looked like a bunch of clueless dolts. I doubt any of the guys will say anything. They'd look stupid, too. But if she says something, and words gets back to the Bureau? I'll never live it down."

"Don't worry," Jason assured her. "Gert Thurogood isn't going to say anything. She can't afford to let a scandal derail the momentum this show is going to give her. Besides, there have been rumors about her before. A cameraman on the set told me she had a thing with Willis Covington in London. They were heavy into the S&M scene. But it started to affect their chef bookings so they parted ways. Publicly, she's been a nun ever since."

Kimberly looked at him. "That confirms what was going on when I followed Willis out to Queens today. The phone call he made before he left made it sound like he was going out to try a restaurant, but when I got to the restaurant there was no sign of him."

"Aunt Tizzie's?" Jason guessed.

"How did you know?"

He had no intention of telling her. He might be a plain-vanilla guy, but that didn't mean he lived under a rock. "I've been asking around, you know—trying to find out background information for you."

She looked at him as if seeing him for the first time. "I owe you one," she said, laying her head on his shoulder.

It was such an unexpectedly feminine move that it disarmed Jason completely. He forgot about how uptight she was. The thought of her being condescending suddenly seemed ludicrous. The bulge from the gun tucked in her side holster did not deter him at all. He was suddenly and utterly in lust.

He put his arm around her and pulled her toward him. "I'm sure it will all blow over," he murmured. He thought that was the safest thing to say. In truth, he wanted to hold his breath. He wanted to stop time so that it stood still. He was suddenly and acutely aware that he was a man, and she was a woman, and they were alone in an elegant hotel room.

"I mean, what is so wrong with regular sex?" Kimberly asked. Her face was inches from his and her breath smelled of peppermint. Had she chewed on gum just for him? Jason was too afraid to hope. "Sex is pretty amazing just the way it is, don't you think?" she whispered.

Jesus. What was he supposed to say? He didn't want to come off as a sex beast, but he didn't want to blow the progress he was starting to make either.

"Sure. Sure, I certainly do," he stammered. It was the best he could do.

"Think about it." She sat up straight but didn't move away. "It's kind of a miracle that men and women can come together at all. I mean, we're all so different from each other. We look at things differently. We feel things differently. We care about different things. But every now and then, you meet someone who's on your wavelength. And you can never tell who it might be. There's no sense in saying you have a type, because the universe will just hand you someone totally different and then— well, you end up thinking about nothing but him. It's like the world uses attraction just to remind you it's in charge. And it's kind of great, right? So why go messing around with that? Why do people need ropes and whips and chains? Answer me that."

She was staring at him like she actually expected an answer, so Jason did the only thing he could think of. He leaned in and kissed her.

He actually kissed her. He conquered thirty-five years of low self-esteem and worries about his weight and hygiene. He stopped wondering whether she was good enough for him or too good for him, a constant dance in his head whenever he got close to women. He just leaned in and put his mouth on hers and felt the shock travel all the way down to the tips of his bare feet.

Her lips were soft as silk pillows and, hallelujah, she was actually kissing him back. Yes, he was sure of it. She moved her head a little so that they fit together better and she wasn't pulling away. In fact, she increased the pressure of her lips on his and opened her mouth a little.

Uh-oh. What did she expect him to do now? He couldn't just ram his tongue into her mouth. She was perfect. For all her toughness, she was a lady. It was too soon.

Plus he'd been jamming hamburgers smothered in grilled onions less than an hour ago. He'd repulse her.

She gave a little sigh and pulled away, smiling. "That wasn't half bad."

"Thanks," Jason managed to say, his thoughts still reeling. But wait. *Half bad?*

"I feel better now," she said. "It really freaked me out. I mean, I truly thought I was stopping a killer. I really thought I'd walk out of that hotel room a hero, killer in tow. I thought that this was going to be over. It's just so frustrating. I feel like we're so close to the truth."

What should he say? He did not want her to go. It was a miracle she was still here. It was a bigger miracle she had actually kissed him back. He wanted her to stay, but he couldn't think of anything to keep her next to him.

"Will you have people at the taping tomorrow?" he asked, rather stupidly.

Of course she would. They both sensed another murder was near, that somehow all the other murders had led to this.

"Yes, at least four agents scattered throughout the audience. We're meeting there at seven a.m ." She looked at her watch, suddenly alarmed, and Jason could have kicked himself for bringing up a topic that only led to her realizing she had to get up early the next day. "Thanks for letting me vent. I was pretty keyed up. I get like that sometimes."

She stood up and her torso unfolded in front of him, a beautiful prize just out of his reach. Jesus, but she looked good in a black shirt and gray pants. She even made her blazer look sexy.

"You'll be there, right?" she asked while he stumbled to his feet, still thinking of their kiss.

Jason snapped to it. She expected an answer.

"Yes, of course," he said. "Freddy's arranged for me to be there as part of the production team. I'll be right by the set, just out of camera range. I'm going to keep a close eye on everyone. I know most of them pretty well. I'll text you if I see anything suspicious."

He had her work number, but when this was over, he had to get her real number, the private one. Damn, he was so off his game. What little game he had. She made him feel like a clumsy fifth-grader.

"Lock the door after me," she ordered him. "And please tell me you're not into whips and chains. I've seen enough to last me a lifetime."

He felt his face grow hot and that only increased his embarrassment.

"No, of course not," he said truthfully. "It's just that the cooking world is pretty intense. People have to let the steam off somehow."

Kimberly shook her head. "I don't think I'll ever be able to look Gert Thurogood in the eye again. And I'm not sure I'll be able to take my mind off other parts of her anatomy." She shivered. "And the guy? You should have seen that guy." Her eyes widened and a smile flitted across her lips.

Now Jason wanted desperately to change the subject. He could only guess how impressive the guy must have been. Gert would not have laid out money for a mere mortal.

"It's all in how you use it," he tried to joke and immediately felt like a fool.

"Exactly," she agreed unexpectedly. "Just like a gun." She patted her holster and walked out the door, looking back over her shoulder to smile at him. Her blonde hair swayed with every step.

He watched, mesmerized, as she strode down the corridor, turned a corner and disappeared.

Damn. What had just happened? And now what could he do? He didn't want to lose the memory of those moments to any activity more mundane. There would be no mediocre television shows for him tonight. No surfing the web. No reading of email. All he wanted to do was lie on the couch and think about what had just happened.

He could still feel that kiss.

Chapter 41

In her prison cell-sized hotel room, Audra DeFord lounged in her pale blue Victoria's Secret bra and panties. She knew she had ridiculous taste in lingerie— she might as well throw her money into the Hudson River. Both items would fall apart after four or five washings. But there were maybe, what, three hundred people in the entire world who actually looked good in Victoria's Secret? Since she was one of them, she would wear what she pleased.

She lay on her stomach on the hard little bed, a swath of newspapers spread out before her to shelter the threadbare comforter from a cardboard boat of cholesterol-loaded goodness: chili fries topped with hot sauce, ketchup and chopped onions.

Audra rolled on her back and lowered three fries dripping in chili into her mouth as if she were eating caviar on a cracker. She was celebrating her first step toward stardom. Tomorrow, she'd be on the set with her new lady love, Beacon, spiritual advisor to Willis Covington. She had no idea what that meant except that Beacon was always present when he competed.

It was the first taping of the new show— and the first rung of the ladder upward for Audra. All she had to do was charm Willis Covington and convince him he needed another assistant. And by "convince" she meant "blackmail" if necessary, though she preferred the less ugly word. Then she could parlay her experience with both him and Fuller Muddlark into a book and brand of her own.

Wiping chili off her chin with a carefully manicured finger, Audra lowered three more fries dripping with goo into her mouth. Three was usually her lucky number.

She concentrated hard on finding a way to ingratiate herself with Covington without having to resort to the unpleasantness of blackmail. She didn't want him to discover she knew who he really was. Surprisingly, she also didn't want to burn Beacon or take her spot on Covington's staff. Covington was her ticket to a book deal, but making an enemy out of Beacon didn't seem right. Audra and Beacon were very similar: They both came from backgrounds any sane person couldn't wait to leave behind.

Sure, Beacon's show was unbearably pretentious and her advice was ludicrous. Half the time you couldn't tell what the hell she was talking about. But anything was better than living your life in a moldy double-wide crawling with cockroaches and a husband who beat you on the days he got his paycheck and could afford an extra six-pack. She got that. Her mother had lived that existence and now her sisters were.

But not Audra.

And not Beacon.

Audra wondered why there wasn't more of a connection between them. She had a gnawing feeling that perhaps she would never feel the spark she'd had with Calista again, that perhaps some better part of her had died.

Making love with Beacon was nothing compared to her golden, long-limbed love. Audra went through the motions with Beacon, but it had been a performance, not an emotional experience. She'd felt as if she were standing across the room watching herself in action, a means to an end and nothing more. She could tell Beacon liked her as the person she was pretending to be, and Audra was starting to feel a little bad about that.

But how could anyone ever recover from Calista, much less in a matter of weeks?

Alone in her hotel room, Audra had no way to escape from herself. Or the memory of Calista.

It was the one thing Audra and Fuller Muddlark had ever had in common. They had both loved Calista and realized she was truly one-of-a-kind, sexually speaking, of course— her uniqueness physically was a secret they had all shared— but also because of her fragility. Calista was like a flower that bloomed in the dark, when it was just the two of you, a flower that you knew could never survive in the sunlight for long.

She made you feel that you were the only one in the world, yet she had also always managed to find a way to be herself, against all odds.

Truth and beauty: an irresistible combination. Beauty and fragility.

Calista's delicate sensibility was why she'd killed herself, Audra was certain. Calista mourned the loss of the three of them together and couldn't live without it. Calista loved Fuller truly, madly, deeply. But she had also loved Audra truly, madly, deeply. Her love was as big as America, powerful enough for the two she loved so fiercely.

The three of them together had been invincible, inseparable, incredible. Until someone killed Fuller and ruined it all.

Audra rolled back onto her stomach and stared at the now-empty container in front of her. Not even three thousand calories could banish the inescapable truth. Calista had killed herself because she couldn't live without Muddlark. She loved Audra too, but without Fuller the light just went out. Whoever had killed Fuller Muddlark had also killed Calista.

Audra knew herself well. She was ambitious to a fault. She would always love Calista but she was selfish. She could live without Calista and Fuller because she loved herself most of all. She wouldn't hesitate to leave anyone behind, just as she had left that boisterous, uncouth, doomed family of hers back in Arkansas. But she would never abandon Calista. Not now, not ever. She would carry the memory of their moments together to her grave and always look at them as the happiest of her life.

She would avenge Calista's death if it was the last thing she did, if she had to die trying. She had to. Even if it meant giving up her dreams.

Now that surprised her. The urge to find out who had killed Muddlark and to bring them to justice was greater than the thirst she felt to be famous one day. Her heart grew a little bigger. She was doing this for Calista, for Fuller, for truth, for justice. It was a need she couldn't ignore.

The killer had to be near. Just as Audra had cultivated a walk like a panther— deliberate, slow and full of menace— she had honed her instincts over the past two decades. She could smell a phony from a half-mile away and see through people's facades as if they were cellophane. The set tomorrow would be filled with more phonies than so-called Willis Covington. It would be crowded with people pretending to be someone they weren't. It was television; everyone was a poseur. She was certain the killer would be there.

All she had to do was watch.

If she stood on the sidelines and observed them all, she'd know who killed her beloved Calista.

And then there would be hell to pay.

Chapter 42

Hannah was seething with frustration.

To see Gert get what she deserved, to imagine herself wielding the whip and choking the life out of the wench, only to be interrupted and then abruptly cut off from what was happening— it was too much to bear. She felt like a Siberian tiger caged in a zoo. She paced back and forth across her hotel room, weighing her bloodthirsty options.

Gert deserved to die. But she needed to die in the most spectacular fashion. She needed to suffer and it needed to be public. Clearly, physical humiliation was not enough. The bitch actually liked that. No, it needed to be professional humiliation. And it needed to happen tomorrow.

Hannah froze, then slowly smiled. How could she have forgotten?

For over ten thousand miles, she'd driven the murdermobile across America with that one very special partition hiding her very special secret weapon. She had taken such care in hiding it that she knew no one would ever be able to detect it. It lay in wait in an envelope wrapped in double plastic bags, hidden behind a false back to her glove compartment. So little space for such a deadly substance. It was perfect for what she had in mind.

Shepherd's pie. Gert had decided to make the meat and potato English standby for the first Nouveau Nostalgia challenge. Would it be the same recipe that Hannah had once had in Des Moines, at Gert's restaurant, the mixture of ground lamb, finely chopped Kobe beef and truffles for the filling? Perfect: the strong flavors of the lamb and truffles would mask anything.

They would certainly mask ricin.

All she had to do was retrieve her secret stash of the poison and find a way onto the set tonight, while everyone else was sleeping. One of Gert's famous hand-blown spice jars would be perfect. It wouldn't take much. It had taken her months to develop the poison— and the rush it had given her to realize she held the power over life and death in her hands had led her to stockpile enough ricin to kill them all.

Salt, pepper, rosemary and maybe the thyme. She'd put a little in each to ensure at least one contaminated spice was chosen. She had learned that Gert always made a big deal out of tasting a competition dish before the judges did, then rolling her eyes in ecstasy for the camera.

This time the script would be a little different. She'd start convulsing instead, foam at the mouth, and then die writhing in agony with the cameras rolling, a victim of her own cooking. Yes, that was fitting. That was just what Gert deserved.

Hannah rubbed her hands together. Her plan was coming together, so easily it was almost ludicrous.

First she dressed all in black— making her the only person in all of midsummer New York City who was dressed in black for a reason. She topped off the ensemble with Ellen Bartkus's dark wig.

Then she retrieved the sample desserts she had been trying and tasting all week for Ricardo Z. There were at least six stored in the mini-fridge in her hotel room, waiting for her to taste and adjust the flavors. The desserts were crucial to her plan.

Next she walked the four blocks to the parking lot where she had stored the murdermobile, glad for the cover of darkness. It only took her three minutes to pry open the false back of the glove compartment and retrieve the envelope that held her precious ricin.

Supplies in hand, she hailed a cab and got out three blocks from Chelsea Market where the studio was located. Only two entrances were open at night. One was the front desk, manned by a geriatric old dragon who made everyone sign in, no matter what, and no doubt had a photographic memory. The other was a side door that opened on an alley. It was often used to haul equipment in and out for various tapings. It was also next to a line of malodorous dumpsters that were emptied every few days in the dead of night.

As she suspected, the side door was open and the only thing between her and the taping studio four floors above was a bored maintenance worker watching movies on an old computer in a dingy office. She was in luck. He was the same guy they had sent in to fix the broken oven a few days before, and she had seen him swipe samples of food when he thought no one was looking.

She now had six, count 'em, six desserts to distract him with. And, if need be, one of them could contain ricin. First she'd see how it went.

The maintenance man was about thirty-five years old with ghastly mutton chop sideburns and a ridiculous Elvis hairdo, the kind favored by urban hipsters these days. It did not serve his beefy face well. In fact, it looked like he had a mound of chocolate pudding melting on his head.

Nonetheless, she took a deep breath and stepped into his office. She sat on the edge of his desk, leaning forward so he could get a look down the front of her black blouse. "Remember me?" she asked.

His feet tumbled off the desk and he sat up abruptly. "No," he said loudly. Instead of staring at her cleavage, he was gazing hungrily at the bag in her hands.

"I'm Jackie," Hannah lied, choosing a name at random. "I'm one of the production assistants. I noticed you the other day when you were fixing our stove. That was pretty handy of you. I like a man who's good with his hands."

"What do you have in those boxes?" he asked, totally ignoring her come-on.

"Nothing much. Some desserts a couple of the chefs have been trying out. Nothing you would want."

He quivered slightly. "I like desserts."

No doubt he did. His gut popped out of his gray maintenance uniform like the rising dough ball from hell. "I could give you a couple of them. No one would notice. If..." Hannah waited, making him ask. She was starting to like it when people begged her, whether it was for food or for their life.

"If what?" he asked, unconsciously licking his lips.

"If you let me scoot upstairs for a few minutes. I forgot to finish set-ting something up in the kitchen, and if I don't have it ready by the time my boss gets here tomorrow, he'll fire me on the spot."

"Sure. Go on." He held out his hand and she handed over three of the desserts. You never know. She might need the others later to bribe her way out— or to kill him.

He already had the first container open and was gobbling banana cream pie with both hands. Good God, she might not have to kill him at all. If he kept that up, he'd have a heart attack by morning.

Hannah took the freight elevator up four floors and stepped out into the fabled series of sets where King Culinary Partners filmed each of their legendary cooking series. The floor was vast and dotted with one state-of-the-art kitchen after another. A series of tracks built into the floor allowed film crews to quickly custom-build walls and arrange for cooking areas as small or as large as they needed.

The set for *A Cut Above* had long since been ready for taping and both cast and crew had been practicing in it all week. It took up the southwest cor-ner of the building and she slipped across the darkened floor, smiling. This was even easier than she had anticipated.

Gert Thurogood had been assigned the end kitchen island in a series of four prepared for tomorrow's taping. Her area was spotless—Herman the German was clearly OCD— but the refrigerator assigned to Gert was actually padlocked. Boy, some people are paranoid. You'd think someone was trying to sabotage her.

Hannah was suddenly afraid that the rest of Gert's cooking supplies would be locked away as well, but the glass spice jars were pushed against the back of the main cooking island, protected only by the shadows of the stainless steel cabinet above it. She worked quickly, shaking out a half teaspoon of the ricin into each of the spice containers, then mixing the top half of each with a toothpick to mix it in and disguise the color.

She had just finished poisoning the rosemary and sliding it back in place when she heard footsteps approaching. She ducked behind the freestanding stove, crouching down so she would not be seen.

Willis Covington emerged out of the shadows and stood in a pool of reddish light cast by an exit sign near the back stairwell. He too was dressed all in black. How he gotten into the building? What the hell he was doing there, the sabotaging little bastard.

She thought of the fast food prank that had been pulled on Ricardo Z and other hazing. Yes, that sounded like Willis Covington all right or rather like that low class, backcountry peckerwood she knew. He slipped off a backpack and set it on one of the counters then pulled out a small jar and began checking the refrigerators.

Hannah squinted at the jar. That little fake British shit. He planned to poison the dairy products with vinegar. It was the oldest trick in the book. Sabotage a competitor by sabotaging their ingredients. How very junior varsity. The fact that Hannah was doing the exact same thing, only with deadly ingredients, did not occur to her. Her disgust of Covington overwhelmed all other emotions.

But Gert Thurogood was not the only chef who had padlocked their refrigerator. Everyone had. Willis had no luck at all. That did not seem to deter him. He simply returned to his knapsack and began rummaging inside it, no doubt looking for some other childish prank to play. He was still hunched over the counter in the dark when Hannah came up behind him, a cast iron skillet held high above her head, and brought the heavy metal down over his skull with every ounce of her weight.

It hit the top of his head with a satisfying thud combined with a sweet crunching sound. Willis Covington dropped like a rock. She immediately checked his pulse— it was fading steadily— and then rummaged around in his knapsack for something she could use to dispose of him.

Perfect. He had rope in the bottom, God knows what for. Perhaps he had intended to rappel down the building once he was done sabotaging his competitors. It was more like clothesline than rope, but it would work for what Hannah had in mind.

She didn't care if his body was found; she just didn't want it found until she had the chance to kill Gert during tomorrow's taping. Besides, an extra dead body might come in handy, she thought. Maybe she could find a way to pin the poisonings on Willis Covington somehow. Yes, that was just the thing.

His round spectacles had fallen off and she held them to the light, noting that they were clear glass, just like her own decoy glasses. Phony as his British accent. She tucked them into his pocket, knelt beside his body and pulled his knees up against his chest to make him more compact. Wrapping it carefully around both feet in a figure eight pattern, she began to intertwine the rope around his legs and arms, encircled his back, and then looped it through his bound arms and legs again until he was trussed as thoroughly as a butchered hog on the way to market.

He had been a small man to start with, but by the time Hannah was done he was bound so tightly she could easily have fit him into one of the industrial ovens displayed in the dark behind her.

It was tempting, and would be ridiculously simple. She could reprise her murder of Byron Peppers, that insufferable kitchen makeover host she'd killed in New Jersey This time she'd season with habanero peppers in memory of Terlingua.

It would be her own version of Nouveau Nostalgia.

Imagine the commotion when everyone arrived for taping tomorrow only to find one of the chefs cooking in his own oven. But, no. She had too much on the line. They'd call off taping and her murder of Gert would inevitably be downgraded into something far more mundane. Besides, Willis Covington wasn't worth the effort.

Her problem now was where to stash the body.

She couldn't leave it on the fourth floor. Too many people would be crawling over it come morning. And there was no way she was going to sneak it out past the maintenance man downstairs. There weren't enough desserts in the world to distract him from the sight of a dead body being dragged past his office.

In the end, she opted to shove Willis onto a rolling kitchen cart and pushed him toward the freight elevators. She wasn't sure what else was on the schedule tomorrow, but she knew that the floor above was seldom used for anything other than storage. Surely she could stash him there for a day or two, until she either came up with a plan or hit the road, victorious once again.

The elevator doors opened soundlessly and she pushed the trussed chef inside. He had ceased twitching and lay on the stainless steel floor of the cart as if he were on his way to the morgue.

The fifth floor was even better than she had hoped. While half of it contained extra appliances and huge boxes of kitchen supplies, part of the floor contained heating and cooling units used to manage the temperature of the building. It was unlikely anyone would come up here for days.

Within minutes, she had trundled Willis to a far corner of the floor and rolled him out on a tarp that covered a small open area next to an air-conditioning unit. She pulled half of the tarp over him and then carefully checked the floor for blood spatters as she wheeled the cart back toward the elevator, making sure she had left no trail behind.

It took her longer to mop up the mess on the bottom of the stainless steel kitchen cart, but there were scads of paper towels and she was meticulous. In the end, it shone like new. She pushed the trash down to the bottom of her bag then left the cart exactly where she had found it, smack dab in the middle of Willis Covington's kitchen set.

She wondered what they would do tomorrow when he didn't show up for taping. Surely the show would go on. Too much money was riding on it. And Freddy Maxwell had been adamant when they received their final briefing. Participants were to be in position and ready to cook at the designated hour, or they were off the show.

No exceptions, no excuses, no tardy slips.

Maybe she could even plant a rumor that she'd seen Willis heading out late at night with a couple of prostitutes. By the time the rumor got around to the producer, it would be embellished to mammoth proportions. They'd attribute his absence to bad behavior and get on with the show.

And then her finest, final revenge would be revealed.

Hannah didn't even have to bribe the maintenance man to keep his mouth shut. Nor did she need the option of killing him just in case.

The slack ass was not even at his station. His office was empty and the action flick he'd been watching played forlornly in the dark, unwatched. She couldn't afford to wait around for him. She'd just have to rely on his stupidity, but the good news was he had plenty of it.

She slipped out into the dark New York night, enjoying the cool breeze that came in off the Hudson. In the alley she removed the paper towels from her bag and pushed them into one of the disgusting dumpsters. Wiping her hands on her slacks, she decided she was like a cat, a big black cat slipping through the dark, supple, confident, sure of its footing. She felt good. She felt strong. It was all coming together.

Killing. Cooking. Copulating. It was all the same to her. You just had to keep all the balls in the air, balls to the wall. It was no world for the weak.

Chapter 43

Jason woke early the next morning, floating to consciousness on a dream he'd been having that made it nearly impossible to wake.

He and Kimberly had been lying in chaise lounges, basking happily on a vast and sunny beach near azure seas, holding hands and toasting one another with boat drinks with tiny umbrellas. In his dream, he was as buff as a teenage movie star, while Kimberly? Well, she was the same as she always was— perfect. She just wasn't packing a gun in her bikini.

He had a couple hours before the taping, so he decided to follow up the perfect kiss of the night before with a perfect cup of coffee this morning. He showered quickly, then donned the terrycloth robe that came with his hotel room and unpacked his Nespresso machine. It had been a pain hauling it over on the subway from Queens at the start of rehearsals, but the idea of subsisting on the swill that passed for in-room hotel coffee was nauseating.

Also, somebody once told him about seeing a hotel maid cleaning an in-room coffee machine with a toilet brush, which settled the matter for all time.

He savored his java while staring out over the Hudson River and New Jersey. He could see his own future as closely as the skyscrapers that now dominated the Jersey side. With Kimberly beside him, and a head start on a sensational series of celebrity crimes, he would emerge not just as America's up-and-coming food blogger but as a force in the writing world to be reckoned with. He would be admired both for his taste in food and his power as a writer.

He would someone to be feared, a sort of Truman Capote meets the love child of Frank Rich and Craig Claiborne.

Because he, Jason Bainbridge, was at the epicenter of it all.

The culinary world was poised today with their digital knives at the ready as Freddy Maxwell's latest effort debuted. Who would be the first chef to go ape-shit on *A Cut Above*? Would Sallie Tam jump on Willis Covington's back and beat him about the head and shoulders with her favorite wok? Would Ricardo Z try to choke Gert Thurogood with a handful of rainbow chard?

Or even more spectacularly, would the killer strike again as Kimberly feared and he suspected?

He decided to wish her luck today. After what had happened between them, surely that was not showing too much desperation? He finally found his iPhone buried deep beneath the cushions of the couch where he had floated in Caribbean island dreams for much of the night. It was just before seven a.m.— the perfect time to wish her luck at the taping and assure her he would keep a close eye on the backstage area.

He tapped in his password and saw that several text messages had arrived in the night without him hearing the notifications. The first was from his mother, asking again when he planned to show up for Sunday dinner. What was the point of her cooking it if he wasn't there to eat it, she wanted to know? She had perfected the art of whining while texting.

He ignored Mom and scrolled down to a message that had come in from an unfamiliar number well past midnight. Maybe it was fan mail from an intrepid follower of his blog who discovered his phone number. He opened the message and froze, mouth agape, re-reading it more carefully, word for incendiary word:

"Dear Jason. I'm quite the fan of your work. You have written of my exploits, even speculated who I might be and what my motivations are on your blog and in interviews. By the way, is that Polo you use as aftershave? It smells good on you, very masculine. I just wanted to let you know I have a fantastic new serving of chef à la fatale planned. This will stand that crazy hair of yours even more on end. Be prepared to write reams about it. You won't see it coming. Not from a mile away."

It wasn't signed but whoever he, or likely she, was, the killer was near. The killer had his phone number. The killer knew how he wore his hair and even what he smelled like. And the killer was planning to strike again— probably very soon.

After a minute, Jason remembered how to breathe and called Kimberly. No answer. He tried again and again, not caring how it would look to her, like some desperate, lovesick kid unable to control himself.

He had to get through to her. The person who had written that message— the killer, obviously the killer— was right in the thick of things, with something spectacular planned.

"Call me ASAP," he finally messaged Kimberly, adding "911" at the end because he'd heard somewhere that was how cops told each other something was really urgent. Then he placed his phone on the bathroom counter so he could hear it if she called while he was in the shower.

But he was dressed and heading out the door before she messaged him back, and once again Jason didn't hear the ping— moisture from the bathroom steam had screwed up his settings. He was already at the studio before he saw what she had written: "Problems on the set. Talk later."

The coffee in his stomach fused into a hard knot of dread. The killer was a step ahead of them all.

Chapter 44

Freddy Maxwell was pissed. He should have known better than to give Willis Covington a spot on the show. There was something funny about that Brit. His teeth were too good. He should have followed his instincts. When would he ever learn?

One of Covington's assistants came running up, out of breath. Freddy couldn't remember his name and didn't care. "Mr. Maxwell, I heard a couple people say that Chef was spotted leaving his hotel room last night in the company of two women who looked, well, you know..." The young man stopped short and looked at him expectantly.

"Spit it out or you'll spend the rest of the day scrubbing toilets in the staff bathroom." Freddy was in no mood to fuck around.

"Whores, sir. You know, p-p-prostitutes. Escorts..."

Freddy cut him off before he segued into *ladies of the night*.

"I get the gist, kid." He looked at his watch. "He's missed the deadline anyway. Tell Roger and the rest of the crew that we're going to be shooting with only three kitchens today. Take Covington's down."

Freddy was disgusted. Not only would they have to rearrange the whole set with Covington gone, his assistants and sous chef would be left standing around with their dicks in their hands. No doubt they'd be such pains in the ass that he'd either have to babysit them backstage the entire time or toss them out, in which case his reputation would take another hit. And if this show tanked?

His career would be over. Christ, he needed to catch a break.

Plus he'd have at least ten minutes of air time to fill in during editing without a fourth chef. He doubted the judges were interesting enough or the other morons competing as chefs skilled enough to fill in all that time without putting demanding viewers to sleep. Damn Willis Covington. When he saw him again, he'd kick his ass back to London.

Freddy stared at the set grumpily, wondering what the hell was wrong with Gert Thurogood. She looked like she had seen a ghost. Just then, two women pushed past Gert, making her jump about two feet. Christ, she was skittish today. The two women ran at him full tilt like they'd just seen someone murdered.

No, he moaned silently. Please, no more dead bodies until they at least got the taping underway.

The women were as different as night and day. One was average height and kind of dumpy, and the other a long, lean goddess. The tall one looked vaguely familiar and not someone you saw once and forgot. Too bad he had no time for cooch today.

"Get out of my way," he barked at them. "I've got problems to solve."

"I'm Willis Covington's spiritual advisor," the plain one blurted out.

Freddy sneered at her, "Then I'd advise him to get a good lawyer. He was supposed to be here an hour ago. We signed a contract."

"I can go on in his place," the taller woman said firmly. "I'm his business partner." She had a low, throaty voice. It would play well on camera. "We have a new restaurant opening in Provincetown."

Her companion looked startled but bit her lip, silent.

Freddy stared at the hottie who claimed she was Covington's partner, letting his eyes trail all the way from her incredible gold-painted toenails a metallic sandals up to her endless legs, past an exquisite torso, to a pair of amazing breasts and a face that, while a little strong for a woman, would nonetheless make viewers drool. Where had she come from? Where had she been all week?

And why the hell had Covington ever been booked on the show in the first place when he and the rest of America could be looking at her?

It was like she could read his mind. "Let me take over for Willis," she said in a confident voice. "If he shows up, great. We can be a team. If he doesn't, I can run his crew. Trust me. I know the way he cooks."

The short, dumpy woman glanced at her companion in surprise again and opened her mouth to speak but Freddy cut her off.

"Fine," he told the tall, good-looking one. "Get dressed and check in with Layla. She's the redhead with the clipboard. She'll need to know your name, your background— just make up some bullshit if your real story's not interesting enough— but leave me out of it. I've got a shitload to do and taping starts in half an hour. I do not intend to wait a minute, even for you."

As the short woman opened her mouth to speak again, Freddy strode off, anxious to stop the crew from removing the fourth kitchen before they got too far. Plus, he had no doubt there would be at least three other disasters to deal with before the show began. He was too old for this shit. All of his friends had struck it big with syndication. Why the hell was he the one always starting over?

Chapter 45

Hannah had not counted on the lights.

Sure, she had been on camera before. But nothing this big since that terrible episode of *86ed*. Don't think about it, she told herself. But the lights were really bothering her. She had prepared herself mentally for this moment but hadn't anticipated the blinding glare. God knew she'd had her hands full keeping Ricky from puking his guts out in nervousness and forgetting his recipes entirely.

Plus, a commotion was unfolding on the side of the set where Freddy Maxwell held court. Hannah assumed everyone was freaking out about Willis Covington being a no-show. Wouldn't they all shit a ton of bricks if they knew he was only a few feet above their heads, trussed up like a pork roll?

She had expected the crew to start rolling away his kitchen, but to her surprise Maxwell barked at them, stopping the transformation. Still the show appeared to be going on without him. Hannah started lining up the ingredients for Ricky's meatloaf filling as she squinted across the set, trying to see what was going on.

Damn those lights. She remembered the klieg lights best about her experience on *86ed*, the incident that had sent her running into the shadows, traveling from one place to the next, never staying long enough for anyone to recognize her or connect her with that humiliating episode, sure she would never live it down. The memory burned through her with paralyzing shock, but she couldn't stop it. The lights took her right back to that ill-fated day. A day that should have been so different.

The hell of it was, she was born to win *86ed*.

She was food royalty. Her father had taught her at his knee, albeit very intermittently. She had been creative even in her nana's stuffy old Iowa country kitchen. She watched every episode of *86ed*, had even practiced in her kitchen so that she could deal with the time constraints and the curveball of a crazy ingredient. After she walked out of culinary school she knew she needed a respectable comeback. Cooking school wasn't the end. It couldn't be. She practiced her cooking techniques until she could have whipped up a sauce or gauged the doneness of meat blindfolded. She memorized the *86ed* judges' peccadilloes and formed a long list in her head of rules to remember to follow:

"Never use truffle oil.

Hash is for losers.

Respect the ingredients or you will go down.

Don't attempt pasta unless you can be sure it is absolutely perfect.

The Hispanic judges like some heat.

Give the Upper Eastside judges dishes they can eat with a knife and fork.

Don't stint on spices if a foreign chef is judging.

Make sure the bites are pretty.

Never let a dish be too acidic or too sweet. Balance is king.

Don't cook the tuna belly or poach the halibut.

And for heaven's sake, transform the ingredients or be prepared to go home.

Just don't use too many pantry ingredients: The basket offered must be the star of the show."

She had known those rules like the back of her burn-marked cook's hand. She prepared to wow them all, to make her father so proud he would no longer hide the fact that she was his daughter.

But those lights. It had all gone wrong because of those lights.

It had been over a year since she'd let herself obsess over those humiliating hours of her life and even longer since she'd had a panic attack over what had happened. She couldn't afford to give in to the memory now.

She took deep breaths, putting her hand on the surface of Ricardo Z's countertops, hoping the cool metal would calm her. None of it helped. The lights were pulling her back in time, then further back, until she was waiting in the wings for her big moment, waiting to hear the host call her name.

And, then, there she was, bouncing down the hallway, rounding the corner, comfortable and cheery in the camera frame, smiling brightly, certain that— though she might be seen by others as just another too young, too chubby and too inexperienced sous chef— she would wow them all by the end. She had hustled out onto the set with a confident smile, the last of four competitor chefs to be introduced, acutely aware that the judges were staring at her and the other contestants blatantly sizing her up.

Her toe caught a rubber mat as she neared her station, but she recovered and thought that no one had noticed. But as she turned to face the judges, ready to gauge how to best play to them, the glare of the track lights above struck her square in her eyes. She winced and moved a little to the left, but the damn lights seemed to follow her. Her eyes were watering, stinging. She started to panic: *What if she couldn't see? What if she mistook the salt for the sugar? What a rookie mistake that would be: instant death.*

These and a thousand other questions raced through her head as the host explained the rules and instructed them to open their baskets. Hannah was finding it hard to breathe. She didn't hear a word as the host intoned the ingredients. By the time she processed her challenge, he had announced that the round was beginning and the other chefs were already moving to the pantry. She felt frozen in place.

Hannah had stared down numbly at the basket before her. All of her practicing and training flew out the window. She felt like an alien trying to puzzle out what strange nutrition these earthlings relied on. Slowly, she lifted each item out of the basket and placed them on the counter, acutely aware the judges were staring at her and murmuring among themselves.

The Pea Guy.

She suddenly knew with certainty they were talking about the Pea Guy, the poor schmuck who, during an early season, had frozen under the pressure, eventually managing to present the judges with plates that held nothing more than two green peas, rolling forlornly around the dish like escaped pinballs. The rest of the basket ingredients were either still cooking on his stove or lay forgotten by his cutting board.

A few minutes later, millions of viewers watched in fascinated horror as, the host raised the silver top from a plate containing two lonely peas and solemnly announcing the Pea Guy had been "*86ed.*" Hannah had laughed and laughed when she first saw that episode, as surely all of America had. But now that it was happening to her, now that she was in danger of becoming the next Pea Guy, she didn't think that she could take it.

Her chest was in a vise. She couldn't breathe. She wanted to run from the set and keep on running, as far from food and lights and cameras as she could get.

Focus, she ordered herself. Just focus. She peered at the items before her. She could do this. If nothing else, she'd throw it all together in a pan and call it hash. What did she have to work with? Canned salmon, mandarin oranges, green onions and borscht. Think, she ordered herself. Just think. She could do this.

The answer came to her like redemption offered by the gods at the last possible moment: She'd make salmon cakes, incorporating the green onion and cracker crumbs, and serve it with a cold soup made from the borscht and orange segments. Perfect. She knew just what to do.

Quickly, she grabbed a frying pan and put it on a lit burner, pouring vegetable oil in it to heat. She was in a hurry and sloshed the oil on the floor and stove top, but had no time to clean it up. She'd just have to hope it didn't catch fire. She dumped the can of salmon into a bowl then quickly chopped the green onions and tossed them in. Next, she needed some celery, onion, sour cream and spices to bring life to the salmon cakes and cold soup.

She lined up stainless steel bowls on her counter top, poured the borscht into one of them, then grabbed a bowl and took off running for the kitchen. She was acutely aware that she was already several minutes behind the other chefs; she'd have to get all of her supplies in one trip. She snatched sour cream and regular cream from the fridge, realized she had grabbed the bowl of borscht instead of an empty one, and jammed the celery and onions into the pockets of her apron instead. Panicking, she tucked a handful of spice jars under one arm and dashed back toward her station.

The other three chefs loomed in her way like football players on a field. Ducking low, she shouted "Behind! Behind!" and darted forward, trying to avoid them. She had to make up for lost time.

She hit the oil patch in front of the stove at full speed. It all happened as if in slow motion. Her feet flew out from underneath her and she seemed to levitate straight upward, the spices and cream skittering to the floor as the bowl of borscht soared up, up, up, hovering above her like a discus as it slowly flipped. Even as she was suspended in midair, knowing she was about to go down hard, she saw the borscht swirl out of the bowl like an angry red bird in flight, pause for a millisecond, and then splash toward her, hitting her face full on, covering her hair, her skin, her eyes, her mouth, her nose, trickling down the front of her chef's jacket like blood.

At that moment, gravity claimed all and she hit the tile floor with a thump that made the judges gasp and rise from their seats as the other con-testants froze.

It was a turning point. Life would never be the same. She had seen it all in her mind's eye: She could become the sole chef in the history of *86ed* to be dragged unceremoniously from the competition— "Bring out your dead! Bring out your dead!" Or she could show them all that she had guts.

She popped up from the floor, shouting, "I'm okay, I'm okay!" and set to work frantically trying to get back on track. But in her haste, just as she got back on her feet, she hit the edge of the stainless steel bowl containing her salmon mixture and it flew straight at her, the pink fish flesh splattering on her forehead, lodging in her ears, dripping down her shoulders and dotting her arms.

It was too much to bear. She closed her eyes and would have sunk to the floor in utter humiliation right there and then, except a calm voice to her left suddenly said, "You can have some of mine. I'm not using it all."

The chef standing next to her pushed forward a partial can of salmon and a tiny portion of borscht. He was a young cook in his early 30s with blonde hair pulled back and a patch of triangular facial hair that she found particularly attractive in those times when she wasn't insanely stressed. She grabbed at his proffered supplies in desperation, forgetting to say thanks.

By then, she had less than ten minutes left to complete her appetizer but, somehow, she managed to produce four plates, each one holding a tiny salmon cake rimmed by a circle of orange-beet sauce with green onions scattered over everything. It was the best she could manage to do under the circumstances, and while it was barely a bite for each judge, when she looked over at her competition she thought that their plates lacked elegance and came off as amateurishly crude.

She held her hands up high, and her head, too, when the host finished the countdown and pronounced the round over.

Until then, Hannah had not even had time to see who would be judging her. As she wiped her hands and joined the queue of cooks waiting to obediently shuffle out from behind their counters and around to the judging area, she saw Byron Peppers, Willow St. Clair and a well-known pastry chef named Candice Kane staring at her, ignoring all the other contestants.

I showed them, she thought triumphantly. I took disaster and turned it into victory. I earned their respect.

As the last chef out of the gate to join the line, she would be the first to introduce herself to the judges. On *86ed* you had thirty seconds to give the judges your sob story, to present some tale so compelling they might feel sympathy for you and judge you a little less harshly. She had searched her life for something, anything, that would paint her in a more sympathetic light and had settled on the perfect approach.

It came rushing out of her even before she introduced her dishes—she was the daughter of Frank White, she blurted out, and it was hard being in his shadow. She was on *86ed* to make him proud of her. He loved restaurants and food and relished being known as a gourmand. She didn't want to let him down.

The judges seemed stunned by this news. No one said a word until Candice Kane said in her most polite, saccharine voice, "You're saying that your father is Frank White?"

"Yes," she said, suddenly panicked that perhaps her father had given them all bad reviews and she had just doomed herself. But, no, they were looking at her with sympathy, and maybe something a little more. It was not until later, she realized with shame, that they had been looking at her with pity.

She couldn't remember what they said about her dish. They had praised it politely, she thought, and pointed out its flaws with monotone precision. In fact, they treated her so nicely she began to get a little suspicious. Perhaps her father's name was working too well? She wanted to win on her own merits, not his. What was the point otherwise?

The next chef up for judging, the one who had given her some of his supplies, was praised profusely for his generosity toward her. This pissed Hannah off to no end. He had just been using her to make himself look better. Rage welled in her, a desire to take him down right then and there, in front of the world, to grab that hair of his for leverage and beat his face against the floor repeatedly until it was reduced to a bloody pulp.

"My father is dying," the blond-haired chef was telling the judges, a mournful look on his face as he fought back tears. "He's in hospice and they say he has less than 48 hours to live. His dying wish is to see me win *86ed*. So

I'm here to make him proud."

Seriously? Hannah couldn't believe her ears. That could not possibly be true. No one would care who her father was now. This poor guy's father was dying.

She would not feel sorry for him. He was the enemy. He stood in between her and triumph.

"If your father is dying, why aren't you with him?" she had asked the competing chef right then and there on camera, in front of the judges and the world.

A long silence followed her question, one of those interminable, endless silences that seemed to last days when, in fact, it was probably only a few seconds.

"So judges, what did you think of Chef Jaime's dish?" the host finally asked brightly, averting his gaze from Hannah.

She'd only said what everyone else had been thinking.

But those lights, always those lights searing into her eyes. She gritted her teeth and endured the rest of the judging, unnaturally aware that the other chefs in the competition were constantly sneaking glances at her. Probably intimidated by her father's name or perhaps by the way she had bounced back from disaster. They knew she was the one to beat.

They had filed out to a small waiting room to await the verdict of the judges, and suddenly it seemed like no one would look at her. She sat on her stool, roundly ignored by the others, head held high and eyes fixed firmly on the camera. She would not be intimidated anymore. She was Hannah White, daughter of food royalty.

They called the chefs back in and Hannah prepared herself for the triumph she would feel when one of the lesser chefs was dismissed. She must not show it on camera. But when the host lifted the metal domed top covering the plate of the soon-to-be eliminated chef, she was stunned to see her own tiny salmon cake sitting there, the orange-beet sauce now looking like blood splashed over it. "Chef Hannah, you have been *86ed.*"

For a moment, Hannah couldn't move. To be chopped in the first round was a humiliation she knew her father would never abide. She winced, thinking of what he would have to say.

Willow St. Clair was speaking then, explaining that Hannah had failed to transform the borscht or green onions, and that the salmon cake had been undercooked and the portion too small. She spoke carefully, precisely, as if afraid Hannah might crumple under harsher criticism.

When she was done and Hannah had heard the dreaded words, "For these reasons, we had to 86 you from the menu," she could find no words in reply and simply stepped forth as if in a dream.

She turned and began her long walk of shame back down the empty hallway. The camera hovered in front of her like some sort of hungry machine, pulling her defeat toward it for the consumption of the television audience. She made herself look straight into the camera. When they asked her to talk about her defeat, she managed to say, with dignity, that she knew she had let her father down and she was sorry for it.

But nothing she could say would have mattered that day. Because her father never spoke to her again.

Not because she had lost, but because of the way she had lost—specifically of how she had looked when she lost. She had never stopped to consider her appearance after she had slipped and splattered borscht all over herself followed by a shower of wet, pink salmon flecks.

The whole time she had waited proudly in line to be judged, the whole time she had sat on her stool with the other contestants trying to look dignified, she looked as if she had stepped straight out of an abattoir.

Splashes of red covered her face and body like she'd been drenched with a bucket of blood, and tiny clumps of pink flesh dangled from her face and arms as if she had just butchered babies. The camera highlighted every inch of her utter humiliation with ruthless clarity, lingering on her appearance, zooming in on the droplets of red and chunks of pink, capturing the expressions of the other chefs and the judges as they stole shocked glances at Hannah every chance they got.

Hannah had stared at the screen when the episode aired, feeling used and abused. They could have called timeout after the appetizer round to allow her to wash up before judging. In fact, they usually did, so that everyone could take a deep breath.

So when the show aired, she suddenly understood why the producer had waved frantically to the cameras to keep rolling. They had wanted to humiliate her. They had wanted to capture her grotesque appearance and loss of dignity. They had reveled in every moment of her disastrous round.

Later, the show would use the shot of her slipping on the oil in slow motion, over and over again in each show's opening credits. For the next three seasons. The image of her levitating up in the air, clearing the edge of the counter to be splattered with borscht in front of all, then dropping like a rock to the floor, became an iconic *86ed* moment.

Her borscht-and-salmon spattered face became a meme on the Internet, with millions of people adding their own captions, making her the poster girl for such sentiments as "Having a bad day?" "*86ed*: Game of Thrones style." "When life gives you lemons, kill everyone." "Chainsaw broken? Craftsman tools are guaranteed for life."

In the cruel, relentless caprice of modern culture, the momentum of Hannah's humiliation only grew. A popular live comedy television show featured a cooking competition between a character who was obviously her and someone playing Hannibal Lecter from *Silence of the Lambs*. The two comedians in the sketch frantically dismembered obviously-fake human bodies to include in their dishes, delighting in the carnage before attacking each other with knives at the end.

The studio audience roared and the show's ratings soared. Hannah was devastated.

She would never live it down. She knew she couldn't endure a life-time as Carnage Girl. So she decided to become somebody else. She starved herself to lose weight, changed her hair color, and began using her mother's name professionally. The memory of that show, of how she had been used, festered inside her. It had ruined her plans to make her father proud, and now— it was all too clear that it would never, ever go away.

So long as there were lights and cameras and more lights, she would always be Carnage Girl.

* * *

"Hannah! Hannah!" Ricardo Z was shaking her hard, like a rag doll, trying to get through to her. She struggled back to the present, blinked her eyes and looked around. His other assistants were staring at her curiously.

"What the hell is going on?" Ricky demanded.

She shrugged. "I'm just tired. I had a long night, thinking of all we had to do today." She fought hard to claw her way back to the present, to leave the memory of her humiliation behind, to focus on her plan to get her revenge in the here and now.

"Well, get it together," Ricky ordered her. He whispered furiously, casting glances over his shoulder to make sure he would not be overheard. "I need you to make the best Cobb salad of your life, got it? Whatever you did in the last testing recipe, do it again. I'm going to start prep for the meatloaf, but I need you on the salad. Got it, Hannah? Do not fuck this up for me."

Hannah wanted to tell him to make his own damn Cobb salad, or better yet, to shove it up his ass, apples first. She felt angry, bristling. Who was he to tell her what to do? Without her, he would never have gotten this far. Without her, he'd be going down in flames in about an hour, using the same lame old recipes he always foisted on the public. She was the brains in their partnership. That was clear.

So why the hell should she let him tell her what to do instead of vice versa?

And why in hell had she ever let Ricky live? She should have killed him when she had the chance. Good thing she had the gun in her apron pocket.

Maybe it wasn't too late.

Chapter 46

Willis Covington was ready to be reborn.

In his lifetime, he had lived under four different names, tried and failed at six careers, and finally made it as a chef— but only after fleeing to the UK and starting over yet again. How cruel was it that, on the cusp of his new fame, he'd been brought down once again, this time by a five-foot-three unknown wielding a cast iron skillet?

He had no consciousness of his situation. His brain had ceased to work in the traditional sense. The gray matter had been pounded into scaloppini with one swift, savage blow. Swelling had set in after the bleeding started and his synapses simply shut down. He was incapable of thought, no longer knew his name and, indeed, his body barely sensed it was alive.

But he had survived. And somewhere deep in his shattered brain, in a long forgotten corner of primal memory, Willis Covington was absolutely sure that he was in the womb.

He floated in a safe, warm place, utterly secure and carefree, a gentle pressure surrounding him. Somewhere nearby, a rhythmic whoosh breathed in and out, lulling him into calm. Soothed by the sound and concealed by the dark, he could have stayed there forever, or at least until the eternal dark overtook him. But as it is the internal drive of his species to progress, to move, what was left of his mind eventually whispered to his body: "It is time to leave this place."

Willis Covington moved his head and wiggled his body, sensing that his arms and legs were still tightly against his torso. He had to move forward to survive. Tentatively at first, then with the growing confidence of muscle memory to guide him, he pushed out of the covering wrapped around him, and wormlike, he inched and rolled his way toward the whooshing sound of the air-conditioning unit that was calling to him. It took hours to reach the lip of the opening beside the machine but by dawn he had made his way there. His shoulder rolled ever so slightly into a circular opening and his body responded instinctually by dipping his head into the shaft. Was this the way out?

Yes, his long ago memories assured him. The tunnel was the way out, his first memories whispered. Go to the tunnel.

Slowly, painstakingly, with unstoppable instinct, Willis Covington inched his way headfirst into the duct system of the taping studio and began his long, exhausting journey toward freedom.

Chapter 47

Jason stood off-camera, huddled in a cluster of production assistants, wondering if the world had lost its damn mind. He had reviewed shows for his blog often enough, and once or twice ventured on set for an interview, but he had never witnessed the filming process before. If this was any indication of what went on, he couldn't wait to get back to his computer.

Freddy Maxwell was barking orders into his headset like a Nazi general on steroids.

Ricardo Z's blue-haired assistant was staring off into space like she had seen a ghost, and that made Jason uneasy. Had the killer threatened her?

Meanwhile, Willis Covington was missing entirely and Audra DeFord, Fuller Muddlark's golden goddess assistant, had appeared out of nowhere to take his place. As for Gert Thurogood? She jumped when anyone so much as sneezed and seemed as nervous as someone trying to smuggle a pound of heroin past Indonesian border officials. Only Sallie Tam remained calm, cool and collected as she moved about her kitchen set, orchestrating the preparation of what looked to be gourmet hamburgers and French fries.

Of course. Someone was bound to go for burgers and fries as part of the Nouveau Nostalgia challenge. But Jason felt an unwelcome twinge of self-awareness nonetheless. He was a foodie, granted, and he loved a good burger as much as anyone— the two he'd scarfed down the night before remained as almost as alluring as Kimberly Douglas's kiss— but God almighty, did the world really need a burger that took two hours to prepare and French fries dusted with truffles?

He was annoyed that Kimberly was ignoring him. He could admit that much to himself. He had been texting and calling her repeatedly all morning without a response. He couldn't see her anywhere on the set.

What the hell? He thought they were partners. Here he was risking his ass for her cause and she couldn't be bothered to return his calls. The not-so-cryptic message from the killer was stored in his phone like a malignant tumor. He was afraid to click on it and read it again. For all he knew, the killer was looking over his shoulder.

He checked his phone yet again to see if Kimberly had called. No such luck. He felt like a loser, checking his phone like a teenager. But he had no choice. The ringer was off on the penalty of expulsion from the set.

Complete silence had been decreed by the officious sound man after he had halted proceedings twice to investigate what he claimed was a strange thumping sound he was picking up on one of the microphones. But his temperamental outbursts had produced no confessing culprit, nor had anyone else heard the thumping sound. Filming had eventually proceeded.

The chefs had dutifully exaggerated each step of dish preparation to give the cameraman an opportunity to get the best shots. Dishes had been placed in ovens with great fanfare. Indeed, no crown anointing the head of a king at his coronation had been given more loving attention than the shepherd pies that Gert Thurogood was baking.

At least the set was starting to smell good. At least most of the time. Every now and then, Jason swore he got a whiff of porta potty. He was afraid to go to the bathroom and check.

Christ. The studio audience must be bored out of their skulls.

Even though the show wasn't live, Freddy Maxwell had insisted on having an audience, saying it added to the "energy" of the show. But any energy in that audience was long gone, probably sapped out of them by the fourth take of Ricardo Z painting his meatloaf with some secret, burgundy-colored ingredient while acting like he was the culinary equivalent of Jackson Pollack.

Jason had looked for Kimberly among the audience members without luck, though he spotted what he thought was another agent.

Why was she was ignoring him? Should he show the text to the other agent? But what if he wasn't actually an agent?

The weird vibe was getting to him. During a rare, eerily calm moment on the set, broken when a production assistant dropped a bottle of fresh cream and Freddy Maxwell screamed, "God dammit!" Jason actually thought he heard a thumping sound, too. He listened carefully, trying to locate where it was coming from, but the sound was gone.

Across the set, he finally spotted Kimberly, dressed in her usual gray slacks and black blazer, moving swiftly through a crowd of staff huddled off-camera. He took off like a shot. Pushing through people and props, he managed to move faster than the flames on a Baked Alaska. He reached her as she was heading toward the stairwell.

"Kimberly! Wait!" he called after her.

She whirled around and stared at him, her expression all business. "For Godsakes, Jason, I'm working. I have an emergency. I don't have time to talk about our relationship."

Jason was incensed. "Relationship? You could fill the Rose Bowl with the fucks I do not give about that kiss," he hissed back. Behind them, a production assistant whirled around and shushed them.

He stepped closer, oblivious to the shocked look on her face. "I've been trying to reach you for hours. The killer sent me a text." He held up his phone. "The killer knows my phone number. They communicated with me."

Without so much as a thank you, she snatched his phone and tried to dash away. He grabbed her arm, refusing to let go. "What's going on?" he demanded. "I'm not letting you go until you tell me."

Heads were turning their way.

Kimberly stepped so close to him he thought for one wild moment they were going to kiss again. But when she spoke, her whisper made it plain she had no time for the likes of him. "Willis Covington is missing. Last night, he bribed the half-ass maintenance guy guarding the side entrance to get lost for an hour and to come back with baking soda and cornstarch, of all things. But Covington was missing when the guard got back and now he's nowhere to be found. His bed was never slept in. And he has some hysterical spiritual advisor who swears something has happened to him. I think the killer has struck again."

"I can help," Jason whispered back. "I know why he wanted the cornstarch and baking soda. He was going to mix it in the flour the other chefs are using today. He was trying to sabotage their dishes."

"Well, someone may have killed him for it."

"Let me help," Jason pleaded.

She shook him off. "I have to go. And I have to take this with me." She held up his phone and hurried down the hall, slipping out the stairwell door. He could hear the drumbeat of her shoes as she raced to another floor.

That went well. It had never been more obvious that Kimberly Douglas was out of his league.

He sidled back to his place on the sidelines. Even shunned by the pros he couldn't stop trying to guess: Who among all these people could be the killer?

The studio audience looked as benign as they looked bored. Clearly, they were tourists straight off the buses at the Port Authority terminal nearby. And they looked like they'd eaten their way across America to get here—there was no way anyone of them would be able to move fast enough to be a threat.

But the crew? Any of them could be the killer. Any at all.

He caught a sudden flurry of activity on the set and realized that the judges were about to take their places behind a long table covered with a white linen cloth. Cameramen rushed to film them. They stepped out onto the set, one by one, the host announcing their names as the audience erupted in applause at the sight of each of them. Jason wondered if the audience knew them and was actually impressed— or just relieved that, after two hours, something was finally happening.

Sallie Tam was barking orders at her staff. Intricately designed plates of hamburgers and French fries were taking form under her watchful eye. Long slim French fries were being woven over and under to create a lattice-work structure that towered above the giant burgers like miniature duck blinds.

Ricardo Z was overseeing the careful removal of individual meatloaf servings from their pans and simultaneously hissing at his assistant, Hannah, to step it up. She was building what looked like classic Cobb salads with mechanical precision while staring off into space like a stereotypical zombie. What in the hell was the matter with her? She had not been that spaced out during rehearsals.

The most interesting performance was at Willis Covington's station, where his crew had forged onward without him. That woman Audra DeFord, who had been Fuller Muddlark's assistant, was gliding through their ranks, murmuring encouragement, without appearing to actually do anything. Jason wondered if she even knew how to cook. Though that wasn't really relevant, he admitted to himself. Covington had a well-trained staff that was efficiently producing steaming platters heaped high with glazed pork chops and sweet potato soufflé.

Gert Thurogood seemed to be falling behind the other chefs and Jason knew why: She liked to make a big deal out of tasting the extra portion she always made for the cameras. She'd been trying for almost a decade to get her signature eye roll and look of bliss to go viral.

Jason thought she looked more constipated than caught in the throes of culinary ecstasy when she did it, but who was he to judge? He wasn't sitting at the long, linen-covered table.

The cameramen had turned their attention to Gert, who stood primed for her moment of glory. She held a large, gleaming silver spoon in one hand and stood with military posture behind the counter. Her head assistant, that insanely meticulous German guy, took a tray of miniature shepherd pies out of the oven with a Teutonic flourish. He held them aloft in front of him, marching toward Gert as if bringing her the Holy Grail.

Unfortunately for him, a cameraman had let one of his power cords trail carelessly behind him across the floor.

Herman the German tripped over it.

As the audience gasped, his proud look and haughty smile melted into an expression of utter horror when his right foot caught the cord and he pitched forward. He thrust the baking sheet of shepherd's pies out in front of him in a desperate attempt to keep them safe.

He almost succeeded. But his discipline in protecting the mission at all costs meant there was nothing he could do to break his own fall. He went straight down, landing flat on his face as the tray holding the pies hit the terra cotta tile floor hard.

Gert Thurogood actually screamed as the pies jumped into the air and tumbled back to the baking sheet. Three of them rocked a little but settled back down unscathed. The fourth bounced again, hit the lip of the baking tray and rolled over the edge, landing face down on the tile floor.

Behind him, Jason could hear Freddy Maxwell muttering into his headset, "Keep filming! This is fantastic. Keep filming!"

Gert sank to her knees as if God and fate had deserted her. She ended up eye-to-eye with Herman as he scrambled to his knees, horrified at what he had done, the blood from his shattered nose dripping down his once-pristine white jacket. Together, the two of them slowly looked down at the three perfect shepherd pies between them. The fourth had exploded on impact and the meat juices were slowly trickling out and running down the tile tracks.

Gert would not have a chance to taste it now. Worse, her expected moment of glory had morphed into a meme that could well haunt the Internet forever, an airborne man appearing to fly through the air behind a tray of pies. It reminded Jason of another such viral video, years before. Back then only the show's cameras had recorded the ass-over-teakettle move. But this time every person in the audience had snatched up phones the moment they sensed something going wrong, and Herman the German's brief flight had been captured on video from a dozen angles.

Holy shit, Jason thought. If Gert wasn't the killer, she might turn into one now. The look in her eyes would have melted elevator cables.

And then an even more remarkable thing happened.

Ricardo Z's assistant Hannah actually left her station and rushed to their aid. It was an unheard-of gesture of generosity in a competitive kitchen. The cameras, professional and amateur, captured every moment, zooming in on Hannah's face as she patted Herman on the back and reached for the ruined shepherd's pie, attempting to push it back into its pan.

What the hell? Jason thought. Surely she didn't expect Gert to taste something that had fallen on the floor in front of a national television audience. Gert's big tasting opportunity was already history.

Gert agreed. She pushed away the fourth pie and seemed to collect herself. She nodded her thanks to Hannah, then slipped on oven mitts and carefully took the baking pan from Herman's now trembling hands. She conveyed her rescued prize to the countertop with the tenderness of a mother. For the first time in history, Gert Thurogood was going to serve the judges a dish without tasting it first.

Jason doubted anyone gave a rat's ass but Gert.

Across the set, Jason noticed that Audra DeFord was staring intently at Hannah. Jason couldn't interpret the odd expression on her face. She was glaring at Hannah as if she wanted to kill her.

That was interesting. Could Audra be... ? Was *she* the killer? He could almost feel her animosity radiating toward Hannah.

He had no idea what to do. He had no way to get in touch with Kimberly and no idea where she had gone. All he could do was stand and watch and hope that nothing more happened.

Sallie Tam's burgers and fries were going to be judged first, but the process was halted midway when the sound man insisted that he was picking up some sort of interference, like a faint thumping or metallic noise. Freddy Maxwell himself strode out onto the set, put on the headphones and made a huge show of listening intently. Within seconds, he handed them back to sound man in disgust and stomped off, muttering about divas.

A second take was ordered and the hamburgers were conveyed in again on silver platters as the cameras rolled. The judges took bites of the high-class burgers and immediately lapsed into paroxysms of ecstasy. Apparently Sallie Tam had used the tender young flesh of Kobe calves, no doubt hand massaged daily by Japanese virgins. The truffle-dusted fries induced even more coos of delight.

Nouveau nostalgia indeed. That Sallie Tam. Did she ever drop the ball?

The other kitchens were bustling with last-minute preparations for their presentation to the judges. Ricardo Z had taken over the assembling of the side salads. Hannah seemed to have stage fright now that her moment of intramural rescue was over. She stood stock still, staring at Gert Thurogood's kitchen staff, one hand in the pocket of her apron.

Meanwhile, Willis Covington's staff was starting to flounder because their new self-proclaimed leader was too busy giving Hannah the evil eye.

Jason frowned. He was obviously missing something. But what? He couldn't quite puzzle it out. Was a cat fight about to erupt on camera— Freddy Maxwell would love that— or were they having a lovers' quarrel? Had a new professional pissing match somehow escaped his attention?

Even the air seemed different, charged with electricity, like a lightning storm was eminent.

Jason watched with longing as the barely touched burger and fries were taken away by tuxedoed waiters, to be placed on a side table in case they needed some fill-in shots later. What he wouldn't give to bury his face in one of those burgers now. He had totally forgotten to eat breakfast.

Gert no longer trusted her assistant Herman, nor would she allow the waiters to get near her precious shepherd's pies. While the waiters distributed plates to the judges and served each one portions of some sort of exotic vegetable medley meant to mimic classic peas and carrots, Gert herself placed a miniature shepherd's pie in front of each judge and made a big show of topping each with a perfect sprig of deep-fried parsley.

"Bon appétit," she murmured, extending her time in camera range.

As Gert stepped back with a smile, Jason saw Hannah leave Ricardo Z's kitchen area to get closer to the judging table. Her mouth was agape, her eyes unnaturally wide. She looked almost... hungry.

The second judge proclaimed that it was his turn to go first and picked up a fork. He broke the crust and lifted a still-steaming heap of shepherd's pie toward his mouth.

But before he could even steal a taste, Willis Covington's cooking team leader, Audra, let out a bloodcurdling, "Nooooooooo!" and launched herself like a panther at the judge's table. She took a running start and then leapt, arms outstretched, sliding down the table and taking the tablecloth with her, as if she were shooting down a luge course, knocking plates and pies out of their reach.

Incredibly, she landed on her feet at the end, tucking and shooting her body upward, raising her hands up high. She nailed her landing like an Olympic gymnastics gold medalist. All hell broke loose.

The judges screamed and jumped back, knocking over their chairs in their haste to get away from the mad woman. Production assistants rushed forward at Freddy Maxwell's hysterical commands, though they didn't seem to have any idea what he expected them to do. Gert Thurogood began wailing, tearing her hair and waving her arms.

In all the chaos, only Jason saw Ricardo Z's assistant Hannah pull the gun from her apron pocket. She aimed the weapon straight at a sobbing Gert Thurogood and there was nothing distant or distracted about her anymore. The zombie-like fog was gone. This was a woman who knew exactly what she was doing.

Holy crap! Was...

Audra DeFord shook off a handful of production assistants attempting to grab her and lunged toward Hannah. She stopped short when she saw the gun. The entire set seemed to freeze as awareness moved in waves through the crew and audience.

"Don't move," Hannah shouted at Audra. Then she turned her head, looked straight into the nearest camera and smiled. It was a ghastly smile, wide and frozen, full of malice and utter madness.

A shiver ran down Jason's spine. Hannah was the one. She was the killer. She had planned this moment, and somehow Audra had figured it out and spoiled it.

Audra didn't move, but she apparently had no intention of staying silent. "She poisoned the pies. Test them. She's trying to kill the judges." She turned her gaze toward Gert. "She was trying to kill you, too. She's already killed Fuller and she killed Calista, too."

Hannah scoffed, a hideous sound. "Calista killed herself."

Out of the corner of his eye, Jason saw a man slip quietly of his front row seat and make his way toward the side of the set. FBI? He could only hope.

Just as Jason thought nothing weirder could happen on set, it appeared to start snowing. A fine white powder drifted down from above, gently, like the fake snowfalls on the sets of vintage Christmas shows. This phenomenon was followed by frantic thumping sounds and a sharp crack as the ceiling above them bulged alarmingly. Audra and Hannah backed away from each other, staring upward.

The fine white powder raining from the ceiling gave to way to acoustic tiles that tumbled down onto Audra's and Hannah's heads. The flapping end of a large aluminum heating duct dangled into view. A large, cylindrical bundle burst from the gaping end of the duct and landed smack on Hannah's head like a giant cannon ball. It slammed her into the ground with a sickening thud, sending her gun flying. The gun hit the side of a metal cabinet, bounced on the tile floor and whirled in a wide circle, finally coming to rest at Sallie Tam's feet.

The famed Asian chef reached down and calmly picked it up. As the rest of the bystanders watched Hannah try to extricate herself from beneath the foul-smelling bundle, Sallie Tam walked over to the groaning, squirming pile of flesh, pointed the gun calmly at Hannah and said, "You move, I kill."

Jason couldn't stand it anymore. He rushed forward, along with nearly everyone else on the set, to see what had landed on Hannah's head.

It was the most grotesque sight Jason had ever seen. At first, the thing on top of Hannah was unrecognizable. The creature's hands and legs were bound against its body with coils of rope. Then Jason realized it was a man, one who had clearly soiled himself during his strange journey through the heating duct system. His eyes had rolled back as if he were in the throes of spiritual ecstasy. A terrible wound had rendered the top of his head nothing more than fragments of bone and clumps of hair. Yet his mouth formed a perfect circle and he was sucking furiously at the air, a beatific smile on his face.

Holy catfish, Jason thought, reeling under the realization. *Willis Covington has turned up after all.*

Epilogue, or How It All Worked Out

Audra DeFord became an overnight sensation.

Footage of her sailing through the air and sweeping the judging table clean in one fell swoop, then landing on her feet like a Russian tumbling star, found its way onto the Internet within seventeen minutes. Within a day, different versions of her feat had been set to such songs as R. Kelly's "I Believe I Can Fly" and "I am Superman" by R.E.M., but the one that really hit it big was "Flash" by Queen. That single 30-second clip had 9 million viewers by the end of the week, all of them cheering as Audra sent poison pies and silver forks flying in slow motion to Freddy Mercury's primal, "Flash, a-ah, savior of the universe."

Audra wasted no time parlaying her virtual notoriety into her own Food Channel show, entitled *Flying High with Audra DeFord.* Each week, she hops on a private plane and jets off to a famous restaurant somewhere exotic. There she enjoys a fantastic meal on her producer's dime, with the viewer joining her as her imaginary companion.

It's like *My Dinner with Andre,* only with a superhot dining companion who offers peeks of her cleavage and always has a fascinating story to share. Audra's limitless capacity to lie has really paid off, and so far she hasn't had to learn how to cook.

She always offers her own shallow, yet somehow irresistible, critique of the food— and people can't get enough of her. Every show ends with a simple credit: *In loving memory of Roland Calhoun.*

Only Audra and Calista's mother know who Roland Calhoun was— and neither one of them is telling. But both see it as a tribute to Calista's unique ability to truly be herself. Or himself. For though Calista had ceased to be Roland long before her jump out a hotel window, she had not been able to leave all of him behind before her death.

Beacon left her radio show and became president of Audra's official fan club. For now, she worships Audra from afar.

Only time will tell if she pulls a Selena.

Willis Covington was shipped back to his home state of Alabama and parked, along with the remaining half of his brain, in a lovely nursing home outside of Mobile. There, surrounded by the scent of magnolia blossoms in spring, he likes to lie on a mat in the sunshine, his arms and legs pulled up against his chest like a baby in the womb, smiling as he dreams of gently swooshing fluids and hears the steady drumbeat of his long-gone mother's heart.

The nurses love him— he never fights or seems embarrassed when they change his diapers, and bottle-feeding him is a snap.

Sallie Tam went on to challenge an Iron Chef and won handily on her first try. She remains unbeaten and, after a few foolish pretenders to the throne risked their pride and failed, she is rarely challenged these days. Otherwise, she leads a quiet life with her husband of forty years and enjoys the companionship of her twelve grandchildren.

She seldom gives interviews because reporters are too afraid to talk to her.

Gert Thurogood suffered a nervous breakdown soon after news of Hannah's arrest hit the press.

The first signs of trouble began on *The View*, when another guest knocked a chair over and the crack of it hitting the floor caused Gert to jump up, scream hysterically and run sobbing from the set. Not even Whoopi could coax her back on.

Soon after, Gert entered a private hospital for an indefinite stay. She intends to specialize in comfort foods when she is finally released.

Ricardo Z parlayed his time with Hannah into an endless series of appearances on talk shows, where no question was deemed too personal to answer. The camera loved him and he hit every daily program except *Sesame Street* and *Today's Bible Study*.

To Hannah's secret delight, Ricky publicly deemed her a sex goddess, capable of arousing him to heights no other woman had ever achieved. His descriptions of their lovemaking usually ended with him confessing that perhaps he had somehow sensed the danger within her and had loved playing with fire.

When the public began flocking to his restaurant in the face of all his newfound publicity, he quickly changed its name and theme to Playing With Fire. The neon rainbow was replaced by flickering neon flames reaching into the Pacific Ocean mists. When word got out about his fire-roasted oysters and his chocolate-fondue dipped butter cake (a recipe Hannah had helped him develop), reservations soared. Soon, limousines lined up on the roadway out to the cliff on weekend nights and Ricardo Z no longer suffered from anxiety.

Diners now arrive at his restaurant as couples, ready to be instructed in the erotic arts as part of their meal. Every meal centers on foods that can be prepared over a private fire pit surrounded by frosted glass walls. Amorous diners sit side-by-side on special flame-retardant mats and waiters always knock before they enter. Side dishes and desserts consist solely of foods you can eat with your fingers, and all food can be delivered on request through special slots reminiscent of maximum security prisons.

Playing With Fire offers a menu heavy on foods with aphrodisiac reputations. Jason Bainbridge's breakout blog on aphrodisiacs was reprinted, with his permission, on the back cover of the menu, which features three of Jason's original dishes.

The rest, of course, were created by Ricardo Z and will be detailed in his forthcoming cookbook, *Ricardo Z Plays With Fire.*

With so many culinary superstars emerging from the debacle of his last show, you might think that Freddy Maxwell had hit it big at last. You would be mistaken.

Turns out that no one even remotely famous was willing to serve as a judge on Freddy's new show once word got out that there had been enough ricin in Gert's shepherd pies to kill an entire town. *A Cut Above* folded before the second episode could be filmed. All that remains of the show are the memes of Herman the German tripping and spilling the pies and the video of Audra clearing the judges' table with her well-toned abs.

Last time anyone saw Freddy, he was tramping the jungles of Bora Bora gathering footage for a proposed pitch to the Food Channel of a new reality show called *Free Range Cannibals.*

Jason Bainbridge didn't have to worry about regaining his blog's momentum. His position at the epicenter of the Great Chef Killings ensured his place in blogging history, not to mention true crime annals and the *New York Times* Bestseller List.

Hannah deemed him her official biographer and gave him every juicy detail of her exploits. Understanding that the families of her victims would receive any profit she got from a book, she let him keep all the royalties. She had more important things to worry about these days than money anyway.

Within nine months of the infamous *A Cut Above* episode, Jason had completed his book, and within three more months it was rushed into stores worldwide— the first book-length tale of the killer who had captured the world's imagination. Written by an insider, no less. Within weeks after its initial release, *Killer Chef* became a blockbuster bestseller that exceeded everyone's already high expectations. And no wonder: *Killer Chef* is juicier than a Sallie Tam roast beef and spicier than Fuller Muddlark's famous hot sauce.

The only person who didn't seem to like *Killer Chef* was the killer chef's father, Frank White. Jason didn't come right out and accuse Hannah's father of molding a killer, but he came close. Frank White had at least poured the gelatin into the mix, the book implied. Which may have been why Frank took early retirement from the culinary world immediately after Hannah's trial. He abandoned his seriously underwater condo on the Upper West Side, donated his papers to the Culinary Institute of America (which politely rejected them) and moved to South America with his fourth wife, Brandi.

But Jason Bainbridge didn't just come out of this with a bestseller. He played his hand with Kimberly Douglas like a master.

For months, though tormented by the memory of their single kiss, he nonetheless refused to contact her. He was a nebbish, perhaps some might say an outright slob, but Jason was no fool. He had glimpsed the expression on Kimberly's face the day they caught Hannah, her look of steely pride. And he had swelled with his own pride as he watched her calmly restore order to a studio brimming with chaos that fateful day of the show's taping. She liked to be in charge, or at the very least, delude herself that she was in charge.

He had decided then that the only way to reel her in would be to wait out her resistance, to make her come to him. A risky proposition, perhaps a foolhardy one, but objectively it seemed his only real shot.

It also had the added benefit of postponing final rejection.

So he knuckled down, lived in the pages of his book, and dreamed of one day being able to kiss her again.

To his astonishment, the strategy worked. The very day he finished the final draft of *Killer Chef,* Kimberly called him and asked if he wanted to go to dinner.

Well, yes. Turns out he did.

After accepting her invitation, he turned into a gibbering idiot. Buoyed by the elation of finishing his magnum opus, a torrent of words about the book tumbled out of him as he blathered on about all he'd discovered while writing it. Delighted to hear from her, he threw all fears of rejection to the wind and simply reveled in being able to talk to her again.

She responded in kind.

That phone call became an epic dinner, which turned into an epic weekend that led to another, and another, and another.

They couldn't have been more different, and yet they complemented one another insanely well. Perhaps the magic survived because they refused to talk about it, just lived it and loved every moment.

By beating all other comers to the punch, Jason had received an astonishingly large advance for *Killer Chef.* He knew just how he wanted to spend part of it. Kimberly took a six-month leave from the Bureau and they went on a gastronomical tour of the world together.

Jason took her to every place he had ever wanted to go, directing her through Turkish spice markets and insisting she sample virtually every food stall they passed. They ate their way through Europe, the Balkans, across the Ukraine, through Italy, and onward to the Far East. Reluctantly leaving India, they traveled onward to Thailand, Vietnam, Japan and China.

On the way home, they stopped in Bali where, after a particularly succulent feast of freshly roasted pig, they found themselves on the edge of a defunct volcano being married by a local magistrate dressed in little more than three yards of brightly colored cloth.

The marriage was legal. The marriage has lasted.

Once they got home, it took Kimberly less than a month to lose all the weight she gained on the trip and to fit back into her FBI slacks and blazer.

Jason has been less lucky. He lives around food and is fast approaching not-quite-obese.

But Kimberly does not seem to mind at all. Jason is her guilty pleasure. When her well-ordered days of impeccably dressed men with razor-cut hair and non-negotiable rules end, she revels in coming home to a man who greets her in a half-buttoned shirt, wearing shorts in the middle of winter, holding a wooden spoon drenched in marinara sauce and too excited to see her for words. Sometimes he even puts dinner on hold when the welcome-home kiss turns into something far more urgent.

Besides, he totally rocks her world in the bedroom. She couldn't possibly leave a man who makes her feel like that. She's even working at being less rigid in her home life, though she maintains an ironclad rule against Jason growing a hipster beard. It is her absolute certainty that bits of food will get caught in it, killing both of her newly-cultivated appetites.

As always, she makes a very good point.

Hannah, oddly, has never been happier.

She rules the New Paltz Correctional Institute for Women with an iron skillet. It took her less than four months to rise through the ranks and take over the prison kitchen, the last obstacle being a stubborn drug smuggler already occupying the enviable position.

That problem was resolved when the then-head cook was found hanging from a bed sheet wrapped around the metal legs of an unused guard tower, having apparently taken her own life. If anyone wondered how a 320-pound Puerto Rican with a fear of heights could have pulled off such a spectacular ending, they didn't ask. Probably because they were too busy enjoying the incredible dishes that Hannah now cranks out day after day in her stead.

Cooking in prison is like being on a perpetual episode of *Chopped.* Every day, Hannah arrives to find that new mystery ingredients have been delivered overnight. Who knows what will be among the boxes? The state seems to ship the prison whatever is surplus, has been seized from the ports, or deemed an incredible bargain at auction.

Utility-grade meat, limp produce, oddball canned goods labeled in foreign languages— it doesn't matter to Hannah. In her mind, an imaginary clock is ticking and she dives right in, working her magic with whatever ingredients she has.

Of course, that imaginary clock is the only clock in her life that matters now. When you're serving consecutive life sentences without possibility of parole, there's only one way you will ever leave confinement and there's no point in counting down those days.

It doesn't matter to Hannah anyway. In prison, she is the star. She's worshiped among the inmates, who fight for her favors and beg her to fix their favorite childhood dishes.

As for the prison staff? The warden began hosting a monthly formal dinner for his twenty closest friends soon after Hannah took over as head of the kitchen. Once word leaked out about her amazing Beef Wellington, Oysters Rockefeller, crème brûlée and roasted red snapper wrapped in banana leaves, the warden couldn't keep up with all of the requests for invitations so he turned the whole business into a regular fundraiser.

It's the hottest ticket in the Northeast.

Tax-deductible donations to the prison foundation now pour in every month and the inmates serving time there enjoy state-of-the-art exercise equipment, a well-stocked library, access to brand new computers and the best recreational room since the Titanic.

Hannah isn't interested in any of those things. But once a month she is allowed to order a modest quantity of any ingredients she wants. Fresh rosemary is always on the list. It reminds her of some of her finest moments during her year of revenge.

Once it became clear that her father was never going to visit, Hannah contents herself with the knowledge that Ricardo Z will be there each month like clockwork, bringing her new dishes to taste and help him fine-tune.

Hannah feels a genuine affection for Ricky, and though the warden has denied them conjugal visits, they share their own version of intimacy over bites of luscious food.

Which is just as well. Hannah has grown plumper than ever in the prison kitchen. She doesn't want to worry about how she looks when she takes off her clothes anymore. She is a queen— and a queen can be as fat as she likes.

Each morning, Hannah takes a star turn through the prison dining room, walking slowly enough to hear the accolades as they rain down on her from all sides. The girls all call her "T.C." for "Top Chef."

"Great job, T.C.!"

"Damn, girl. You are the best."

"I never want to get out of here, T.C. I'd miss your cooking too much."

"T.C., girl, you put the T.L.C. in this shit."

"You the best cook I ever tasted, T.C."

And she is.

She has always been the best. She always knew it, too. At last she has found her people, those who adore her and acknowledge her greatness. And if that ever changes— well, Hannah has a plan. She has started training the short-timers in the culinary arts, and already she's produced some of the best line cooks and sous chefs the world has ever seen. Restaurants line up to hire the inmates who have worked with her once they are released. Best of all, she's schooled them on what to expect when they start their new jobs, including how to protect their honor and dignity.

It's a dirty, macho world when it comes to pro cooking, and women always get a lot of shit in restaurant kitchens. But Hannah is taking care of that. Word is out that you do not mess with Hannah's girls— or you will pay the price. She's taught them to go for the pinky, because a pinky can be sacrificed but still sends a very clear message.

It only took a few near misses to convince the culinary world that, chauvinist or not, the only good pig is a roasted one. Hannah's training of her girls in culinary self-defense has put the fear of god in lecherous chefs everywhere. Female chefs are finally getting the respect they deserve.

Oh, yes, Hannah thinks at the end of each and every day. *I have changed the world. I am the very best at what I do, and if ever that changes? Well, I've got my girls, and they can always do something about it.*

And then, lying in the darkness of her private cell, Hannah pulls out the 80% dark chocolate bar the warden orders for her by the case and takes her first bite of the night, letting it melt slowly onto her tongue, savoring its smooth, bitter sweetness.

This life isn't so bad, she thinks to herself. *In fact, it's not bad at all.*

Read more mystery, suspense and crime tales
from Thalia Press

Visit us on the web at
ThaliaPress.com

Made in the USA
Middletown, DE
13 October 2015